THE EFFECTS OF FEMINIST APPROACHES ON RESEARCH METHODOLOGIES

THE EFFECTS OF FEMINIST APPROACHES ON RESEARCH METHODOLOGIES

Edited by

Winnie Tomm

Essays by

Margaret Lowe Benston
Naomi Black
Kathleen Driscoll
and Joan McFarland
Micheline Dumont
Anne Flynn
Marsha Hanen

Jeanne Lapointe
Hilary M. Lips
Pamela McCallum
Thelma McCormack
Rosemary Nielsen and
E. D. Blodgett
Lynn Smith

Published by Wilfrid Laurier University Press
for The Calgary Institute for the Humanities

Canadian Cataloguing in Publication Data

Main entry under title:
The Effects of feminist approaches on research methodologies

Papers presented at a conference held on
Jan. 22-24, 1987 at the University of Calgary.
Bibliography: p.
Includes index.
ISBN 0-88920-986-3

1. Women's studies — Research — Congresses.
2. Feminism — Research — Congresses. 3. Research —
Methodology — Congresses. I. Tomm, Winnie, 1944-
II. Calgary Institute for the Humanities.

HQ1180.E44 1989   305.4'2'072   C88-095228-8

Cover design by Rachelle Longtin

Printed in Canada

The Effects of Feminist Approaches on Research Methodologies has been
produced from a manuscript supplied in camera-ready form by The Calgary
Institute for the Humanities.

TABLE OF CONTENTS

FROM THE DIRECTOR

The Calgary Institute for the Humanities was established at The University of Calgary in 1976 for the purpose of fostering advanced study and research in a broad range of subject areas. It supports work in the traditional humanities disciplines such as languages and literatures, philosophy, history, etc., as well as the philosophical and historical aspects of the social sciences, sciences, arts, and professional studies.

The Institute's programs in support of advanced study attempt to provide scholars with time to carry out their work. In addition, the Institute sponsors formal and informal gatherings among persons who share common interests, in order to promote intellectual dialogue and discussion. Recently, the Institute has moved to foster the application of humanistic knowledge to contemporary social problems.

The Calgary Institute for the Humanities was pleased to sponsor "The Effects of Feminist Approaches on Research Methodologies" conference (January 22-24, 1987). Credit for the idea and organization of this conference is due to Winnifred Tomm. To study this issue further, the papers given in the conference are now published by the Institute through Wilfrid Laurier University Press.

Harold Coward,
Director,
The Calgary Institute
for the Humanities.

ACKNOWLEDGMENTS

Dr. Harold G. Coward, Director of The Calgary Institute for the Humanities, The University of Calgary, is gratefully acknowledged for his unqualified support of the conference on "The Effects of Feminist Approaches on Research Methodologies" from which this anthology follows.

Mrs. Geraldine Dyer, Mrs. Jennifer Bailey, Mrs. Paty Poulton and Mrs. Cindy Atkinson have graciously worked with efficiency and supportive attitudes in the preparation of this volume. It was always a pleasure to work with them and I thank each one for that.

Professor Terence Penelhum's comments, in his response to Thelma McCormack's keynote address, provided a useful perspective in regard to the difficulties involved in reformulating the relation between objectivity and subjectivity in a theory of knowledge. I wish to express our appreciation for his generous contribution.

The task of selecting specialists from various disciplines in different parts of Canada was made possible through the assistance of several people. I wish especially to thank Gisele Thibault, who was a Post-doctoral Fellow in General Studies at The University of Calgary.

I am indebted to Karl, Jill, and Karma for their unfailing interest and supportive corrective feedback.

INTRODUCTION

Winnie Tomm

What difference does feminist methodology make to other methodologies? Is there a single feminist methodology or a multiplicity of feminist methodologies? Or are feminists simply adding new perspectives to existing approaches, rather than developing a separate feminist methodology or several distinct feminist methodologies? The papers in this volume address these issues. They were presented at a conference, held at The University of Calgary, which was organized for the purpose of responding to these questions. The authors explore ways in which feminist scholars conduct their research, paying particular attention to the gender factor and gender relations in the selection, interpretation, and communication of their material.

Since feminism emerged on the horizons of academe in the 1960s many critical paths have been laid across the landscape of academic research. Feminist hermeneutics begins with a guarded approach regarding "received wisdom" passed down to us through the ages since the beginning of recorded history. Received wisdom has been characterized by pervasive cultural assumptions including those made about the different roles men and women play in the symbol-making processes which give meaning to historical occurrences. It has informed us about which topics are important to research, who the appropriate subjects of research are, the kinds of people who are suitable for conducting research, the kinds of interpretations to be applied to the material selected for research, and the implications of the research to be communicated to the public. This received wisdom has, for the most part, been formulated by men. Hence, there is good reason for feminists in academia to proceed with caution.

Historically there has been a fairly close connection between the values which shape the nature of research and the dominant values of the society in which the research is conducted. That is, there is a reciprocal relation between social context and academic research. The notion of pure research which is free from value-laden theories is viewed with a skeptical eye by feminists. However, this skepticism is not unique to feminism. It is widespread in other approaches as well, especially in phenomenology—a perspective with which feminism has much in common. The distinguishing feature of feminism is the focus on gender-related values which have tended to privilege males in both the society at large and in academic research.

Two influential and apparently contradictory beliefs about the relation between men and women have co-existed throughout history. These two beliefs are: (1) men's and women's natures are complementary and equal to each other; and (2) men are more representative of the essential characteristic of human nature (i.e., rationality) and thus women's difference from men is associated with inferiority. The prejudice inherent in the second belief is now widely recognized. However, the fact that there is a slippery slope between the "different but equal" view of the sexes and the inferior status of women is not so obvious. Even when the "different but equal" view is maintained, the different spheres of male and female activities have usually been unequally valued. The domestic sphere of women's activities in which feminine qualities are extolled is still given less value than the public sphere in which masculine qualities are rewarded. These separate spheres of activity, involving different psychological attributes, have generally been argued for in terms of biological differences. These arguments have appeared in contrasting guises ranging from scientific fact (e.g. Aristotle) to romantic idealism (e.g. Rousseau). Traditional academic research has often added the influential weight of research authority to common sense opinion about the differential nature of males and females and the hierarchical relations between them.

In the 1960s academic women, like other populations of women, began to react to the ways in which dominant male interests dictated how women were supposed to think, feel, and act. Male subjectivity was examined. The so-called objectivity of male-defined rationality was found to be replete with unexamined pervasive prejudice against women's interests, especially with regard to academic research. The topics were defined by male interests, the methods used to illuminate the topics were devised by men, the messages communicated to the public were those which reflected the interests of the powerful who were usually men. The interests of the powerful have seldom included the interests of women.

In situations where women's interests coincide with those of men of influence, women have generally not been granted the same kind of authority that men have. Even when it is clear that a woman can produce a good argument, the decision about whether it is a good argument, i.e., whether it is to be listened to, is usually made by men.[1] Acceptance of women is too often contingent upon men's approval. It is the same for women doing research. The value of particular research endeavors has often been determined by those who are under the influence of historical biases (received wisdom) about that which is significant and that which is trivial. Women's interests which do not coincide with those of the ruling group are very often ignored. Even when good research is done in those areas it is not acknowledged in the way good research in traditional areas would be. The long-standing mythology about the importance and correctness of men's ideas and activities underpins the trivialization of women's participation in academic research.

In the early stages of feminist research there were attempts to "bring women into history," using traditional methodologies. A useful consequence of that approach was that feminists became more aware of significant women in history and of their significance to history. As a result of paying more attention to women as subjects of research, an important methodological insight emerged. It became clear that some of the techniques used in eliciting data were inappropriate when applied to women and that new approaches would have to be developed. An example of this kind of insight is found in the well-known work of Carol Gilligan (*In a Different Voice*). Her research shows that there are "two ways of speaking about moral problems" (1982: 1) and that "categories of knowledge are human constructions" (p. 6), depending upon contextualized experience. She emphasized the need to include women's descriptions of moral dilemmas and of conflict resolutions as they applied to their own lives. Gilligan illustrated the inappropriateness of applying theories of moral development based solely on men's experiences to the interpretation of women's descriptions of moral conflicts and their responses to them. As a result of her work we are more aware of gender specificity with regard to moral theory and the importance of devising questions appropriate to the social reality of the subject being questioned. The same principle can be applied to class or race; it is not specific to gender. However, gender is the focus in this book. Taking both genders into account is leading to the development of more appropriate methods of data collection and data interpretation, and, thereby, to greater acceptance of differences without the association of deficiency.

Another significant topic in feminist research that has had methodological implications is that of subjectivity vs objectivity, or qualitative vs quantitative. Objective, quantitative data-gathering methods depend on prior information which shapes the questions asked. They elicit answers that are interpreted according to the sets of pre-established questions. There is little space for new information categories to arise from questionnaire or statistical responses. There is no allowance for the effects of the questioner on the one who is questioned. The notion of objective research requires the assumptions that information is independent of personal influences and that the one asking the questions knows better than the subject what the important questions are. That is the case sometimes, but very often quantitative-type questions do not tap important information. That may be because the researcher has overlooked an area of interest, has deemed it unimportant, or merely assumes it is too "messy" to incorporate it into the determined categories. The categories of knowledge are determined independently of the subjects' responses. Often they do not relate to the actual circumstances of those being questioned. Objective, quantitative research methods are not usually successful, for example, in obtaining information about women's nurturing activities in the home. There are no established categories of knowledge into which such information would comfortably fit. That activity, therefore, is generally overlooked by researchers governed by the belief that research must be objective and quantifiable. This is not to say that quantitative methods are to be discarded. Rather, the process of unstructured information gathering on a large scale must precede the use of structured questions in order to increase the probability that the information which is to be quantified reflects the circumstances of the lives of the respondents. The lives of women have been largely overlooked in the interests of objective and quantitative research. In order to find out more about women's modes of experience and interpretation, it is necessary to observe their responses and listen to their descriptions.

The use of qualitative methods in research involves more generative interaction between the researcher and the researched. This necessitates greater self-scrutiny, especially on the part of the researcher. The researcher becomes more aware of the ways in which one's presuppositions about the subject as well as the methods of interacting with that individual shape the findings of the research. As one pays more attention to the experiences of the person with whom one is engaged one is likely to be more careful about assumptions regarding the other's reality. Erroneous assumptions about women have often been made because of lack of attention to what women themselves report. For example, Hilary Lips points out that the widespread belief that pregnant women are more emotionally labile than the general adult population, is not actually substantiated when the same questions are asked to pregnant women, nonpregnant women, and to men. Empirical testing showed pregnant women to be the least emotionally unstable. Belief in pregnant women's emotional instability was an assumption that had never been properly tested because of the mythology associated with pregnancy — mythology which includes many untested assumptions about women's physiology in general. These assumptions have often been made independently of careful observation or else on the basis of a small number which is mistakenly taken to reflect the majority's experiences. It is now acknowledged that good, objective research includes spelling out the subjective components such as reasons for the choice of research, the interests of the researcher which shape the interpretation of the data collected or text analyzed, and the impact of the research on the lives of individuals. The notion of pure research, which is free from the influence of the politically powerful, is strongly questioned by feminists.

This raises questions about the direction of influence of feminist politics. It may be the case, as Thelma McCormack points out in this volume, that the agendas of political, activist feminists and academic feminists differ more now than they did ten years ago. It cannot be denied, however, that feminist research is fundamentally oriented toward social change.

Much of the work of the late 1960s and 1970s was in response to a new awakening to the omission of women either as subjects of research or as designers of research. There was a recognition of institutionalized social patterns which render women's lives inconsequential in the traditional historical picture — characterized by accounts of wars, political parties, nuclear arms, ownership of property, church and state relations, competing ideologies, theoretical paradigms which reflect the highest orders of objective truths, and so on. Women were (and still are) esteemed for providing a safe home atmosphere apart from the public arena of competition. Because of their "privatization," women, as active subjects, were largely omitted from the political and social history we read about prior to the advent of feminism.

Feminist responses of the 1960s and '70s derived from two fundamental causes: (1) the systematic exclusion of women from history and (2) the fact that men's activities were overvalued while women's activities were undervalued. Feminist political activism and feminist research were motivated by both causes. Activism and research went hand in hand. The strong political activism which accompanied the awakening to the exclusion of women and to their trivialization has, as McCormack indicates, been transformed among feminist academics into a more quiet, determined program of providing substantive evidence of exclusion and of overcoming it. This is not to say that feminist research is independent of political interests; on the contrary, the implications of feminist research are necessarily political. According to Naomi Black, academic feminists of the late 1980s remain politically active while carefully deconstructing old myths and reconstructing new social and political structures, based on redefinitions of gender relations as outlined by the authors in this anthology.

All feminist academic researchers struggle with the difficult task of critiquing the androcentric framework from within which they are operating. Despite this handicap, feminists are developing new ways of bringing women into clearer focus, not as actors in a play directed by men on a stage which is designed by men but, rather, as creators and directors in their own right. As the authors in this volume make clear, it is necessary to hear women's own voices, uninterpreted by men, if they are to contribute significantly to the meaning-giving process of history, which is so heavily influenced by the authoritative voice of academic research.

The possibility for change comes from the fact that apparently we are not chained to the old framework. A loose analogy can be made between Plato's Allegory of the Cave (Bk. VII, *The Republic*) and the feminist awakening. In the Allegory, one man escaped outside the cave and saw the sun and real objects, such as trees, rather than mere reflections on the wall which he had thought were real objects when he was still chained inside the cave. Similarly, feminists have escaped, in part, the influence of the gender-biased groves of academe and see a new kind of knowledge. The problem that contemporary feminists face is similar to that encountered by the man who escaped from the cave. Both have been accused of making claims that are "off the wall." Their new reality is so radically different from that of others that it is difficult to communicate. Their way of knowing has changed to the extent that it is impossible to know as they knew before. The twelve authors in this anthology demonstrate the kinds of struggles which feminists are engaged in as they reveal to us the ways in which feminist approaches may improve and change research methods which allow us to know in ways that have not been part of more traditional accounts of knowledge.

In chapter 1, Thelma McCormack (sociology) raises concerns about current feminist emphasis on subjective knowledge. She claims that the existence of some form of objective evaluation is in the interests of feminists. Without recourse to an objective judgment women's views would most often be overruled by those of men. The problem, as I alluded to earlier, is that often the objective measure is largely a reflection of male subjectivity. The task entails a revision of the meaning of objectivity.

In chapter 2, Marsha Hanen (philosophy) examines the use of reason as it is used in the philosophical pursuit of objectivity. Because objectivity has been closely associated with rationality, re-evaluation of one term includes re-evaluation of the other. Hanen is not in favor of discarding the notion of objectivity and accepting complete relativism. She argues that there is an integral connection between objectivity and subjectivity that needs to be spelled out and which will allow for ways of knowing that have previously been excluded from accounts of knowledge. Feminist approaches promise to provide new avenues for a reformulation of knowledge.

In the search for a more adequate basis for knowledge, Hilary Lips (psychology), in chapter 3, stresses the importance of describing multi-causal, interdependent factors rather than isolating out single causes in any particular situation. Multicausal analysis can be done using statistical, quantitative methods or using qualitative interviews. Whichever method or combination of methods is used, it is important to spell out one's own values and dispositions, which are to be included in any causal account. There is no attempt to devalue causal determinism, but rather to include more interrelated factors in the explanation. A rational explanation includes nonrational factors. Nonrational factors such as feelings, interests, and dispositions belong in causal explanations. These include feelings, interests, and dispositions as described by the women who experience them, rather than only descriptions of them by a third party.

Third-party descriptions are appreciated by feminists, but they are to be placed in relation to first-person accounts. A major issue is that of including the testimony of more women in the research enterprise. Historically, the testimony of women has been valued less than that of men, accordingly women have not been considered as good research subjects as men. Men have, therefore, been the spokes*men* for human consciousness. Feminist approaches are overturning these assumptions about whose knowledge we accept, or rather, whose way of knowing, especially with regard to women.

Lynn Smith (law), in chapter 4, finds that the same kind of assumptions which privilege men are built into the legal system. In view of that, it is unlikely that reform within the existing system will allow for equally just treatment of men and women. The notion of special treatment for women arises in such cases as pregnancy, rape, and pornography. When men are taken as the norm, laws dealing with these issues, which are either exclusively or predominantly relevant to women, are seen to involve special treatment for women. The notion of special treatment for women relies on the androcentric view of person, i.e., that male is normative and female difference is associated with deviation from the norm. Feminist legal researchers have the difficult task of ensuring that laws which appear fair because they deal with men and women equally do not assume the androcentric view of person.

Whether one is doing scientific research, philosophical analysis, legal research, or literary textual analysis the overriding feminist orientation is the same—to include the voices of women in a significant way, to add women's history rather than merely add women to history. In chapter 5, Micheline Dumont (history) stresses the need to look at the relations between the sexes in cultural history in order to give a re-evaluation of human experience. It is not enough to look at the themes of equality and differences between the sexes in order to study the subordination and oppression of women. The issue of power relations between the sexes in political history is seen by Dumont as an important focus of feminist historiographical research and one which will change the study of history as a result of changing the notion of history. New interpretations of human experience are emerging from the study of the historical social relationships between the sexes. Feminists do not see history only in terms of wars, the evolution of men's activities, the developments in men's theories of knowledge, the establishment of new countries with fathers of confederation, and in general the changing of power from the hands of one set of patriarchs to those of another. Feminists aim to interpret history in a way that includes women's history as well as men's, through studying the social relationship between the sexes as it is experienced from both perspectives.

Pamela McCallum (English), in chapter 6, attempts to bring women's history into clearer focus through highlighting women's texts which have been excluded from the canon of great literature. She questions the value of maintaining a literary canon, which by definition is exclusive of genres which do not reflect the dominant orientation of the canonical texts selected by the established gatekeepers. The issue of bringing women into focus in literature is not just a matter of classification of literature, it is also a question of interpretation. Both McCallum's paper and that co-written by Rosemary Nielsen and E.D. Blodgett (classics), for chapter 7, describe the feminist task as that of reading a text from a woman's point of view so the women in literature can be responded to from the standpoint of women's realities rather than from the standpoint of male constructions of women's realities. A major problem in such a reader response approach from the classics perspective is to get past the barriers of classical languages which are believed to represent the male standpoint without giving adequate expression to the female's.

In chapter 8, Jeanne Lapointe (comparative literature) discusses ways in which literature is ultra-conservative in its portrayals of the male/female relationship. She describes six methods used by feminists to uncover these portrayals. Like Dumont, she places more emphasis on the relationship between the sexes than on the separate sex roles. Lapointe maintains that through the use of one or more of the six methods the ideology of male/female domination in literature becomes more visible. A characteristic feature of feminist literary works is that they are free from the conservative depictions of a hierarchical relationship between the sexes. A feminist heroine acts through her own power and gives direction to her own destiny rather than being directed primarily by her complementary relation to the dominant man (or men) in her life.

The history of dualisms (e.g., mind/body, reason/emotion, culture/nature, transcendence/immanence, men/women) influences our attitudes about what constitutes proper academic disciplines. In chapter 9, Anne Flynn (dance) claims that the practice of dance is not separate from the study of philosophy. She maintains that dance enables one to cultivate new ways of knowing, as discussed in earlier chapters, because it is fundamentally a holistic form of activity. Her discussion of knowledge from the perspective of dance provides a valuable balance to the other chapters in the discourse on redefining knowledge, which is the central theme connecting the chapters in this volume.

The orientation towards "ways of knowing" rather than on "having knowledge" is characteristic of the feminist approaches presented in this collection. The significance of the distinction between "ways of knowing" and "having knowledge" is that participation by the knower in the known is recognized as affecting the known and vice versa. The mutually informing effect of knower and known makes the separation of the two impossible. One does not really have knowledge, rather one knows about something in a particular way. This point is central to chapter 10, written jointly by Kathleen Driscoll (sociology) and Joan McFarland (economics). Gathering information is regarded more as a process of listening and describing rather than of fitting the data to the "objective" structure of inquiry. This approach is largely incompatible with the neo-classical tradition in economics which values pure theory above applied theory. The greater value placed on applied theory than on pure, ahistorical theory by feminists is a major point of difference between feminists and many nonfeminist researchers. Apart from any other reason that one may favor applied theory over pure theory, feminists claim that so-called pure ahistorical theory privileges male knowledge. Women's participation in such theory construction is minimal. In addition, these theories have the effect of increasing the importance of "objective" knowledge which has little or nothing to do with the average everyday world.

The question of whose knowledge prevails is examined in chapter 11 by Margaret Benston (computing science) as it applies to the domain of technology. Who controls the kind of knowledge that is programmed into central data systems? Who controls the terminology used in the network of controls? Who controls the methods of distribution of knowledge? Benston describes how gender-related knowledge is currently shaping the development of technology. These systems tend to be hierarchical in structure. There are, however, alternative system designs which will allow for greater sharing of input and usage of information. Like the other authors, Benston helps us see that there are many ways of knowing which can help to bring all of us together in a shared reality rather than to separate the authorities, who have knowledge, from those of us who do not.

Naomi Black (political science), in the last chapter, claims that a feminist perspective in politics and the study of politics is primarily oriented toward including women's voices in the records of history. This may involve redefining the notion of political so that it includes activities which are of particular interest to women, such as women's reform movements (which includes feminist movements). When women go public with their concerns, the separation between the private and public spheres is blurred. That obscuration changes the nature of both spheres. Politics is about power relations. When the gender factor is included in an analysis of power relations then gender relations must be a part of politics. Thus the private is political. Feminist approaches, as Black points out, are bringing women's agendas into the political arena. Feminists are sometimes criticized for having an agenda and finding the statistics to support it. McCormack, in the initial chapter, argues that feminist scholars cannot be accused of that today because of the improved scholarly standards of feminist scholarship since the 1960s. Black aptly points out that such a criticism is more appropriately placed at the door of sexist scholarship which assumes the privilege of male knowledge and interests and excludes women's knowledge and interests. Feminist scholarship, as described in the following pages, is changing the territory where knowledge is located. The old distinctions between that which is significant and that which is trivial are being challenged and new symbols of knowledge are emerging.

The authors of this volume are not only bringing women's voices into research, they are reformulating the guidelines for what constitutes good research. Ultimately they are contributing to a new theory of knowledge which begins with the assumption that research originates from an individual's particular set of interests and is invariably tied to the historical location of that individual. This assumption does not reflect feminist approaches exclusively. An additional assumption, tying the first to feminism, is that women's location in history is as important as that of men. This means that women's interpretations of social reality, literary works, historical perspectives, philosophical reasoning, and technological innovations are to be considered of equal importance in the selection, interpretation, and communication of research material. Feminist approaches are compatible with all other research approaches in so far as they acknowledge those two assumptions and their implications.

Endnote

1. I wish to acknowledge my debt to Judith Hughes, Philosophy Department, Newcastle-on-Tyne, for this account of authority and women.

Chapter 1

FEMINISM AND THE NEW CRISIS IN METHODOLOGY

Thelma McCormack

I

Insider and Outsider Knowledge

A few years ago the Toronto *Globe and Mail* sent one of its younger reporters up to Sudbury, a mining community in northern Ontario. When he returned, he wrote two or three feature-length articles that were a model of good social journalism. Interesting, critical, informative, they were well researched and well written. Sudbury was described as a wasteland. The physical environment was also unhealthy as evidenced by the statistics on the lifespan of residents. And the cultural life was no better; it was as impoverished as the land. He attributed much of this to the International Nickel Company, the corporation which dominated the economy, the culture, and the lives of people in the area. All in all, it was an excellent report in the best tradition of muckraking journalism.

But a few days later a letter appeared in the paper by a resident of Sudbury who was very disturbed, if not angry, by what he regarded as false information. He discussed his own life in Sudbury which covered over half a century, and he described his garden listing the various trees, shrubs, and flowers he had cultivated. So much for the suggestion that nothing can grow in Sudbury. As for health, he himself, he said, was in good health and now well over seventy years of age, thus giving the lie to the statement that people were plagued by health problems and their lives cut short by the environment either inside the nickel mines or outside of them. And, he continued, he had worked in the front offices of INCO for nearly fifty years before retiring. Therefore, he could say without reservation that INCO was one of the finest corporate citizens in Canada and possibly one of the great companies in the world.

I cite this case because it is not a hypothetical one on which we can reflect in a leisurely way. There are real consequences depending on which of the two accounts you believe, whose knowledge you trust. If you are an environmentalist, a union organizer, a public health officer or interested in social policy, the insider's knowledge may be too biased, too restricted by his own occupational history and lifestyle. But if you are a writer and want to explore the subjective dimension or are looking for a more personal vocabulary, the outsider's knowledge will be too distant, too removed from the everyday flux of experience, and the style too impersonal.

All of us are both; we are insiders and outsiders, shifting back and forth between these two modes of cognition just as, on another level, we involve ourselves in some issues and remain apart and satisfied to observe others. At the same time we are capable of reflecting on ourselves, correcting our own errors, recognizing our own biases, and selecting future directions. What we do then in our professional roles in the sciences is a more reflexive and systematic version of processes which go on normally and naturally throughout our lives.

Liberal and Post Liberal critiques of Science and Scientific Method

Nevertheless, if we look at the recent history and sociology of knowledge there has been a major criticism of the demands and austerity of nineteenth-century logical positivism. Within the social sciences with which I am most familiar, the canons of logical positivism were too restricting; we could not hope to be as objective as the natural sciences, nor could we build our knowledge in a social vacuum. Value-free knowledge was neither possible nor desirable. There were some who tried and claimed that we could and should aim to be as rigorous as the natural sciences, to adapt its rules for operational definitions and mathematical expression, to remain detached and disinterested.

But there were others who disagreed and who saw social science actively contributing in a positive way to social change. This liberal tradition in the social sciences, influenced, no doubt, by the collapse of democracy in Europe and the rise of Fascism, was sensitive to the larger world and had a strong sense of social responsibility. It was empirical rather than dogmatic, qualified in its judgments rather than absolute, disaggregating ideologies into testable hypotheses, for there was an underlying conviction that means and ends could not be separated. Liberal social science was to be the rational basis for a humane social change. Thus, in this liberal tradition, social science had one foot in the sciences, one foot in the humanities but was different from either.

In the post-liberal period, however, the two versions were conflated, and liberal social science stood accused of all the sins of logical positivism plus a few more. It was, from this more radical perspective, a mentality that shared a drive to control and to manipulate others, a way of apprehending the world that led inexorably to "body counts" in Vietnam and depoliticizing of political events. The differences then between the liberal and conservative traditions in the social sciences were minimal and, from this point of view, irrelevant, for they both accepted a concept of causality that was itself problematic.

Against this intellectual background, the insider's knowledge acquired a special privileged status. Authenticity became more important than truth claims.[1] No matter how deranged, according to R.D. Laing, the patient saw more clearly and more truly than the therapist. For many feminists who came into the social sciences, not in the 1940s but in the 1960s at the height of this debate, liberation from sexist knowledge was equated with a liberation from liberal social science and its logic. A new kind of knowledge which did not attempt to be objective, and was no longer attempting to "predict and control," knowledge without social causation and without looking for regularities that might lead to "laws," would obliterate the line between subject and object and create both a richer knowledge and a more ethical one. Knowledge would be consciousness-raising for both the people who carried out the studies and those who were studied. The investigator was also the one investigated, the interviewer became the respondent, and we could not objectify others because we could not objectify ourselves. Thus feminists were not only creating a distinctive epistemology, but providing a prototype for other epistemologies.

The impact of this critique was to create a distinction between a methodology for feminists and a feminist methodology. The new feminist methodology was not, then, a refinement of an older tradition of social research, it was a quantum leap, a Kuhn-ian passage from one paradigm to another. In the future, three hundred years from now we would look back at knowledge before feminism the way we look back at medieval scholasticism. For the present we are looking ahead to a postmodern research, a vision of a great step somewhat like the Reformation in the sixteenth century. Indeed, there is an interesting parallel between the emphasis feminist methodologists put on subjectivity and the emphasis Luther put on the inner voice. And just as people across Europe—some of whom were victimized by the breakdown of feudalism, others liberated by it—were drawn toward the new ideas of Luther, so women in the present era are looking for a postmodern knowledge that would restore both their identity and credibility, that would validate their intuitive knowledge about themselves and their ability to reason.

In Defense of Method

Feminist epistemology was anti-method and anti-rational. But it is not quite so simple, for if we look again at the case cited, and if we had two insiders, one of them a woman whose perceptions of the community were different from the man who wrote the letter, there is no question that in a patriarchal society, his views would be more credible than hers. In theory the two are equally valid; there is no reason to choose her account over his, but politically they are not; his views would carry more weight and be regarded as more credible. Feminist methodology in a patriarchal society and without the "controls" of a conventional scientific methodology may be more interesting and more therapeutic, but not less biased. The choice, then, was either to do no research, qualitative or quantitative, or to engage in critical examination of the discourse. Many who followed this through to its logical conclusion found themselves cut-off from the "do-ers," the knowledge builders who were incorporating some of this criticism into their own methods but were unwilling to remain on the outside.

A second concern was with the misunderstanding of science. Feminists who equate a conventional scientific methodology with rationalism and rationalism with phallocentric discourse, seriously misrepresent and overstate the rationality of scientific activity. The ideology of science is rational, and the final work is subject to logical criteria, but the doing involves a creativity and space for the imagination, so that the line between science and art is blurred. Descartes may have fled, as one writer put it, the "organic female universe of the Middle Ages and the Renaissance" but modern science has travelled a long way from the Cartesian vision of objective knowledge (Bordo 1986). This is true of the social sciences as well as the older physical and natural sciences. There, too, creativity calls for a less rigid system. And in the case of the social sciences where people study attitudes, values, opinions and other forms of subjective data, the analysis is expected to follow certain rules, but the processes of hypothesizing and data collection are nine-tenths intuitive and one-tenth reason.

That one-tenth, however, is important, for it is in the interests of all persons and especially women to protect a rationalist tradition. The alternate approaches are best suited to small groups, dyads, to families and other primary groups, but they are ineffective in large scale organizations where conflicts are structural. In a large-scale complex society we would need every bit of empiricism and careful reasoning we could muster to deal with the problems being faced by the community, the nation, and the world. Surrendering rationality in this domain leads only to charismatic leaders and counting the number of angels who can dance on the head of a pin. Hence, there has developed within the feminist community of scholars a division about method. And I am going to touch on some of these problems in my comments. I want to start by discussing the feminist critique of science and scientific method. I'm going to suggest that it is often based on a nineteenth-century model of scientific method and not the reality of twentieth-century social science. Second, I want to look at two approaches to a feminist methodology: a psychological approach based on the uniqueness of women's minds, and a structural approach based on research as a form of activity or work within organizations. I'm going to suggest that our present controversy over subjective vs objective knowledge reflects a distortion created by the organization of scientific activity and the marginality of women within those organizations. Following that I am going to suggest that the challenge to feminists is to find a methodology that avoids the "we-they" bias, and I am going to suggest, further, that in Canada because of our multicultural experience and history we are uniquely situated to provide that methodology; or at least, we have the right conditions for moving in that direction.

II

Feminist research began as a response to the feminist movement which had a strong will and deeply felt aspirations but little ideology and evidential knowledge to back up its claims. Feminist research was, then, highly political, the agit-prop arm of the movement. It was intended to persuade and mobilize, to raise the consciousness of women and to create a climate of opinion which would make the achievement of feminist goals that much easier. As feminist thinking became part of our "common sense," part of our folklore, there would be less resistance to its objectives. And it did that. We have been successful in sensitizing our neighbors to feminist issues. Often the research that was done had more impact on the people who did it than on the others who read it. In recent years that closeness between our research and our politics has changed; there is more distance between the activists and the academics, between theory and praxis, between polemics and scientific knowledge. Feminist scholarship has its own agenda, and feminist activists who turn to the literature find too many caveats and qualifications, too many "on the one hand this and on the other hand that" for their purposes. The pornography issue is a case in point where the research findings and the slogans point in different directions. The most famous and most often cited statement by Robin Morgan: "Pornography is the theory, rape is the practice" is not and never has been supported by research on either rape or pornography. Many similar assertions made about the effects of pornography on behavior are contradicted by the research. The result is, as you may have noticed, that feminists who are pushing for censorship legislation on pornography are citing research less and less; increasingly, they make their case on other grounds, e.g. "quality of life." But a decade ago, the political agenda and the academic agenda were more unified.

Then and now the goals of the movement were the same: equality and liberation, equity and self-determination. They were the same goals as the Civil Rights movement, and the same goals as the nationalist movements in the third world. Closer to home one could recognize the same aspirations among Quebecois. Indeed, feminism could be conceived of as part of a larger worldwide movement for justice and autonomy.

The first wave of feminist scholarship was preoccupied with documenting the discrimination against women in educational and research organizations. Professional women were either not employed or underemployed; unpaid or underpaid. A serious scandal was revealed in the case of Rosalind Franklin, a British scientist, who made a major contribution to the discovery of DNA but, who, according to her biographer, never knew it (Sayre 1975). Her work had been stolen, removed from her locked desk without her permission. Anne Sayre quotes a graduate student who had read *The Double Helix* and said that "the way to get on was to keep your mouth and your desk drawers locked..." (1975:195). In his amusing and vastly popular book on the discovery of DNA, Watson who received the Nobel Prize, dismissed Franklin's work and spoke of her in disparaging and stereotypic terms: the difficult neurotic woman (Watson 1968). It is probably more accurate to say that a crucial part of the DNA puzzle was discovered by Rosalind Franklin, and was given to Watson and Crick without her knowledge or authorization by Maurice Wilkins, the Director of her laboratory. Watson (1968:151) discusses the fact that he did not get her permission. He states:

> That her work had contributed very significantly to Crick and Watson's structure ... Rosalind never quite realized, and for the simple reason that she had no notion at all that anyone outside King's had access to her unpublished results, much less that anyone had used them (1968:171).

In short, it is safe to say that Franklin made an important contribution to the work on DNA by Watson and Crick who not only did not acknowledge her work, but gave the impression that she was another neurotic female who was difficult to work with and had no great capacity for science. They ignore completely the ethical issues involved in the way they procured her work surreptitiously and how they used it.

Along with exposés of the extent of gender discrimination within the scientific community, feminist scholars were engaged in disclosing the bias in the literature which claimed to be objective. These included the failure to mention women, as if they were invisible, or misrepresenting women in ways that emphasized their dependency. History, psychology, biology, philosophy, religion, law, sociology, political theory, fine arts, the humanities, as well as the more practical applications of these such as psychotherapy and social work, were all found to be seriously flawed. There were exceptions; women were not entirely missing, and there were outstanding women, like Margaret Mead, writing on women. The role-models were few but they existed. In spite of this, the overwhelming fact was that Canadian women confronted a large and prestigious body of knowledge which justified a subordinate status for women, a traditional division of labor along gender lines, and labelled as deviant women who chose careers or whose lifestyles, sexual or otherwise, were in any way a departure from these class-based norms. The real reason why R.E.A.L. women do not need research funds is that their research already exists; it has been done for them.[2]

We are in the minority. But I do not want to exaggerate this invisibility. We were not totally ignored in the past. However, what was damaging here was that the existing studies of women were often unpublished reports by social agencies of work left out of summaries and reviews of the literature because it did not seem important. Or they were misfiled. For example, a student interested in women's social movements would have found almost nothing, for the social movement literature is almost exclusively about men's movements and written by men. Women's movements are classified as voluntary organizations, a category that presumes leisure, or as collective behavior, a category that assumes hysteria. There was, then, work done on women but it went nowhere. Particular studies dropped out of sight and did not become a part of knowledge-building. Good or bad, these studies and monographs were isolated or subsumed under some other rubric. There was, then, no incentive, no professional pay-off in doing research on women, and no cumulative development. Nowadays, that is being turned around, and as we recover women's history by rediscovering some of these earlier studies and by doing original research on women's history, the new knowledge will become its own body of knowledge, its own intellectual domain.

Men sometimes have difficulty understanding this point; they recognize the injustice done to women in scholarship that barely mentions women; they understand, too, the resentment women feel about stereotypes and the general androcentric bias. But with good will on both sides, they argue, these past errors of omission and errors of commission can be corrected. What they do not grasp is that we are engaged in building a new knowledge with its own internal coherence and its own Gestalt. This is the rationale for special university-based research institutes in women's studies.

The early feminist scholars who demonstrated the extent of androcentric or sexist bias in our knowledge wanted corrections made but they were satisfied with a method which contained within it a mechanism for self correction. The challenge was elsewhere. In sociology, for example, we had two types of androcentricity. The first was the theory that the inferiority of women was based in biology. Sociobiology equated the inferior status of women in society with the inferior status of women in nature. Thus, there could be no change without endangering the species. The second type of androcentricity emphasized the social environment and the way it impacted on sex through the mechanisms of socialization and sex-role differentiation. In principle, the status of women, then, could be changed for it was not immutable. But so could everything else, and gender had no special status. Poverty and racism were the major problems for a liberal tradition so that gender as a variable never had the same preeminence as class or race. Thus feminist scholars were forced either to disregard class and race or push gender into the shade.

However, many feminists began to question the method itself. Male hegemony, they said, was not so much in the concepts of science or in its theoretical orientations, but in the method, in its logic which was equated with nineteenth-century positivism. What they meant by positivism was vague; the term itself had become a code word meaning, at best, "bourgeois" and, at worst, "reactionary" and supporting the status quo. In any case there have not been many pure positivists in the social sciences, and I am not sure there ever were, but the myth persists and recurs over and over again so that anyone who does any kind of quantitative research is called a positivist and accused of abetting patriarchy.

The same critique of positivism is sometimes applied to science. It too has become a scapegoat for all the problems of the modern world:

violence, hierarchy, exploitation, coercion. The more obscure or esoteric science is to the layperson, the easier it is to manipulate our anxieties about it, and displace our worries over other things on to science. But the critics of science and scientific method often confuse what it does with its misuses. Efforts made to demystify science can never keep up with the development of new knowledge. In any case, there is a tendency to attribute to science evil intentions and insensitivity about the social world as well as irresponsibility for the consequences of work.

Another fallacy is to equate the scientific method with nineteenth-century science, usually chemistry. But the social sciences have developed their own interpretation and applications of scientific method, and it is we who are influencing the physical and natural sciences today rather than the other way around. We tend to be interdisciplinary. Social psychology, political sociology, economic anthropology are examples of the interchange between disciplines, and within these disciplines we often synthesize both the methods of physical science and those of the humanities. In any case, the critiques of science are often unaware of the methods used in either natural or social science, and are basing their objections on an anachronism. Rejecting positivism, then, is beating a dead horse, while rejecting scientific method is uninformed criticism about the nature of scientific research in the natural sciences and the difference between them and the social sciences.

In recent years, however, this critique of science has become much more refined by scholars in linguistics who look not only at the method of science but the deeper structures of language and reasoning. Their work has questioned the central concept of scientific reasoning: *causality*. In the extreme, causality is described as a myth within a myth, a naive view which is not to be accorded any higher status than any other myth. But without a concept of causality (and in my own case a concept of *social* causality), there is little we can do in the social sciences except to talk about talk, and record how different people construct causality. No research can be done, for inevitably the doing of research is compromising.

III

The alternative is to develop a feminist science and a feminist way of knowing. Sandra Harding (1986) would add that we also need a feminist history of science. Like many others, she is not prepared to reject science and concentrate only on its discourse. Her goal and that of many women who are actively engaged in research is to set up criteria for a feminist philosophy of science.

The problem she identifies as central is the knower, the person or persons who initiate the research, carry it out, interpret its findings, and communicate them to others. If there is a feminist way of doing research it begins here. One model of the knower is based on a theory of a woman's mode of cognition. Another is based on the position of women in the structure and organization of science. I want to look at both and contrast them.

First the psychological approach. The main premise is that some women are as rational as some men and neither gender has an exclusive claim on rational thought. But the rationalism is itself different arising out of the experience of gender. An example of a work in this direction is a study done by a group of developmental psychologists, all of them trained in empirical methods and quite capable of computing a Chi-square (Belenky *et al.* 1986). But their method in this study is exploratory and entirely qualitative, consisting of 135 in-depth interviews with women, women who had very different backgrounds in terms of education and socio-economic status. The interviewers asked them how they would describe themselves, what being a woman meant to them, what their important relationships were, and about education. In addition, the interviews included some of the area covered by Carol Gilligan on how moral dilemmas were resolved (Gilligan 1982). But the main part of the interview concerned "ways of knowing"; that is, cognitive styles. In other words, the authors were not dealing with women's motivation, but with their intellectual or mental habits which become involved in responding to situations.

The categories for describing these modes of reasoning are based on the work of William Perry, and ranged from an extreme negative denial, which they call silence and where the women feel "deaf and dumb," to the highest level where subjective and objective kinds of knowledge are integrated. Between these points are, first, the type of person who takes on faith, without any criticism of the views of authorities which are held to be absolute and beyond question. Typically, each person believes that the views they have, based on authority, are held by everyone else. In any case, there are no competing authorities and no room for dissent.

But at the next stage are two forms of subjectivism where women begin to listen to themselves — indeed, may listen only to themselves — and are less deferential toward authority. They may, in fact, be hostile toward authority figures whom they distrust. Women in this group have very little doubt about their own felt truth, an experiential truth, and they feel no need to test it against some external reference or against the views of others like themselves. They have a kind of narrow self-sufficiency. "Subjectivist women," the authors say, "distrust logic, analysis, abstraction, and even language itself. They see these methods as alien territory belonging to men."

> It is not that these women have become familiar with logic and theory as tools for knowing and have chosen to reject them; they have only vague and untested prejudices against a mode of thought that they sense is unfeminine and inhuman and may be detrimental to their capacity for feeling (1986: 71).

A more advanced stage is what the authors call "procedural knowledge" or the voice of reason, and it is in this classification that we see people standing back from their feelings, testing different interpretations on what they observe, checking their own responses with others, and carrying out the different activities which we think of as rational discourse. They hold their personal opinions in abeyance, and are prepared to change them if and when they are convinced by the evidence. It is in this context that we see the cognitive styles of the professional scientists, but the authors maintain that this style of thinking is not limited to academic study. In their discussion of procedural thinking, they make an interesting observation about feminist thinking. "Women who rely on procedural knowledge," they say, "are systematic thinkers in more than one sense of the term. Their thinking is encapsulated within system. They can criticize a system, but only in the system's terms, only according to the system's standards. Women at this position may be liberals or conservatives, but they cannot be radicals. *If, for example, they are feminists, they want equal opportunities for women within the capitalistic structure. . . .When these women speak of 'beating the system' they do not mean violating its expectations but rather exceeding them"* [emphasis mine] (1986: 127).

Procedural knowledge, however, is only the penultimate stage. The final and highest form is "constructed knowing" where the two voices, inner and outer, subjective and objective, are integrated so that persons may be, as the authors say, "passionate about formal knowledge and analytic about one's personal life."

Procedural knowledge is where we have been; constructed knowledge is where we are going, and feminist scholars are, as Marxists say, in the vanguard. Bear in mind that we have seen two categories of feminists who are not likely to shift; nevertheless, I think we can see in the paradigm of constructed knowledge a kind of ideal feminist research.

If we have been unable to attain it, it is because of another factor. Our science, our knowledge-building is embedded in a patriarchal social structure and is carried out in bureaucratic organizations. The result of this combination is a deformation. Instead of moving toward "constructed knowing" which integrates the two voices, subjective and objective, feminist research has become polarized with procedural knowledge at one extreme and subjective knowledge at the other. This situation is not a psychological defect on our part, not a problem with the intellectual skills of feminist scholars who have failed to advance, as the developmental psychologists seem to imply. Rather, it is a consequence of the organization of scientific research. Bureaucratic structures with their built-in preference for easily processed research are conducive to procedural knowledge, while our marginalization within these structures produces a micro-scale subjectivism. Thus, the polarization is not an arrested development at an earlier stage but a counter-scientific culture.

If we start, then, from an organizational perspective rather than a psychological one, the feminist scholar who is marginalized at all levels — the immediate laboratory, the university or research institute, and the wider professional circles — brings to her work the insights and habits of the marginalized professional. Being a women defines her research agenda; being a marginal determines how she goes about it.

IV

One lesson feminists can learn from Marxist analysis is that unless we own and control the means of production, we do not determine either our own agenda or how we engage in the research. As I indicated earlier, we are currently building not a systematic body of feminist knowledge but a patchy counter-scientific culture which we hope will be magically transformed. Yet, under ideal circumstances there is no guarantee that good feminists will do good research.

Lately we have become more critical of feminist research and have insisted on higher standards in our own journals. Younger feminist scholars are experiencing more difficulty in getting published in feminist publications because of the stricter application of standards. Feminist gatekeeping is sometimes as frustrating and unfair as sexist gatekeeping. But the truth is that feminist research has moved from being celebratory to becoming more self-critical, while some of the ideological conflicts in the past have been replaced by eclecticism.

In the long run, however, the objectivity of scientific knowledge which determines its credibility lies in its cumulative form, and this is a matter of many scholars and many generations. The major control, then, and the only control that works in scientific research, is the system we use in recruiting people into research. If we are all white, middle-class feminists, if we replicate ourselves, feminist research will be biased even though our individual studies are beyond reproach. Our first concern, then, must be broadening the base of our recruitment from the ranks of women and insuring that we maintain a pluralism in our research designs: quantitative and qualitative, comparative and longitudinal, laboratory and field, experimental and survey, case histories and group studies, participant observation and interview studies.

A second bias is a narrow parochialism, of studying Canadian women as if they had no connections with women elsewhere. We attend international conferences, and we do research in other countries, and in cultures different from our own. But we do not bring them together so that we have a better understanding of how these cultures impact on us, and how we impact on them. We have no sense of our *interdependency* as women. We know we belong to a world community, but we have very little notion of the lines which connect us in different ways.

One reason for this blind spot is the misperceptions that develop out of modernization or development studies which project a vertical model of underdeveloped, less developed, developed, and highly developed. Within this framework, we come to see ourselves as victims within our own culture but privileged by world standards. Unconsciously, we have internalized a model of progress or modernization which puts us close to the top on a wide range of social indicators. Women at the lower levels of the modernization scale become our pupils, our dependents. Thus, the enemy within us is a "we-they" attitude which runs contrary to our ethic, and is in addition counterproductive. It undermines our ability to communicate and relate to others as equals. Needless to say, the problem of "we-they" is no better in its reverse form of "they-we" where any culture seems superior to our own. Until we can begin to see ourselves through a different imagery, one that is more horizontal and less sequential, an imagery which recognizes the validity of historical and cultural differences, we are condemned to studying only ourselves though we may place ourselves somewhere else — in South East Asia, in the Middle East, Latin America, the Caribbean, or Africa. Women in those countries are quick to sense our patronizing attitude and either conceal their own behavior or conform to our expectations. In effect we become both *egocentric* and *ethnocentric*.

How do we think ourselves out of this? In a recent article (1985), Susan Mann Trofimenkoff talks about the role of feminist biography and its place in feminist social history. Biography is not popular with feminists, she notes, who prefer to think in terms of aggregates and social collectivities rather than individuals. We are ambivalent about the study of biography even when the persons in question are, as Trofimenkoff says, women on our side, one of our "worthies." She outlines three major advantages in studying biographies, and these seem to me relevant to our self-education in studying other cultures.

The first is that when we research or read a biography, we are examining the lifecycle of the woman, the transitions she makes in a maturing and aging process, and how these transitions are mediated by the culture. Second, biographies allow us to study at close range the patterns of relationships women have both within families and outside of them. Third, we can see in the texture of a person's life how she confronts the constraints placed on her by roles and rules which may be formal or informal. It seems to me if we begin to study women in all cultures through the three categories which she describes, our understanding of women would be both less egocentric and ethnocentric. Biographical studies by feminist historians create a resource for other social scientists who want to understand the value systems and the ways of Being in different cultures and at different times.

Along with this we need to develop a world model based on feminist indicators and the connections of women to women. What would the economic map look like if we traced only women producers and women consumers? Would the regional disparities be as wide? Does the metaphor of North/South apply or do we need something with less slope?

Canadian feminists have an advantage. Our multiculturalism is a microcosm of the world which makes it possible for us to work through a method that is feminist and sensitive to cultural differences. The method would begin by recognizing the right of all cultures or ethnic groups to set their own agendas. That is a basic principle for any horizontal paradigm, but also incorporates the feminist value of self-determination. When these different agendas are assembled, we can begin to see how we relate to each other economically, politically, and culturally. We may find there are greater differences within ethnic groups than between them but that is a straight empirical question.

We should expect that as we look at the priorities of women in the various subcultures of Canada that there may be conflict. For one group to achieve its goals, it might be at the expense of another. Conversely, we may discover that what we have thought was a conflict was not. In any case, resolving these differences provides us with experiences and techniques that can be used on a larger scale. Canada's unique contribution to feminist research is, I suggest, in the way we have turned our *given* multiculturalism into a *feminist* multiculturalism.

V

A feminist methodology is not radically different from other methodologies in the social sciences: in part, because there has been a tradition in the social sciences of studying stratification and disadvantaged groups, and in part, because our methods have been varied and flexible. In the early days of feminist research we were really drawing on an existing methodology based on a liberal tradition. But as our attention focused more sharply on gender we began to sense some of the limitations of a method which had ignored gender. This, in combination with the strong conviction that research ought to do more than describe the world, that it ought to change it, or at least change us, led to a crisis in our thinking about methodology and a search for some creative solutions.

Many of the criticisms feminists made about methodology in the social sciences had already been made by others, in particular, by critical theorists. Some were coming out of a new emphasis on consciousness and semiotics. The resulting disarray within the feminist community left one feminist, Evelyn Fox Keller, who had done pioneering work in exposing the sexist biases in science, to wonder whether she would have to choose between feminism and science (Keller 1982). She warned that women who rejected concepts of objectivity and rationality would soon find themselves not laying the foundations for a New Jerusalem but writing a script that "dooms women to residing outside of the realpolitik modern culture." (1982: 593). I have arrived at a similar conclusion: that women would go from a marginal position in the scientific establishment to no position.

I was suspicious, too, that if I agreed to give up a model of research reflected in the newspaper articles on Sudbury, and chose, instead, the spectrum of insider perceptions, that the man from Sudbury's views would not be equal to that of women in Sudbury; his would count for more. If I had to choose between male subjectivity and male objectivity with all of its limitations, I would infinitely prefer the latter if only because it was more accountable and vulnerable to the criticism of bias. But it was not a choice I was comfortable with.

What I have suggested here is that when that choice is translated into feminist terms, subjective feminism vs objective feminism, it is a no-win situation. It polarizes us and distorts what we are trying to do. Neither of the options can do what needs to be done: (1) to prove the unprovable, (2) to demonstrate that gender equality is a viable option in modern social life and (3) that the oppression of women through symbolic systems destroys the richness and decency of culture.

We have typically seen our methodology as a way of discovery with a certain value framework and a system of communication. But as we began to question the status of methodology, as more feminist scholars wrote more articles about epistemology, methodology became an end-in-itself. And it seemed as if we would have to solve the methodology problem first before we could carry on. It looked, too, as if the methodology would determine the direction of research. That period is now over and we no longer think of methodology as an end-in-itself; it is the means. But in the discussion that has been taking place within the feminist movement and among its friends we have also learned that the meaning of methodology is not static, and that like the content of science, methodology grows and changes; it, too, reflects the social structure. The impact of feminist research on methodology, then, was to challenge the received meaning of methodology, but the new feminist methodology, that goes beyond either procedural or subjective knowledge, will serve all of us who care about social justice.

Endnotes

1. I want to thank Professor Terence Penelhum of The University of Calgary whose comments on this paper have helped me to clarify my thinking on this point.

2. R.E.A.L. (an acronym for Realistic, Equal, Active and for Life) is a national organization of Canadian women which supports traditional values with respect to gender, the family, and sex roles. Its members oppose abortion, pay equity, day care, and other feminist goals. Recently, when the organization applied to the Secretary of State for a grant under the Women's Program, it was turned down on the grounds that it was not furthering equality as envisioned by Section 15 of the Charter of Human Rights. Hence, my comments that since we have inherited a body of knowledge that is deeply patriarchal, conservative women like R.E.A.L. do not need funding for research; it has already been done for them.

References

Belenky, Mary Field; Clinchy, Blythe McVicker; Goldberger, Nancy Rule; and Tarule, Jill Mattuck.
    1986   *Women's Ways of Knowing*. New York: Basic.

Bordo, Susan.
    1986   The Cartesian Masculinization of Thought. *Signs* 11: 439-56.

Gilligan, Carol.
    1982   *In a Different Voice*. Cambridge, Mass: Harvard.

Harding, Sandra.
    1986   *The Science Question in Feminism*. Ithaca: Cornell University.

Keller, Evelyn Fox.
    1982   Feminism and Science. *Signs* 7: 589-602.

Sayre, Anne.
    1975   *Rosalind Franklin and DNA*. New York: Norton.

Trofimenkoff, Susan Mann.
    1985   Feminist Biography. *Atlantis* 10: 1-9.

Watson, James.
    1968   *The Double Helix*. New York: Signet.

Chapter 2

FEMINISM, REASON, AND PHILOSOPHICAL METHOD

Marsha Hanen

If I were asked what effect feminist methods, approaches, and concerns have had in philosophy, I would say: "relatively little." There has been some recognition of the standard point about nonsexist language, so that fewer journal articles these days use the male pronoun and pretend it is neutral, and the various divisions of the American Philosophical Association are in the process of adopting a policy on this matter. The Canadian Philosophical Association, however, has so far done nothing, nor do any of the Canadian philosophical journals have a policy, so far as I know. Still, pockets of recalcitrance notwithstanding, I would say that the reform of language has been fairly general, though important books that proceed as though all persons were male, as though the discussions about sexist language of the past fifteen years had not occurred, are still regularly published.[1]

The deeper point, though, is that most feminist work in philosophy is done, read, and discussed by women. Few male philosophers, in my experience, are interested in it, and it is not uncommon even today to hear them opine that it is not philosophy. Furthermore, much of the feminist work that has been done has been in one of two modes: in epistemology we have seen critiques of traditional dualistic ways of thinking (Bleier 1984); in ethics we have seen attempts to incorporate women into the dominant ethical/political paradigms such as liberalism or Marxism (Jaggar and Rothenberg 1984). This has been very valuable work, but it has only recently reached the point of attempting to reconstruct philosophical categories in a way that takes account of women's experience. That most of the constructive work is yet to be done is hardly surprising, of course, given the relative newness of the concerns; but one hopes that now that sustained works of feminist philosophy are beginning to appear (Grimshaw 1986; Harding 1986; Jaggar 1983; Lloyd 1984), they will receive more general attention in the philosophical community.

Two things make me pessimistic. First, there appears to be a widespread belief that feminist philosophy has to do with ethics and politics only, so that those who do epistemology, metaphysics, or philosophy of language have a license simply to go on as before. That our ideas of rationality are neutral and apply to everyone, regardless of circumstance, is an article of faith which most philosophers still find hard to examine. Second, even where there appears to be recognition that the feminist critique is broader than just an examination of political philosophy, the essentially radical nature of the critique has not been recognized (or, perhaps, has been recognized but has been suppressed). Thus we have believed that it is enough to have more women in the professoriate as role models for female students, or that it is enough to provide a course or two in each department that incorporates feminist research and that is taken primarily by women. These things are important, but they are not enough. Feminist research is providing some of the most exciting ideas in philosophy today and we need to have far more of the best minds, female and male, engaged in examining them and building upon them.

In order to indicate some of what I have in mind, I want to discuss briefly two recent contributions to the philosophical literature. These are very different from one another in style, method, and subject matter; what they have in common besides being feminist works is that neither is explicitly concerned with problems of ethics or politics, though both have profound implications for those areas.

The first work I want to say a bit about is Genevieve Lloyd's *The Man of Reason* (1984). Drawing on work spanning virtually the entire history of philosophy from Plato through Philo, Augustine, Aquinas, Bacon, Descartes, and Hume to Kant, Rousseau, Hegel, Sartre, and Beauvoir, Lloyd tries to show that

> the maleness of the Man of Reason. . .is no superficial linguistic bias. It lies deep in our philosophical tradition. This is not to say that women have their own truth or that there are distinctively female criteria for reasonable belief. It is, however, to make a claim which is no less a scandal to the pretensions of Reason. Gender, after all, is one of the things from which truly rational thought is supposed to prescind. . . . The aspiration to a Reason common to all, transcending the contingent historical circumstances which differentiate minds from one another, lies at the very heart of our philosophical heritage. The conviction that minds, in so far as they are rational, are fundamentally alike underlies many of our moral and political ideals. And the aspiration has inspired, too, our ideals of objective knowledge. The claim, repudiated by relativism, that Reason delivers to us a single objective truth has often been substantiated by appeal to

Reason's supposed transcendence of all that differentiates minds from one another (Lloyd 1984: ix).

Lloyd is very careful to distinguish her claims from more extravagant ones involving sexual relativism about truth or the suggestion that the principles of logical thought are somehow sexually relative. Nevertheless, she finds that the philosophical tradition which forms the intellectual context within which we all work has formed our ideas of rationality in relation to what is conceived of as male.

What is valued — whether it be. . .'aggressive' as against 'nurturing' skills and capacities, or Reason as against emotion — has been readily identified with maleness. Within the context of this association of maleness with preferred traits, it is not just incidental to the feminine that female traits have been construed as inferior — or, more subtly, as 'complementary' — to male norms of human excellence. Rationality has been conceived as transcendence of the feminine; and the 'feminine' itself has been partly constituted by its occurrence within this structure (1984: 104).

These are profound claims which need both to be taken seriously and to be developed further. One of the things Lloyd shows is that philosophy's pretensions to timeless truth have done the discipline a considerable disservice. The history of philosophy, like any history, is a reflection of "the characteristic preoccupations and self-perceptions of the kinds of people who have at any time had access to the activity" (1984: 108). Though most of us, trained as analytic philosophers of whatever particular persuasion, were taught to examine the views of philosophers of other ages quite apart from their historical and social context, this activity has now come to be seen as providing at best a partial and distorted picture of these views and of those who held them. That reason has been taken to be involved with abstract thought, transcending the particular, the merely contingent, the private realm associated with female thought and activity is viewed by Lloyd as no accident.

Philosophers have at different periods been churchmen, men of letters, university professors. But there is one thing they have had in common throughout the history of the activity: they have been predominantly male; and the absence of women from the philosophical tradition has meant that the conceptualization of Reason has been done exclusively by men. It is not surprising that the results should reflect their sense of Philosophy as a male activity (1984: 108).

What Lloyd tries to show, then, is that our ideas of femininity have themselves been partly constituted through this exclusion. This, of course, tells us nothing at all about whether there are distinctively female ways of thinking or knowing; indeed Lloyd herself seems more inclined to look for ways of reconceptualizing reason and thinking in a way that will not be exclusionary of either men or women. Clearly, though, this is an area that requires much work, for we are still far from having an analysis of rationality that is integrative in the way that Lloyd wants.

The second book I want to speak about briefly is Sandra Harding's *The Science Question in Feminism* (1986). It provides a sharp contrast with Lloyd's book, thus underscoring what we all know anyway—that feminism is not monolithic and that there is no such thing as *the* feminist standpoint, method, or view. Harding begins by asking how science, and especially philosophy of science, can incorporate women's experience—a question which is quickly transformed into the question of whether a feminist outlook can incorporate science as we know it. Harding's science, like Lloyd's reason, is largely a male construction whose pretensions to objectivity have excluded women, their questions, and their approaches.

Harding discusses five interrelated research programs that have both expressed a number of feminist critiques of science and have raised questions for one another. None of these constitutes a developed feminist theory: it is Harding's contention that it is too early in the evolutionary process of feminist theorizing for that. The first program she identifies concerns itself with equity issues—the "massive historical resistance to women's getting the education, credentials, and jobs available to similarly talented men" and also "the psychological and social mechanisms through which discrimination is informally maintained even when formal barriers have been eliminated" (1986: 21). Second, we have studies of the abuses of biology, technology, and the social sciences in the service of sexist (not to mention racist) social projects. As Harding points out, there are often questionable assumptions underlying each of these research programs—in the first case the assumption that equality with men in science as it is should be our goal, and in the second case that pure science is value free and distinguishable from its social uses, and that there is somehow a clear distinction between the proper and improper uses of science. The third program raises just these questions about the fundamental value-ladenness of all knowledge-seeking—not least in the selection and definition of what requires explanation, what is to be seen to be of interest and so on.

Fourth, we have studies that use historical interpretation, literary criticism and psychoanalysis to "reveal the social meanings – the hidden symbolic and structural agendas – of purportedly value-neutral claims and practices" (1986: 23). And fifth, we have the development of alternative epistemologies – Harding identifies them as feminist empiricism, the feminist standpoint, and feminist postmodernism. According to feminist empiricism, sexism in science can be corrected by stricter adherence to proper scientific methodology. Feminist standpoint epistemologies argue that "men's dominating position in social life results in partial and perverse understandings, whereas women's subjugated position provides the possibility of more complete and less perverse understandings" (1986: 26). One serious question here is whether there can be a single feminist standpoint, given the variety of women's experience in relation to culture, class, race, and other factors. Feminist postmodernism is closely related to a number of intellectual movements in philosophy and criticism which "share a profound skepticism regarding universal (or universalizing) claims about the existence, nature and powers of reason, progress, science, language and the 'subject/self'" (1986: 27-28).[2]

As she develops her exposition and criticism of these five strains in feminist thought (and we should remember that her particular five are not necessarily the only ones possible), Harding points to a number of things that are interesting for our purposes. One is that there is much in common between the developments in feminist theorizing about science, especially in relation to the last two research agendas, and recent developments in what some like to think of as more "mainstream" post-Kuhnian philosophy and sociology of science. I develop this point shortly in another connection.

The other feature that I find most challenging and worthy of further thought arises from Harding's identification of various tensions and even incoherences not only in traditional thought about science, but in the feminist critiques themselves. The central strain in recent epistemology has treated as valuable without question simple, coherent theories that attempt to make sense of all the available relevant data. What seems not to fit must be explained away – the "dirty test tubes" model – but the possibility is rarely considered that the tensions between the pressures for a totalizing theory and our recognition of differences and specificities that resist bringing together under one non-trivial theoretical umbrella are somehow irresolvable at this time. It makes us very uneasy not to have a theory, an answer, but Harding suggests that we may be in such a position and that it may not be such a bad thing to recognize it. She writes:

> Instead of fidelity to the assumption of patriarchal discourse that coherent theory is not only a desirable end in itself but also the only reliable guide to desirable action, we can take as our standard of adequate theorizing a fidelity to certain parameters of dissonance with and between the assumptions of these discourses. This approach to theorizing captures the feminist emphasis on contextual thinking and decision-making, and on the processes necessary for gaining understanding in a world not of our own making—that is, where we recognize that we cannot order reality into the forms we might desire. We need to be able to cherish certain kinds of intellectual, political, and psychic discomforts, to see as inappropriate and even dangerous certain kinds of clear solutions to the problems we have been posing (1986: 246).

This sort of suggestion does not sit comfortably with any of our standard philosophical presuppositions. After all, philosophy takes itself to be the paradigm of the rational enterprise, and the *sine qua non* of rationality is consistency. But such tensions are not unknown in philosophy or even in science, and it appears to be Harding's point that attempts at resolution at this historical moment may be premature. She is not, so far as I can see, arguing that there is any positive virtue in inconsistency. Nor would I. Her point, I think, is that neat and tidy theories that also take account of the multiplicity of information we have are not now available; and to insist on them may result in a distortion of what we know and experience to the point of rendering the theories at best irrelevant, and probably false. The argument on the other side, of course, is that there is value in trying to achieve order and coherence—indeed human beings can hardly avoid doing this—even if this means that our theories require almost constant revision. Harding's point about accepting incoherence if we must, seems quite compelling, at least in the short run; but one cannot help worrying that accepting it will paralyze us into giving up the attempt to achieve coherence and reconciliation, and that seems self-defeating.

One interesting thing that emerges from the work of both Lloyd and Harding (and one could cite a larger number of others) is that developments in feminist philosophy have paralleled certain developments in philosophy more generally, so that some of the themes can be said to be part of the philosophical *zeitgeist*. I wish to cite here just three of the most obvious examples. Before I do, let me mention that much recent European philosophy pursues these themes even more fruitfully than the work I am about to discuss, but I confine myself to English-speaking writers for reasons of familiarity.

Perhaps the most discussed work in this vein, both within and without philosophical circles, has been that of Richard Rorty. In both *Philosophy and the Mirror of Nature* (1979) and *Consequences of Pragmatism* (1982) Rorty criticizes the standard philosophical claim to provide a timelessly true representation of reality. He sees the historical embeddedness of all thought and recognizes that this affects our conception of reason as much as it does our conception of the nature of reality. Interestingly enough, Rorty is much cited not only in the philosophical tradition often thought to have emerged from the work of Kuhn and Hanson, but also by literary critics and scholars seeking a philosophical basis for the "anything goes" approach to postmodernist literary interpretation.

Rorty attempts a very wide-ranging dissolution of the philosophical tradition, particularly with respect to the centrality of epistemology and the search for a theory of the nature of truth. He argues that there is no such thing as a natural starting point: all are bound up with historical and cultural traditions, and there are no neutral terms in which to formulate philosophical or any other problems. There is not even one thing that is meant by the term "philosophy." "Philosophy," he says, "is not the name of a natural kind, but just the name of one of the pigeonholes into which humanistic culture is divided for administrative and bibliographical purposes" (1982: 266). Radical thoughts, these.

Rorty argues for a pragmatist conception of philosophy that is related to recent movements in literary criticism and hermeneutical approaches to the social sciences. Pragmatism, he says,

> views science as one genre of literature — or, put the other way around, literature and the arts as inquiries, on the same footing as scientific inquiries. Thus it sees ethics as neither more "relative" or "subjective" than scientific theory, nor as needing to be made "scientific." Physics is a way of trying to cope with various bits of the universe; ethics is a matter of trying to cope with other bits. Mathematics helps physics do its job; literature and the arts help ethics do its. Some of these inquiries come up with propositions, some with narratives, some with paintings. The question of what propositions to assert, which pictures to look at, what narratives to listen to and comment on and retell, are all questions about what will help us get what we want (or about what we *should* want) (1982: xliii).

Needless to say, these views are extremely controversial, and there is in any case no explicit attention paid to feminist concerns. But some of the approach and sense of what is or is not problematic is certainly closely related to what we have seen so far of feminist philosophy. The point is that feminist philosophy, like any number of other recent developments, participates in general culture both as cause and effect of changing ideas and ideologies. For all its frequently being ignored by what is often called "mainstream" philosophy, feminist thought is in some (though by no means all) respects on the same track.

Another interesting connection to recent work in literary interpretation comes through the work of Ronald Dworkin on interpretation in law. Dworkin, who has been developing an anti-positivist theory of law over the past twenty years argues, in his most recent book *Law's Empire* (1986), that law is fundamentally interpretive: there is no text "out there" whose meaning appears on its face. Meanings have to be constructed in the same way that the meaning of a work of art or literature is constructed — by construing it in the way that makes of it the best possible work of art. Dworkin actually believes there is a single best such interpretation, and he believes the same thing of the law. A hard case in civil law has a uniquely correct answer even though what that answer is may be controversial among equally well-trained, intelligent and sincere lawyers and judges. The best answer is the one that exhibits law as integrity: coherence with the main thread of past decisions as well as the principles of justice and fairness.

The feature of Dworkin's view that is interesting for our purposes is its holistic character — its emphasis on the connectedness of law both historically and doctrinally. A decision in a hard case requires that we interpret past decisions (or legislation or constitutional provisions) in a way that makes the best sense of the historical record of cases while at the same time cohering with our political morality. There are, of course, troubling features about this way of conceiving coherence. It embodies strong conservative pressures arising from institutional legal history, so that it is not clear how we can ever expect to transcend a background that has excluded women from so many of the realms over which law has had control. Certainly many feminists have questioned whether any standard liberal political framework, however subtly conceived, can be adequate to account for women's concerns (MacKinnon 1982). I shall return to this point shortly. For the moment it is important just to see the Dworkinian approach as one that attempts to see law as a holistic, developing, integrative enterprise rather than one in which timeless abstract truths are articulated without connection to social context.

Another interesting feature of Dworkin's approach is his conception of objectivity. Interpretive claims in law and literature are more like scientific judgments in that they are parts of very complex systems of beliefs with many levels and "internal tensions, checks and balances" (1985: 170) than they are like simple judgments of taste.[3] Furthermore, interpretive judgments can be objective without our being able to claim that everyone agrees to them. Objectivity does not require correspondence with some external reality though it does require that we be prepared to offer arguments for our judgments. Still, at least in principle, this view of objectivity does not require the non-involved stance that abstracts from all particular features of the case in question. Hilary Putnam argues, in a similar vein, that

> much of the emptiness of current social science arises from the attempt to study social and psychological questions with an entirely false ideal of "objectivity" which misses even the connections of the social sciences with each other, in addition to missing the questions of the greatest importance to moral reflection (1978: 93).

On the other hand, that there is a correct or "best" interpretation of any legal text even if there is no theory-independent fact of the matter against which to check our interpretations is hard to reconcile with more relativistic approaches to literature which always presume a point of view. Dworkin insists, of course, that the existence of a single best interpretation does not imply that all sensible judges or literary critics will agree about that interpretation; nor does the existence of controversy go any way toward showing that there is no best interpretation. Legal or literary interpreters can only attempt to persuade one another but, where no unique interpretation emerges, substantive political theory (or artistic theory, in the literary case) will be decisive. Thus conservative, liberal, or radical interpretations of crucial and difficult parts of law may be expected to differ, and the interpretive question concerns which conception is the best in the context of the whole of law.

Still, when it is interpretation we have in mind rather than legislation, Dworkin would argue that existing law must be preserved, and thus that it is not open to us simply to declare vast portions of the law to be wrong and in need of reform if not even more drastic change, as many feminists would wish to do. He claims that his conception of interpretation based on principle accounts for the shift from Plessy v. Ferguson (separate facilities for whites and blacks are acceptable as long as they are equal) to Brown v. Board of Education[4] (separate facilities are inherently unequal); and presumably he would argue that similar shifts away from sexism in law could equally well be accounted for and, indeed, would be required by the principles that underlie constitutional adjudication.[5]

Feminists would surely be skeptical of this claim. Part of the difficulty, I suspect, is that Dworkin's approach, like that of many philosophers in the Anglo-American tradition, is in a deep sense ahistorical. Although he makes frequent appeal to previous legal decisions, he makes little effort to place them in their social or historical context, or to understand them as the product of social forces which include but are not limited to doctrinal matters or "black letter law." It is this failure that makes his work seem to lack a clear tie to the realities of the social relations that produced the law at particular times; and his insistence on a single best interpretation closely tied to existing law does not appear to leave sufficient scope for the kind of social change many feminists advocate. Still, these difficulties should not blind us to the possible helpfulness of Dworkin's conceptions of interpretation and coherence in pursuing a revision of philosophy along feminist lines.

The third development in recent philosophy that parallels some of the concerns of feminist philosophers is the challenge to realism that we find in the writings of people like Hilary Putnam and Nelson Goodman. Goodman, for example, argues in his two most recent books for a view he calls "irrealism," which is even more radical than the original anti-realism of Dummett (1978) or van Fraassen (1980). Thus he says:

> I am convinced that there is not one correct way of describing or picturing or perceiving "*the world*," but rather that there are many equally right but conflicting ways — and thus, in effect, many actual worlds. We must, then, inquire into the standards, compatible with such multiplicity, of rightness of rendering of all sorts, in all media, in symbol systems of every variety (Goodman 1984: 14).

Goodman claims that there is no independent world against which to match a version or description. "Any notion of a reality consisting of objects and events and kinds established independently of discourse and unaffected by how they are described or otherwise presented must give way to the recognition that these, too, are parts of the story" (1984: 67). Thus reality depends upon discourse and other means of symbolization, the correctness of which derives not from correspondence with the "external world," but from appropriate categorization and related things.

Similarly, Bas van Fraassen argues for a view he calls "constructive empiricism." He says "scientific activity is one of construction rather than discovery: construction of models that must be adequate to the phenomena, and not discovery of truth concerning the unobservable" (1980: 5). And Hilary Putnam tell us that there is

> nothing in the history of science to suggest that it either aims at or should aim at one single *absolute* version of "the world." On the contrary, such an aim, which would require science itself to decide which of the empirically equivalent successful theories in any given context was "really true," is contrary to the whole spirit of an enterprise whose strategy from the first has been to confine itself to claims with clear *empirical* significance (1983: 228).

The existence of these various positions suggests, then, that we can identify a variety of stances about truth or correctness in interpretation ranging from the absolutism of Dworkin's "one right answer" thesis to a complete relativism to the point of arbitrariness — a sort of "anything goes" attitude that denies the possibility of any selection criteria that are anything but purely subjective.

Such a view is familiar to us in philosophy of science from the work of Paul Feyerabend (1975) and in literature from that of the radical literary critics. In law, too, there has been much recent discussion of various respects in which law is to be seen as pure ideology rather than as rational and principle-governed. Thus law is sometimes seen as the tool of a particular social class, or of commercial or political interests rather than as a working out of underlying principles that express the moral fabric of society.

An intermediate possibility that attempts to avoid both absolutism and arbitrariness is the alternative that there are many right or acceptable interpretations, some of which may even be incompatible with one another, though this does not imply that we cannot identify some interpretations as wrong. Perhaps the simplest example of such a state of affairs occurs in the theatre, where many different and even incompatible versions of *Hamlet* or *Hedda Gabler* may strike us as interesting, illuminating, and correct while yet others will be totally unacceptable.[6] We have seen that Goodman adopts this sort of view. Putnam too, while accepting that we cannot expect agreement on the one correct moral theory or conception of rationality any more than on political conceptions or interpretations of history, nonetheless maintains that this need not lead us into a self-refuting relativism. "The correct moral to draw is not that nothing is right or wrong, rational or irrational, true or false, and so on, but. . .that there is no neutral place to stand, no external vantage point from which to judge what is right or wrong, rational or irrational, true or false" (1983: 202-3).

So the argument that any claim to knowledge or to truth is always from some point of view is familiar in the philosophical literature of the past twenty years or so. What is missing, however, from most of these "mainstream" discussions is any explicit recognition of gender, particularly in epistemology. Race, class, and gender are sometimes part of discussions in ethics and politics concerned with justice, equity, and distribution; but rarely does this carry over into considerations about reasoning, evidence, or knowing. These considerations are central mainly only in feminist writing and even here there has been relatively little integration of ethics and epistemology. Most of the feminist epistemological literature has concerned itself with a critique of dualistic or dichotomous thinking and a call for greater connectedness and wholeness, and this is, of course, a necessary first step. But to date there has been little constructive feminist epistemology, partly, I think, because of the difficulty that people trained to accept traditional notions of scientific objectivity have in introducing "subjective" elements without feeling that they have fallen into an unacceptable relativism. The problem of adducing grounds for rejecting certain views as incorrect while at the same time allowing that we cannot tell which from among remaining uneliminated positions is correct, even when these are incompatible with one another, is one for which we have no clear methodology. Perhaps different ones of these positions are acceptable in different contexts and for different purposes, and we do not have to choose. Women are sometimes said to be better able to deal with ambiguity and inconsistency than are men, and this is often attributed to women's greater involvement in the complexities of day to day living and personal relationships. Whatever its basis, recognition of incompatible pressures on one's life and thought rather than abstracting from these in order to produce a coherent picture may at least give a more accurate, if more complex, representation of reality.

By and large, it is mainly only in explicitly feminist philosophy where issues of gender have been taken to be central. For all the turn to more holistic and more concrete approaches, there are still relatively few philosophers doing work that might lead to a greater understanding of problems associated with gender, or even taking explicit account of such work, beyond care with pronouns and using women's names as often as men's in examples. As unsurprising as this is, it is nonetheless unfortunate for a number of reasons. First, it leaves feminist philosophy still outside the so-called mainstream and so still relegated to separate courses taken primarily by women, to separate meetings, and even to separate journals, thereby perpetuating its inaccessibility to male students and thus to men generally. Second, there is the unfortunate tendency of male philosophers who do try to gain access to this material to reformulate it in more traditional terms, to explain us to ourselves and to the world at large, and in general to be rendered extremely uncomfortable by the less adversarial and more cooperative style we try to employ. The intellectually revolutionary nature of the enterprise is often not seen, nor is the way in which it is in its infancy and requires continuing investigation and building in almost every aspect.

One other feature is, I think, extremely important in all of this, and this is the ideology of interdisciplinarity on which women's studies has been built. The academic milieu is not one in which genuine interdisciplinarity flourishes easily. Academic departments still tend to exhibit extreme territoriality, even though the boundaries of that territory are constantly shifting with new knowledge and new categorizations. Most of us are still very uncomfortable speaking about any matter on which we do not consider ourselves expert, and we are often touchingly willing to accept the claimed expertise of others, both in other disciplines or in remote parts of our own, forgetting momentarily the familiar spectacle in our own disciplines of experts disagreeing and the extent to which we are split into opposing camps. The typical effect in philosophy of this parochialism has been to brand feminist work as "not philosophy," often because it tackles different problems from the conventional ones and employs different and more eclectic means for solving them. If the work is "not philosophy" then it need not be taken seriously by serious philosophers.

Even feminist philosophy has not always fulfilled the promise of a more holistic outlook. After all, none of us is immune from our background, education, or academic environment: we are all trained within the philosophical tradition and we all do our work within a departmental structure that values separateness and that treats knowledge as bits of intellectual property. Small wonder, then, that so much feminist philosophy is no more adventurous than most philosophy done by men, being often confined to a rather narrow conception of what is truly philosophical.

One important breakthrough, however, seems to have occurred around the work of Carol Gilligan (1982). Gilligan's discussion of moral development, and especially of what she calls an ethic of responsibility in contrast to an ethic of rights has captured the imagination of feminist academics in virtually all areas—whether psychology, philosophy, law, education, or whatever. In philosophy of education Nel Noddings, in her book *Caring* (1985), has tried to develop some of these ideas further, and numerous feminist writers have commented, both positively and negatively, on Gilligan's representation of the two distinct moral "voices." Most recently this thread is developed by a group of four psychologists in a book entitled *Women's Ways of Knowing* (Belenky *et al.*), published in 1986. Developing their conclusions from in-depth interviews with 135 women, the authors describe "five different perspectives from which women view reality and draw conclusions about truth, knowledge and authority" (1986: 3). Besides being based entirely on interviews with women, one of the most interesting features of this work is that it deals with women from a wide variety of ages, socio-economic circumstances, and educational backgrounds. Unlike the work of Gilligan with women (and, with men, of Kohlberg 1981, 1984 and Perry 1970 before her) we do not find conclusions about thinking and knowing drawn only from research with an educationally privileged elite. Another interesting feature of this work is that the authors try to connect particular styles of knowing with particular kinds of family background, and to draw some conclusions about educational practices that appear to be more conducive to women's learning than traditional ones.

The five major epistemological categories are as follows:

1. silence, where women experience themselves as mindless and voiceless;

2. received knowledge, where women conceive themselves as capable of receiving knowledge from external authority, but not creating it themselves;

3. subjective knowledge, where truth is thought to be personal and private;

4. procedural knowledge, where women use traditional "objective" procedures; and

5. constructed knowledge, which is contextual and where both objective and subjective strategies are employed (1986: 15).

Irrespective of the particular epistemological perspective employed, the metaphor of voice seems to be pervasive.

The tendency for women to ground their epistemological premises in metaphors suggesting speaking and listening is at odds with the visual metaphors (such as equating knowledge with illumination, knowing with seeing, and truth with light) that scientists and philosophers most often use to express their sense of mind. . . . Visual metaphors encourage standing at a distance to get a proper view, removing. . .subject and object from a sphere of possible intercourse. . . . Unlike the eye, the ear requires closeness between subject and object. Unlike seeing, speaking and listening suggest dialogue and interaction (1986: 18).

The authors also note that metaphors of "blind justice," "double blind" tests and the "veil of ignorance" are intended to remove the scientist, the judge, and the moralist from the influence of the particular, and of the knower on what is known. Only recently have these influences come to be seen as inevitable and even positive.

There is much about this research that requires questioning and further investigation, including the extent to which these categories apply to both women and men, and even the extent to which the categories make sense. Here I wish to raise just one question about what appears to be an underlying assumption of the research. The authors speak throughout the book of truth as relative, of meaning as context-dependent, and of knowledge as constructed rather than given. There is no effort made to distinguish among these positions but surely it is possible for knowledge to be constructed without its also being the case that truth is relative, if that means that every belief about any topic is as good as every other. This is important because clearly the authors do want to make judgments about certain modes of knowing being more adequate than others. Furthermore, we all want to claim that an epistemology that incorporates feminist concerns is both more objective and more likely to yield truths than one that does not, even if we grant at the same time that we cannot be certain which of our claims is true. Another way to put this is to note that not every position is acceptable, nor should every point of view be expected to yield truth. Some views are based on bigotry or bias and need be given no credence at all, and it would be odd for a feminist epistemology, of all things, to deny this. This is not, of course, to say that we cannot understand the source of bias or the historical reasons for its having held sway; nor is it necessarily to condemn those who may have held the biased view within a particular historical or social framework. But to understand racism or sexism is not to condone it, or to believe that its claims are true.

It is important also to distinguish this claim about truth from one which insists that we must achieve consistency among all our beliefs at any particular time. As has often been pointed out, there may be a certain strength and adaptiveness in intellectual flexibility, in being able to tolerate ambiguity and even contradiction. But this is different from the view that "anything goes"—that whatever I believe is "true for me" and thus that there are no standards for assessing the reasonableness of a position. I do not claim that the authors believe there are no such standards; rather, I'm concerned that they talk in places as though a thoroughgoing relativism is the only intellectually responsible stance. And I think this just is not so. But whatever its flaws, exploration in this book of ways of thinking, and coming to know that they differ somewhat from the ways we had come to accept as standard, opens up new vistas not only in psychology but in our understanding of knowledge more generally. The authors use material from a wide variety of disciplines but even more importantly, they are, I think, like Gilligan, destined to be read and discussed much more widely than in their own field. And others will modify and build upon their work. This is, I think the real value of feminist research and methodology; and the more narrowly it is conceived, the further it is from fulfilling its potential. The issue is not so much whether there is a specifically feminist methodology but rather how well our new approaches can help in reorienting knowledge to human and humane ends.

Endnotes

1. A nice example is Ronald Dworkin's *Law's Empire* (1986) which discusses concepts of justice, fairness, and the like at length and which nevertheless uses the male pronoun almost throughout.

2. This is a quote from Jane Flax. See reference.

3. In earlier work, Dworkin was not so ready to see similarities between science on the one hand and law on the other. See Dworkin 1977: 150-168 and Hanen 1983: 67-83.

4. Plessy v. Ferguson, 163 U.S. 537 (1986).
   Brown v. Board of Education of Topeka, Shawnee County, Kansas, 347 U.S. 483, 74 S.Ct. 686, 98 L. Ed. 873 (1954).

5. Dworkin has in mind, of course, constitutional adjudication in the U.S. To what extent similar arguments can be made about post-Charter Canadian constitutional adjudication remains to be seen.

6. Portions of the last two paragraphs are taken from Hanen 1988.

References

Belenky, Mary Field; Clinchy, Blythe McVicker; Goldberger, Nancy Rule; and Tarule, Jill Mattuck.
    1986   *Women's Ways of Knowing*. New York: Basic Books.

Bleier, Ruth.
    1984   *Science and Gender: A Critique of Biology and Its Theories on Women*. New York: Pergamon.

Dummett, Michael.
    1978   Truth. Pp. 1-24 in *Truth and Other Enigmas*. Cambridge, Mass.: Harvard University.

Dworkin, Ronald.
    1977   *Taking Rights Seriously*. Cambridge, Mass.: Harvard University.

    1985   *A Matter of Principle*. Cambridge, Mass.: Harvard University.

    1986   *Law's Empire*. Cambridge, Mass.: Harvard University.

Feyerabend, Paul.
    1975   *Against Method*. Atlantic Highlands, New York: Humanities.

Flax, Jane.
    1986   Gender as a Social Problem: In and For Feminist Theory. Pp. 193-213 in *American Studies/Amerika Studien*, Journal of the German Association for American Studies.

Gilligan, Carol.
    1982   *In A Different Voice*. Cambridge, Mass.: Harvard University.

Goodman, Nelson.
    1978   *Ways of Worldmaking*. Indianapolis: Hackett.

    1984   *Of Mind and Other Matters*. Cambridge, Mass.: Harvard University.

Grimshaw, Jean.
    1986 *Philosophy and Feminist Thinking.* Minneapolis: University of Minnesota.

Hanen, Marsha.
    1983 Justification as Coherence. Pp. 67-92 in *Law, Morality and Rights*, ed. M.A. Stewart. Dordrecht: D. Reidel.

    1988 Feminism, Objectivity and Legal Truth. In *Feminist Perspectives, Philosophical Essays on Method and Morals*, ed. L. Code, S. Mullet, and C. Overall. Toronto: University of Toronto.

Harding, Sandra.
    1986 *The Science Question in Feminism.* Ithaca, N.Y.: Cornell University.

Harding, Sandra, and Hintikka, Merrill B.
    1983 *Discovering Reality.* Dordrecht: D. Reidel.

Jaggar, Alison M.
    1983 *Feminist Politics and Human Nature.* Totowa, New Jersey: Rowman and Allanheld.

Jaggar, Alison M., and Rothenberg, Paula S. (eds.).
    1984 *Feminist Frameworks.* 2nd ed. New York: McGraw-Hill.

Kohlberg, L.
    1981 *The Philosophy of Moral Development.* New York: Harper and Row.

    1984 *The Psychology of Moral Development.* New York: Harper and Row.

Lloyd, Genevieve.
    1984 *The Man of Reason.* Minneapolis: University of Minnesota.

MacKinnon, Catharine.
    1982 Feminism, Marxism, Method, and the State: An Agenda for Theory. *Signs* 7: 515-44.

Noddings, Nel.
    1984 *Caring.* Berkeley: University of California.

Perry, W.G.
> 1970 *Forms of Intellectual and Ethical Development in the College Years*. New York: Holt Rinehart and Winston.

Putnam, Hilary.
> 1978 Literature, Science, and Reflection. Pp. 83-94 in *Meaning and the Moral Sciences*. London: Routledge and Kegan Paul.

> 1983 *Realism and Reason*. Cambridge: Cambridge University.

Rorty, Richard.
> 1979 *Philosophy and the Mirror of Nature*. Princeton: Princeton University.

> 1982 *Consequences of Pragmatism*. Minneapolis: University of Minnesota.

van Fraassen, B.
> 1980 *The Scientific Image*. Oxford: Clarendon.

Chapter 3

TOWARD A NEW SCIENCE OF HUMAN BEING AND BEHAVIOR[1]

Hilary M. Lips

More than eighty years ago, Helen Thompson, one of the first female graduate students in psychology at the University of Chicago, embarked on an ambitious thesis project. Her goal – to "obtain a complete and systematic statement of the psychological likenesses and differences of the sexes by the experimental method." Her extensive review of the literature on sex differences in mental abilities had unearthed a tangle of inconsistencies and contradictions. She believed that only a careful experimental investigation could produce the evidence needed to resolve the disputes about female/male psychological differences (Thompson [Woolley] 1903: 1, 3-6).

Using fifty Chicago undergraduates, half of them female and half of them male, Thompson tested a long list of motor skills and sensory abilities: auditory and visual reaction times, ability to hit a target, rapidity of finger movement, pain threshold, ability to discriminate heat and cold. It was the first time that anyone had systematically compared women and men on a wide variety of abilities measured in a controlled laboratory setting.

What Thompson found was a striking *lack* of evidence for gender differences in mental abilities. Women and men did perform differently on some tests, but it was the similarities rather than the differences between the sexes that were most impressive. These similarities were obvious when Thompson graphed her data: the distribution curve of scores on any particular test for the women in her sample overlapped almost completely with the distribution curve of scores on the same test for men. Her research thus provided the first experimental basis on which to question the popular assumption that women's and men's different mental abilities made different social roles suitable for the two sexes.

Helen Thompson's research is one of the earliest examples of the very first, and perhaps still primary, impact of feminism on research methodology in psychology: an increased sensitivity to sexist bias in theory and research and attempts to minimize such bias by doing better, more careful research. She and her contemporary, Leta Hollingworth, used the research skills they had been taught as graduate students to gather data that challenged the views of women held by many of their professors. They hoped, by a careful gathering of solid evidence, to challenge the mistaken beliefs about the differences between women and men. However, they found that, even in the supposedly "value-neutral" academic environment, carefully collected data were not enough to shake people's adherence to gender stereotypes. Leta Hollingworth (1914) was moved in frustration to accuse her male colleagues in psychology of adopting a double standard of scientific proof, refusing to subject their assumptions about sex differences to the same careful criticism as they devoted to other assumptions. Her exasperation is quite understandable: her own advisor, the eminent Edward Thorndike, held fast, in the absence of data, to the notion of a "maternal instinct" in women, long after he had concluded that, in general, the notion of "instinct" was too vague and mentalistic to be useful to psychology (Rosenberg 1984: 93-95).

What the early feminist psychologists did not reckon with was that their own research endeavors and their own academic discipline could not be isolated from the sea of gender prejudice in which it struggled to stay afloat. Possibilities for bias were built into the very processes of data collection used by psychologists; indeed, no data collected by human beings about human behavior could be completely "pure" or unaffected by the researchers. Moreover, the pervasive cultural ideology concerning gender was so nonconscious and accepted that most psychologists were unaware of the extent to which it limited their framing of research questions and their interpretation of data. It has now been years since feminist psychologists' early loss of innocence with respect to the notion that all that must be done to undermine gender bias is to do the right research carefully enough to eliminate biased conclusions. Feminists in my discipline have for years been focusing on the research process itself, and on the cultural assumptions surrounding both research and gender, in their efforts to transform psychology into a science of truly human being and behavior.

Conducting Nonsexist Research

Under the influence of feminism, there has been a major emphasis within psychology on "cleaning up" research methods so as to avoid gender bias as much as possible. As far as it goes, this attempt has been reasonably successful. For example, over fifty years ago, Saul Rosenweig (1933), in a pioneering paper on the social psychology of the psychology experiment, mentioned gender as a "personal quality" of the experimenter that could introduce what he called "errors of personality influence" into the laboratory. In other words, the sex of the experimenter might make a difference to experimental results simply because people react differently to men and women. Rosenweig's point was largely lost on his contemporaries (Adair 1973), but in recent years, partly under the influence of the new consciousness instilled by feminism, the researcher's gender has become an accepted factor of consideration in research design. "Sex-of-experimenter effects," while still sometimes overlooked, have been found in virtually every area of psychological research, from hypnosis (Johnson, Smith, Whatley, and DeVoge 1973) to eyeblink conditioning (Gold 1969). There are many complex effects: some indications are that female experimenters tend to *disconfirm* their hypotheses, whereas male experimenters *confirm* theirs (Rosenthal, Persinger, Mulry, Vikan-Kline, and Grothe 1964). It has also been suggested that male and female researchers each tend, without realizing it, to design research in ways that favor the portrayal of their own gender (Eagly and Carli 1981).

Psychologists have now become aware that the social psychology of the psychological experiment is rife with aspects that can interact with sex or gender, causing artifactual findings. It has been found, for instance, that females are more likely than males to comply with the demand characteristics of an experimental situation — to be sensitive to cues that suggest what behavior is appropriate (Rosenthal 1966). Thus, for instance, in a laboratory setting that is arranged to allow plenty of opportunity for nurturant behavior, so that the behavior can be studied, women may be more likely than men to fit their behavior to the setting by behaving in a nurturant way. Reported male-female differences in such a study of nurturant behavior may simply reflect the fact that women are more likely than men to respond to the demand characteristics of the experiment: to act nurturant, as they perceive the situation requires.

Since research on human behavior is, by its very nature, a social endeavor taking place in a particular social context, it would be unrealistic to expect that the interactions between researcher and subject or the interpretation of the data would be "uncontaminated" by the gender stereotypes and gender-related habits predominant in the surrounding culture. This does not mean, however, that structural sources of bias built into the research process should not be sought out and eliminated where possible. While recognizing that a "value-free" science conducted by human beings is an impossibility, feminist psychologists have nevertheless striven mightily to document the sources of bias in the research process and to work within the psychological establishment to make the discipline less sexist. In so doing, they have tried to draw a distinction between bias, as a source of error or distortion, and values — commitments to particular goals (Wittig 1985: 806-807). In essence, they are arguing that a feminist psychologist can be committed to values such as the personal dignity of women and fair treatment of the sexes, while still striving for unbiased knowledge. The distinction between bias and value presuppositions is admittedly a difficult and fuzzy one, and it carries the risk of being self-serving (i.e., my "value" is your "bias"). However, in an intellectual environment of criticism, researchers can work to maintain a consciousness of their own values, and of how these values influence their work. At any rate, committed feminist psychologists have seen no inconsistency between their strong values and their work against sexist bias in research.

In psychology, the fight against sexist research was spearheaded by the Task Force on the Status of Women in Canadian Psychology, of the Canadian Psychological Association (Wand 1977). A decade ago, Olga Favreau (1977) documented the possibility of sexist bias at every stage of the research process, from the review of the literature to the interpretation of the results. More recently, the Canadian Psychological Association adopted and published a position paper prepared for its Status of Women Committee, in which sexist research is labelled as "bad" research, and the support, conduct, and publication of sexist research is termed unethical (Stark-Adamec and Kimball 1984). This position paper, titled "Science Free of Sexism," comprises a guide to the conduct of nonsexist research, outlining the potential pitfalls in reviewing background literature, formulating the research question, designing and conducting the research, analyzing and reporting the results, and interpreting the findings. The paper is now used as a guideline for students learning to do psychological research in many Canadian universities. Some students have indicated to me, however, that their professors belittle the importance of this position paper and make it clear that adherence to the guidelines for nonsexist research and nonsexist language is done strictly in order to stay out of trouble. Be that as it may, the fact that blatant sexism in their research can now be a source of trouble for academic psychologists in Canada is cause for feminist rejoicing.

The issues raised by critics of sex bias in psychological research are too numerous to cover here. I will focus briefly on one issue that is especially problematic for psychologists: the choice of subjects or respondents. Who should be studied, and with whom should they be compared? An important guideline is that the people to be studied should be representative of those about whom the researcher wishes to draw conclusions. Obvious though this may seem, it has been common practice for researchers to study one sex (usually males) while drawing conclusions about people in general (Prescott 1978). An interesting case in point is a frequently cited finding in social psychology: the way that watching oneself on videotape affects one's judgments about the causes of one's own behavior. Research on men led to the conclusion that the videotape experience causes people to feel more like external observers of their own behavior, rather than like actors, and to judge their own behavior in the way that an external observer would (Storms 1973). Seeing themselves on videotape, men tend to shift their causal attributions for their own behavior in an internal direction, paying less attention to social context and environmental constraints on their behavior and more attention to individual personality and motivation as reasons for their actions. Although this pattern is often presented as one that holds for people in general, efforts to replicate it with female subjects have failed (Scott and Webster 1984).

Another problem in subject selection occurs when researchers study people who are having difficulties with a normal process (e.g., menopause or the menstrual cycle) and then generalize their conclusions to all people who are experiencing the process. Thus, information gathered about the female patient has often been generalized unthinkingly to females in general (Stark-Adamec and Kimball 1984). In this era of media attention to the Premenstrual Syndrome, feminist psychologists find themselves once again crying in the wilderness as they remind people that the occurrence of severe premenstrual difficulties in a small percentage of women says little about the menstrual experience of women in general.

In order to put information about a particular group into perspective, it is often necessary to make comparisons with other groups. Without such comparisons, information about the group being studied is too easily assimilated into an existing stereotype. For instance, in a culture that views pregnancy as a time of emotional instability, the finding that 24 percent of a sample of pregnant women agreed with the statement that "I sometimes feel as if I am going to have a nervous breakdown" might easily be taken as supporting that stereotype — unless, as was the case in the study in question, it was balanced by the finding that the comparison group (female university students) showed an agreement rate of 57 percent with the same item (Barclay and Barclay 1976). When the symptoms reported by pregnant women are compared with those reported by their husbands, nonpregnant women, and husbands of nonpregnant women, the myth that pregnancy is a time of emotional instability for most women receives little support (Lips 1982; 1985a).

Feminist psychologists have alerted the psychological research community that not only must researchers use comparison or control groups, they must also choose such groups, and examine the assumptions governing their choices, with care (Parlee 1981). For example, when comparing males and females, it may not always be appropriate to equate the two groups for age, since women and men order some of their activities differently across their lifespans (McHugh *et al.* 1981). Lifespan researchers have noted, for instance, that North American women often find themselves shifting their life priorities at middle age toward more agentic concerns with education and employment, at an age when their male counterparts are making a reverse shift—toward more affiliative and intimate concerns (Rossi 1980).

One obvious comparison that needs to be made if researchers are to understand gender is the comparison between social contexts. Psychology as a discipline has long acknowledged that behavior is a function of the person and the environment, but until recently researchers in psychology have behaved as if gender were a powerful built-in force that transcends social context. As both Naomi Weisstein (1971) and Sandra and Daryl Bem (1970) noted in early widely-circulated feminist critiques of psychology, this behavior stemmed from an immersion in the social context that was so profound as to render it invisible. So automatic was the assumption that women and men were naturally different, based on their biology, that no attempt was made to examine the degree to which the differing social contexts in which they functioned might help to produce these differences. Researchers who have turned their attention to the impact of social context on gender-related behaviors are now finding that gender by situation interactions (i.e. instances in which a gender difference in a particular behavior, such as nurturance, appears in one type of situation but not another or takes a different form or magnitude in different circumstances) are more common than simple gender differences (Deaux 1984), and that traditional findings such as those that women are less self-confident or less aggressive than men hold up only in particular kinds of situations (e.g., Frodi *et al.* 1977; Lenny 1977). This type of finding is very significant for understanding gender, since women and men often differ in the kinds of situations they encounter and in the proportion of their lives they spend in particular situations.

Getting Beyond Cultural Gender Bias

The science of psychology has been accused of furnishing support for stereotypic beliefs about women and men — beliefs that, in turn, have supported patriarchal ideology and political, legal, and economic inequalities between the sexes (Parlee 1975; Weisstein 1971). Many have argued that seeking out and eradicating specific sources of bias in the psychological research process is an inadequate approach to the problem of sexism in research. Not just the process, but the world view in which it is embedded, makes it difficult to conduct research that is feminist — or at least free of sexism. In recent years, feminist psychologists have turned their attention to the culture, evaluating its impact on the assumptions that shape the entire research climate in psychology.

Cultural attitudes toward gender. Kenneth Gergen (1973) began arguing years ago that social psychology should be characterized as a historical rather than a scientific enterprise, in part because psychology has a tendency to reflect the accepted values of society when labelling behavior at any given period in time. Moreover, the labels psychology applies to behavior in turn affect society's evaluative biases, in a kind of vicious circle. In other words, there is bidirectionality of knowledge and behavior. Gergen's analysis is useful in illustrating the interaction between psychology and the culture in which it exists: how culture influences the biases psychologists bring to the study of behavior, and how the evaluative biases built into the way we report our findings influence the way the public views certain behaviors and tries to tailor its own behavior.

One way in which psychology has interacted with the larger culture is in the re-valuing and re-labelling of certain aspects of women's experience. One impact of feminism on psychology's approach to knowledge has been the beginnings of awareness that, when differences are found between women and men, such differences do not have to represent a hierarchy in which the masculine version of a particular behavior or quality is seen as superior to the feminine one. Feminist psychologists have learned to ask, for example, not just "How can women learn to be more assertive and dominant?" but also, "How can men learn to be more sensitive and able to compromise?"; not just "How can more women be encouraged to enter the scientific professions?" but also, "How can more men be encouraged to spend more time on their parenting responsibilities?"

Perhaps the most well known example of this particular impact of feminism on psychological research is the work of Carol Gilligan (1982a,

1982b). Gilligan noted that data gathered from males formed the basis for the most widely accepted theory of moral development in psychology. She noted, furthermore, that, using this male-based developmental scale, some studies found females' moral development to be lower than that of males. Troubled by this finding, she embarked on an investigation of moral development in girls and women. Her investigation revealed new dimensions of moral development that had been ignored in earlier research. The girls and women she studied tended to analyze moral problems in terms of conflicting responsibilities rather than, or at least as much as, conflicting rights. Some have been quick to interpret these findings as evidence that women's moral development and moral reasoning is qualitatively different from that of men, perhaps due to early differences in upbringing in which females but not males are primarily parented by a person of the same gender. However, there has been no convincing demonstration that women and men differ on either the rights (Walker 1984) or responsibility (Ford and Lowery 1986) dimension of moral development. The real importance of Gilligan's work is the acknowledgment that qualities stereotypically associated with women, such as attachment, intimacy, and concern with relationships, are associated with positive growth and development, with strength rather than weakness. While earlier students of moral development, beginning with Sigmund Freud (1925/1974), argued that women were handicapped in their ability to be highly moral because their concern with relationships made it difficult for them to make detached, principled moral judgments, Gilligan's work has made it clear that this relationship-oriented sense of responsibility is not a liability, but is itself an important dimension of morality. Within psychology, Gilligan, along with Jean Baker Miller (1976), has probably made the greatest impact on the re-labelling and re-valuing of qualities traditionally associated with women — making it clear that, where gender differences do exist, there is no reason why the onus to change should be on women and not on men. It would be unwise, however, to use their work as a basis for claiming that women are "naturally" more caring or more responsible in relationships than men. Such conclusions are not warranted by the evidence; furthermore, they lead back into the quicksand of gender stereotypes.

Science as culture. Feminism has challenged, not only the culturally-shaped attitudes toward gender that pervade our research questions, but also some of the basic assumptions about the proper conduct of scientific research. Within psychology, which has a long tradition of experimenter-subject interactions in which the experimenter knows what is going on and the subject does not, a major aspect of the feminist approach has been to change the definition of the experimenter-subject relationship. According to the Task Force on Issues in Research in the Psychology of Women (1977) set up by the American Psychological Association's Division on the Psychology of Women, feminist research tends to be "cooperative, participative. . . (and) nonhierarchical," with a focus on the personal experience of the participants and a recognition that "truth is not separate from the person who 'speaks' it" (1977: 3). Even in the context of a reliance on empirical methods, psychologists can use "procedures that recognize and respect the common humanity of the investigator and the subjects of the investigation" (Wittig 1985: 805).

Attempts to move in the direction of participative, experience-based research have had a number of consequences. One documentable example is the movement of feminist researchers away from heavy reliance on traditional experimental methods of data gathering, and from the exclusive use of first-year university students as subjects. A comparison between articles published in the *Psychology of Women Quarterly* and the *Journal of Personality and Social Psychology* for the years 1978 and 1983 showed that research reported in the psychology of women journal was more likely to be based on populations outside the typical college group (83% in *PWQ* vs 33% in *JSP*) (Lykes and Stewart 1983). As well, "fewer than 20% of the *PWQ* studies used traditional experimental methods while 68% of the *JPSP* studies did" (1983: 13). Bernice Lott states that:

Feminist scholarship rejects no careful, rigorous, intersubjective, repeatable method of inquiry. . . . The new research questions posed by feminist psychologists demand expansion in our field of inquiry, in acceptable sources of data, and in research techniques. Thus, issues of content become issues of method.

Feminists have been critical of a model and vocabulary of science that emphasizes "objectivity," "control," and the search for prime causes rather than the exploration of complex interactions, interdependence, and the dynamics of process (Keller 1982; Lott 1985). Within psychology, this critique has clearly led to the exploration of new methods for studying human behavior. Thus, for instance, a small but significant minority of feminist psychologists has adopted explicitly phenomenological research methods — methods that demand that the researcher begin with no theoretical preconceptions and then proceed to construct a theory based on information provided by the individuals being studied (e.g., Fischer 1984). This method, while problematic in its assumption that the researcher *can*, in fact, start out with no theoretical preconceptions, provides a needed corrective to traditional approaches.

Feminist psychologists will be interested in new approaches to phenomenological methodology that are currently being developed (Andrew 1985, 1986)—approaches that can incorporate experimental variations without compromising the qualitative approach. Such methods allow for an inclusion of the investigator's standpoint as a variable to be studied as part of the research process. In addition, these methods allow the possibility of involving subjects as true participants—conscious, intentional collaborators with the researcher—who systematically respond to a particular research situation, provide reflections about their own responses, and respond to externally-derived presentations of their own responses (e.g., a videotape or an observer's account). This type of research makes possible the study of processes that can elude other methods, and emphasizes the idea that the research enterprise cannot be separated from the persons/behaviors it examines.

While a strict phenomenological approach is still rarely used in psychology, many feminist psychologists begin their research by questioning participants about their experiences rather than by assuming a rigid theoretical framework (e.g., Lips 1985a; Lips and Morrison 1986; Peplau *et al.* 1978). For example, in their research on value orientations in lesbian relationships, Anne Peplau and her colleagues used a twenty-three-page questionnaire. The questionnaire was developed not just on the basis of their own theories about what factors were important in these relationships, but on extensive interviews with a small sample of lesbian women about their relationships and on group discussions with lesbian students.

In the attempt to depart from the focus on finding single primary causes of behavior in favor of an approach that explores the way that many variables interact to describe a process, feminist psychologists are also turning increasingly to sophisticated data-analytic methods such as path analysis and the development of complex causal models to describe behavior. For example, the search for explanations of women's career decisions with respect to science and mathematics has leaned heavily on this approach, in recognition that there is no single factor but a multitude of interdependent factors that influence women away from science and mathematics in this culture (e.g., Eccles (Parsons) *et al.* 1985; Lips and Davidson 1987). Such research attempts to be truly descriptive of the situation as it exists, rather than isolating a part of the situation and manipulating variables separately to see what happens.

There has been a tendency among some feminists to move away from quantitative research, arguing that it objectifies and dehumanizes people. It is very important that women in psychology who embrace feminism do *not* dismiss quantitative approaches as representative of a "masculine" model of science. First of all, there is really no such thing as masculinity, except as our own cultural construction (see, for example, Lott 1985: 159). Secondly, there is no reason why the entire quantitative approach to knowledge should be assigned to men as their special territory. Rather, women must make special efforts to become skilled in the use of the nontraditional and powerful statistical tools that allow for a holistic and deeply exploratory approach to research. These methods can sometimes provide a vision of an overall pattern of social behavior that cannot be glimpsed using in-depth interviews with a few people.

Finally, feminism has helped to push psychology to grapple with the problem of explanation—with the dilemma that, try as we may to do good, careful research, that research will always be shaped by our individual and social values. This development has perhaps been highlighted best by Michelle Wittig in an article based on her 1983 presidential address to the Psychology of Women Division of the American Psychological Association. Wittig (1985: 800) points out that a psychology of gender has been established concurrently with a growing attention to metatheoretical issues in psychology and that such metatheoretical questions have taken a central place in the new discipline. The psychology of gender has often provided a forum for the application and refinement of an emerging constructionist perspective in psychology—a perspective that assumes that "knowledge about behavior is [subjectively] constructed, not merely deduced [from objective facts]...[that the] constructions are affected by the historical, personal, social, and cultural context" (Wittig 1985: 803). The constructionist perspective encompasses a number of arguments, several of which have already been raised in this paper. It proposes that complete explanations of human behavior cannot be discovered by studying individuals under controlled conditions, in the absence of knowledge about their social contexts. It argues that behavior has multiple causes, and that behavior and knowledge about behavior are reciprocally linked, each influencing the other. Therefore, methods sensitive to reciprocal and multiple causality are important tools for the advancement of our understanding of human psychology.

In attempting to apply this constructionist perspective to psychological research on gender, Wittig explicates possible feminist resolutions of four "metatheoretical dilemmas": scholarship vs advocacy, science vs humanism, orthodoxy vs schism, and subjectivity vs objectivity. Constraints of space forbid me from trying to elaborate on all of these, but I conclude this paper with a description of her suggestions on dealing with the tension between orthodoxy and schism. This tension arises from the question of whether a feminist psychology of gender can be part of the discipline of psychology, or whether traditional psychology must be rejected by feminists as being simply a reflection of cultural sexism. Wittig argues that *both* choices in the dilemma — approaching the study of gender by simply adopting the theories, methods, and explanations used by traditional psychology *or* rejecting the whole approach used by traditional psychology as illegitimate — are insufficiently self-critical. She suggests that neither psychology as a discipline nor the feminist concern with gender bias in psychology should be considered illegitimate (Wittig 1985: 806). The psychology of gender should not be a subdiscipline of traditional psychology, nor should feminist psychologists withdraw in frustration or despair from mainstream psychology. Rather, she suggests, feminists need to develop a "transformational psychology of gender" — one that attempts to "construct a nonsexist psychology from within the discipline, so as to avoid both gender bias and dissociation from psychology." Such a transformational psychology would have to be self-critical and subject to reevaluation, not locked into dogmatic conceptions of, for example, which specification of gender equality or which conception of the self is ideal for all people in all situations.

Wittig's analysis suggests to me that the very tension, uncomfortable though it may be, inherent in refusing to choose one side or the other of these dilemmas: orthodoxy vs schism, subjectivity vs objectivity, and others, is what may best motivate and inform self-criticism in feminist theory and research. It makes us skeptical of the explanations we derive, no matter what methodology we are using. It makes us critical of our own work and that of our colleagues — and it is to be hoped that the criticism springs from knowing and caring about one another's work rather than from the intolerance, lack of respect, or defensiveness that characterizes so much of the modern day academic environment. Wittig (1985: 809) has argued that "a constructionist psychology of gender uses knowledge of what is as a means of understanding what could be." I believe that, while we are still a long way from understanding either what is *or* what could be, the dialogue and self-criticism that derives from the tensions between the traditional and feminist approaches will move us more quickly in the direction of that understanding.

Endnotes

1.   Parts of this paper are adapted from Chapter 3 of *Sex and Gender: An Introduction*, by Hilary M. Lips, to be published in 1988 by Mayfield Publishing Company. This material is used here with permission. I am grateful to Dena Davidson and Sharon Jeanson for their helpful comments on an earlier draft of this manuscript.

References

_____.

1977   Task Force on Issues in Research in the Psychology of Women — Final Report. *Division 35 Newsletter* 4: 3-6.

Adair, John G.
1973   *The Human Subject: The Social Psychology of the Psychological Experiment.* Boston: Little Brown.

Andrew, Wayne K.
1985   The Phenomenological Foundations for Empirical Methodology I: The Method of Optional Variations. *Journal of Phenomenological Psychology* 16: 1-29.

1986   The Phenomenological Foundations for Empirical Methodology II: Experimental Phenomenological Psychology. *Journal of Phenomenological Psychology* 17: 77-97.

Barclay, R.I., and Barclay, M.L.
1976   Aspects of the Normal Psychology of Pregnancy: The Midtrimester. *American Journal of Obstetrics and Gynecology* 125: 207.

Bem, Sandra L., and Bem, Daryl J.
1970   Case Study of a Nonconscious Ideology: Teaching the Woman to Know Her Place. Pp. 89-99 in *Beliefs, Attitudes and Human Affairs*, ed. D.J. Bem. Monterey, CA: Brooks/ Cole.

Deaux, Kay.
1984   From Individual Differences to Social Categories. Analysis of a Decade's Research on Gender. *American Psychologist* 39: 105-116.

Eagly, Alice H., and Carli, Linda L.
1981   Sex of Researchers and Sex-Typed Communications as Determinants of Sex Differences in Influenceability: A Meta-Analysis of Social Influence Studies. *Psychological Bulletin* 90: 1-20.

Eccles (Parsons), Jacquelynne; Adler, Terry F.; Futterman, Robert; Goff, Susan B.; Kaczala, Caroline M.; Meece, Judith L.; and Midgley, Carol.
    1985   Self-Perceptions, Task Perceptions, Socializing Influences, and the Decision to Enroll in Mathematics. Pp. 95-122 in *Women in Mathematics: Balancing the Equation*, ed. S.F. Chipman, L.R. Brush, and D.M. Wilson. Hillsdale, NJ: Erlbaum.

Favreau, Olga E.
    1977   Sex Bias in Psychological Research. *Canadian Psychological Review* 18: 56-65.

Fischer, Constance T.
    1984   A Phenomenological Study of Being Criminally Victimized: Contributions and Constraints of Qualitative Research. *Journal of Social Issues* 40: 161-178.

Freud, Sigmund.
    1925   Some Psychical Consequences of the Anatomical Distinction between the Sexes. *The Standard Edition of the Complete Psychological Works of Sigmund Freud*. London: Hogarth [1974].

Ford, Maureen R., and Lowery, Carol R.
    1986   Gender Differences in Moral Reasoning: A Comparison of the Use of Justice and Care Orientations. *Journal of Personality and Social Psychology* 50: 777-783.

Frodi, Ann; Macaulay, Jacqueline; and Thome, Pauline R.
    1977   Are Women Always Less Aggressive Than Men? *Psychological Bulletin* 84: 634-660.

Gergen, Kenneth.
    1973   Social Psychology as History. *Journal of Personality and Social Psychology* 26: 309-320.

Gilligan, Carol.
    1982a   *In a Different Voice: Psychological Theory and Women's Development*. Cambridge: Harvard University.

    1982b   Why Should a Woman be More Like a Man? *Psychology Today* 16: 68, 70-71, 73-74, 77.

Gold, D.P.
    1969   Effect of Experimenter in Eyeblink Conditioning.
                Psychonomic Science 17: 232-233.

Hollingworth, Leta.
    1914   *Functional Periodicity: An Experimental Study of the
                Mental and Motor Abilities of Women during
                Menstruation.* New York: Teachers College, Columbia
                University.

Johnson, C.A.; Smith, D.E.; Whatley, J.L.; and DeVoge, T.
    1973   The Effects of Sex and Personalism Factors on Subjects'
                Responses to Hypnotic Suggestions. *Proceedings of the
                81st Annual Convention of the American Psychological
                Association*, Montreal, 8: 1077-78.

Keller, Evelyn Fox.
    1982   Feminism and Science. *Signs* 7: 589-602.

Lenny, Ellen.
    1977   Women's Self-Confidence in Achievement Settings.
                Psychological Bulletin 84: 1-13.

Lips, Hilary M.
    1982   Somatic and Emotional Aspects of the Normal
                Pregnancy Experience: the First Five Months.
                American Journal of Obstetrics and Gynecology 142: 524-
                31.

    1985a   A Longitudinal Study of the Reporting of Emotional
                and Somatic Symptoms during Pregnancy. *Social
                Science and Medicine* 21: 631-40.

    1985b   Gender and the Sense of Power: Where are We and
                Where are We Going? *International Journal of
                Women's Studies* 8: 483-89.

Lips, Hilary M., and Morrison, Anne.
    1986   Changes in the Sense of Family among Couples Having
                Their First Child. *Journal of Social and Personal
                Relationships* 3: 393-400.

Lips, Hilary M., and Davidson, Dena.
    1987   Predicting University Women's Participation in Mathematics and Science: A Causal Model. Paper presented at the annual convention of the Canadian Psychological Association, June, Vancouver.

Lott, Bernice.
    1985   The Potential Enrichment of Social/Personality Psychology through Feminist Research and Vice Versa. *American Psychologist* 40: 155-64.

Lykes, M. Brinton, and Stewart, Abigail J.
    1983   Evaluating the Feminist Challenge in Psychology: 1963-1983. Presented at the Annual Convention of the American Psychological Association, Anaheim, August.

McHugh, Maureen C.; Koeske, Randi D.; and Frieze, Irene H.
    1981   *Guidelines for Nonsexist Research.* American Psychological Association Division 35 TaskForce Report, December, available from the American Psychological Association, 1200 Seventeenth St. N.W., Washington, D.C., U.S.A. 20036.

Miller, Jean B.
    1976   *Toward a New Psychology of Women.* Boston: Beacon.

Parlee, Mary B.
    1975   Psychology: Review Essay. *Signs* 1: 119-38.

    1981   Appropriate Control Groups in Feminist Research. *Psychology of Women Quarterly* 5: 637-44.

Peplau, Letitia Anne; Cochran, Susan; Rook, Karen; and Padesky, Christine.
    1978   Loving Women: Attachment and Autonomy in Lesbian Relationships. *Journal of Social Issues* 34: 7-27.

Prescott, Suzanne.
    1978   Why Researchers Don't Study Women: The Responses of 62 Researchers. *Sex Roles* 4: 899-905.

Rosenberg, Rosalind.
    1984   Leta Hollingworth: Toward a Sexless Intelligence. Pp.
            77-96 in *In The Shadow of the Past: Psychology Portrays
            the Sexes*, ed. Miriam Lewin. New York: Columbia
            University.

Rosenthal, Robert.
    1966   *Experimenter Effects in Behavioral Research*. New York:
            Appleton-Century-Crofts.

Rosenthal, Robert; Persinger, G.W.; Mulry, R.C.; Vikan-Kline, L.; and
Grothe, M.
    1964   Changes in Experimental Hypotheses as Determinants
            of Experimental Results. *Journal of Projective
            Techniques and Personality Assessments* 28: 465-69.

Rosenweig, Saul.
    1933   The Experimental Situation as a Psychological Problem.
            Psychological Reivew 40: 337-469.

Rossi, Alice.
    1980   Life-Span Theories and Women's Lives. *Signs* 6: 4-32.

Scott, William B., and Webster, Sandra K.
    1984   Gender Differences in the Attributional Effects of
            Videotape Self-Observation. Presented at the Annual
            Convention of the American Psychological Association,
            August, Toronto.

Stark-Adamec, Cannie, and Kimball, Meredith.
    1984   Science Free of Sexism: A Guide to the Conduct of
            Nonsexist Research. *Canadian Psychology* 25: 23-34.

Storms, Michael D.
    1973   Videotape and the Attribution Process: Reversing
            Actors' and Observers' Points of View. *Journal of
            Personality and Social Psychology* 27: 165-75.

Thompson (Woolley), Helen B.
    1903   *The Mental Traits of Sex: An Experimental Investigation
            of the Normal Mind in Men and Women*. Chicago:
            University of Chicago.

Walker, Lawrence.
    1984   Sex Differences in the Development of Moral Reasoning: A Critical Review. *Child Development* 55: 677-91.

Wand, Barbara (ed.).
    1977   Report of the Task Force on the Status of Women in Canadian Psychology. *Canadian Psychological Review* 18, entire issue.

Weisstein, Naomi.
    1971   *Psychology Constructs the Female, or the Fantasy Life of the Male Psychologist.* Boston: New England Free Press.

Wittig, Michelle A.
    1985   Metatheoretical Issues in the Psychology of Gender. *American Psychologist* 40: 800-11.

Chapter 4

WHAT IS FEMINIST LEGAL RESEARCH?

Lynn Smith

Feminist approaches to legal research differ from the standard approach to legal research in two respects. First, they are informed, to a greater or lesser extent, by an understanding that our legal system (and therefore the language of discourse or range of arguments which our legal system permits) is patriarchal in origin and spirit (Smith and Weisstub 1983). Second, they tend to be oriented toward changing the legal system in ways which will improve the position of women in the society. However, because feminist legal scholars differ in their analyses of the existing legal system, and in their views of the ways in which legal changes will improve the position of women (Du Bois *et al.* 1985) there are differing approaches to research.

Applications of feminist theory to legal change have formed an important part of the work of feminist legal researchers. They have seen the results when their theories are put into practice through legislative change or through arguments in court (Atcheson *et al.* 1984.) Two notable examples of this in the last decade are the development of a remedy for sexual harassment (MacKinnon 1979; Goodman 1981)[1] and statutory reform of the evidentiary rules applicable in rape cases (Clark and Lewis 1977; Backhouse and Schoenroth 1983; Estrich 1986.)

I will argue in this paper that there have been relatively distinct phases in feminist legal theory which have resulted in different ways of defining the issues concerning women in our legal system, and consequently, different ways of researching and arguing cases, and proposing solutions. Although "phases" suggests a notion of historical progress, this is somewhat inaccurate: these phases all continue into the present time and their development did not take place completely in the neat chronological order in which I discuss them. Before attempting to describe feminist legal research, I will briefly describe standard legal research, by way of contrast.

What is standard legal research?

Three main groups of people conduct legal research: academics, practitioners, and persons interested in law reform and policy review (law reform commissions, government departments, interest groups).[2] The research focus and methodology vary, depending upon the area of law and the purpose of the research, but the following description of legal research in terms of a particular problem should be generally accurate.

Research Problem

A young woman has applied for a job with a small business as a receptionist/secretary. She has been referred by her local Canada Employment Office. She is on Unemployment Insurance and five months pregnant when she goes for the job interview. She does not mention that she is pregnant, and is hired for the job, for which she is well qualified. It will consist of answering the telephone, and doing some typing. When the employer learns that she is pregnant, on her first day of work, he fires her. She brings a complaint under the Human Rights Act of the province, alleging sex discrimination in employment. The Human Rights Act does not mention pregnancy, but says: "No employer shall discriminate by reason of sex in hiring or terminating employees, or in setting terms and conditions of employment, except where the gender of the employee is a bona fide occupational requirement or where public decency would be affected."[3] The issue requiring research is whether the Human Rights Act prohibition against sex discrimination extends to cover discrimination based on pregnancy.

Standard Research Agenda

The checklist for research into this problem in most contexts would look like this:

1. Check the accuracy of the statutory language (i.e., make sure there have been no recent amendments.) Check recent legislative history (e.g., was there previously a section in the statute, addressing the issue of pregnancy discrimination, which was removed after a report from a legislative committee recommending that pregnancy discrimination be permitted?)
2. Search for previous, decided cases about whether sex discrimination includes pregnancy discrimination:
   A. under that province's Human Rights Act;
   B. under comparable human rights statutes in Canada;
   C. under the Canadian Bill of Rights and the Canadian Charter of Rights and Freedoms, which also refer to discrimination based on sex.

3. Sort the cases according to level of tribunal or court and jurisdiction, as well as according to the degree of similarity in the facts and statutory wording between the previous case and the instant case, and (informally) according to the stature of the jurist or Court in the previous decisions.

In many cases, research would stop here and the arguments would be formulated. The arguments generated would include arguments about the meaning of the words in the statute, bringing to bear legislative history and various "canons" of statutory construction, such as the "golden rule"[4] and the "mischief rule."[5] They would also include arguments about the previous cases, bringing to bear the rules of *stare decisis*[6] and analyses of the cases designed to show their similarity or difference from the instant one. This is the research model consistent with legal positivism, in which the answers to legal problems are thought to be discoverable through examination of statutory instruments and previous decided cases, in a quasi-scientific endeavor which takes those materials as the raw data and derives inferences about "the law" from them. It is a view of legal research consistent with some law practice and law reform goals, but inconsistent in some serious ways with the study of law as an academic discipline (*Law and Learning* 1983). The assumptions upon which legal positivism is based are among the matters most seriously questioned by feminists (see Hanen in this volume), as will be discussed later in this paper.

In other cases, either because the case is "big" enough to warrant an examination of "policy" issues and a review of the experience in other places, or because the purpose of the research is not adversarial but connected with an academic or law reform project, research would continue and could include:

4. A deeper and more long-term look into the sources of the legislation. This might include a review of the other legislative provisions affecting pregnant women in the jurisdiction in which the case arose.
5. A review of comparable provisions outside Canada, for example in the United Kingdom, the United States, or under the European Human Rights Convention.
6. A review of the legal academic literature.
7. Some review of the available empirical data on women and pregnancy in employment.

In summary, standard legal research consists of a conscientious and careful review of what legislatures and judges have said on the subject at hand, a task which is not at all easy or straightforward (Banks

1985; Yogis and Christie 1974; MacEllven 1983) but which leaves fundamental questions unasked. It may also include looking at comparable provisions or legal rules in other jurisdictions, at proposals for law reform, and at academic commentary.

Arguments in court often turn on establishing similarities or finding differences between one case and another. In order to know what counts as a similarity or a difference, one looks at previous cases to see what counts there. There are no clear principles under which similarities and differences will be determined, outside of particular contexts, and sometimes not even there. For example, with respect to the problem we are considering, the researcher would find a 1978 Supreme Court of Canada decision (*Bliss v. A.G. Canada*)[7] in which the Court found that section 1(b) of the Canadian Bill of Rights,[8] guaranteeing equality before the law without discrimination based on sex, does not extend to discrimination based on pregnancy. That case involved a challenge to the denial of regular unemployment insurance benefits to pregnant women (during a period of time around their expected date of confinement) whether or not they were ready and available to work. Among other things, the Court said (Dominion Law Reports 422):

> Any inequality between the sexes in this area is not created by legislation, but by nature.

The outcome of the game "Similarities and Differences" is highly unpredictable, as may be seen in the fact that, since the *Bliss* case, there have been seriously divergent views among courts and human rights tribunals about whether sex discrimination indeed includes pregnancy discrimination. Some judicial decisions have followed *Bliss* in interpreting human rights legislation,[9] while some human rights tribunals have not.[10] One of the most popular reasons for not following *Bliss* has been that it did not arise under a human rights statute, and the interpretation of human rights legislation should be "broad and liberal," according to Supreme Court of Canada cases in that area. On the other hand, those courts which have followed *Bliss* have pointed out that it is a Supreme Court of Canada statement about whether pregnancy discrimination is sex discrimination, and that the views of that court must be followed.[11]

Academics have been known to play "Similarities and Differences" with the best of them, although academic analysis sometimes focuses on showing that an original common law principle has been misconstrued or misapplied, or that the judicial decisions are inconsistent with one another, and suggesting a new principle which will reconcile as many of the decisions as possible and permit the derivation of decisions in future cases. Part of this exercise may include looking at public policy considerations and at the experience in other jurisdictions. Some academic work is much more theoretical, empirical, or interdisciplinary, but I believe that my description still fits a good deal of Canadian legal research today (*Law and Learning* 1983).

The point of most legal research, then, is to discover "what the law *is*" (what judges and legislatures have said) and extrapolate from that information to particular cases. Where there are gaps or inconsistencies, there is an appeal to higher-order principles derived from the existing body of law. The neutrality and universalizability of the principles are presumed.

First Phase of Feminist Legal Research

Explanation of Approach

Under this approach, the overall objectivity of the legal system, and its general principles, are accepted, but exceptions made from those general principles in areas involving women are challenged. Research consists in finding those exceptional areas where the law singles out women for disadvantageous treatment. The issue is typically defined to be whether these exceptions are "rational," meaning consistent with biological and social realities, or whether they can be eliminated and a gender-neutral state achieved. The British common law (judge-made and statutory) was full of such express distinctions, a few of which still persist and many of which have persisted until very recently. For example, many of the recommendations in the 1970 *Report of the Royal Commission on the Status of Women in Canada*, directed themselves toward such matters as different minimum wages for men and women, the married woman's loss of separate domicile, and Indian women's loss of Indian status for themselves and their children upon marriage. (Some of the Royal Commission's recommendations, on the other hand, concerned matters such as government support for child care and abortion, where there were no express distinctions between men and women.)

It will be useful to give examples, in the discussion of each of these "phases," of the problems which were defined and the solutions which were proposed. Examples of the first phase follow.

Examples

Admission to the legal profession. Women were not permitted to practice law in any Canadian jurisdiction until 1897 and have been permitted to practice in every jurisdiction only since 1941[12] (Backhouse 1985; Smith, Stephenson, and Quijano 1973). This was a clear case of differential treatment, which did not require much research to discover. That it was disadvantageous was contested by some, for example the editor of the *Canadian Law Journal* in 1879 who is quoted by Backhouse (1985: 14) as saying:

> As conveyancers or as compilers of text-books, there may be no reason why some women should not succeed as well as some men: but to refuse to allow them to embark upon the rough and troubled sea of actual legal practice, is, as it appears to us, being cruel only to be kind.

The cases in which the exclusion of women was challenged provide an excellent illustration of the construction of statutory language in an allegedly "neutral" system. The statutes typically provided that "persons" who met the requirements would be eligible for call and admission to the Bar, and the Interpretation Acts provided that "words importing the masculine gender" would include females as well as males except where the context indicated otherwise. Nevertheless, law societies argued, and courts agreed, that women were not within the contemplation of the legislature as potential lawyers: in other words, that the statutory wording should not be taken at face value. The proviso allowing for the context to indicate otherwise provided the escape hatch which was necessary to achieve this result. Such a result did not seem to be dictated by the wording of legislation or by previously decided cases; rather, it flowed directly from judicial views about what was right and proper in the world (Sachs and Wilson 1978).[13] It was by and large through legislative, rather than judicial, action that women gained entry to the legal profession, over the opposition of the profession in most places (Sachs and Wilson 1978; Smith *et al.* 1973).

Prostitution laws. Until 1972, the Criminal Code prohibited a "common prostitute or nightwalker" from being found on the streets and unable to give a good account of "herself." This can appear to be an equality issue when (a) the existence of men who sell sexual favors is contemplated, and (b) the decision is made to use the word "prostitute" to describe them. It was not until the end of the 1960s that the contemplation and the decision about word usage came to be relatively widely shared. At that point arguments began about the discriminatory nature of the law in that it failed to treat male and female prostitutes equally (*Report of the Royal Commission on the Status of Women*: 369-71; Smith 1971.) As well, the role of the vagrancy law (and its predecessors) in controlling female conduct had been criticized by feminists for a considerable time (*Report of the Royal Commission on the Status of Women*) and the radical notion that the consumer and provider of the services should be treated the same way (i.e., that if prostitutes were to be charged with an offense, so should be their customers), began to be widely discussed.

Matrimonial property laws. At common law, ownership of all of a married woman's personal property was vested in her husband. As well, the husband acquired control of all her land (McCaughan 1977: 5). The rationale for this position was found in the notional "unity of person of husband and wife"; they were one person, and that person was the husband. According to Backhouse (1985: 37), Clara Brett Martin (the first woman lawyer in the Commonwealth)[14] commented on this:

> This notion of unity of husband and wife, meaning thereby the suspension of the wife and lordship of the husband, seems to have been particularly agreeable to the whole race of English jurists, tickling their grim humor and gratifying their very limited sense of the fitness of things. How pleasantly, how good humoredly does the great Blackstone handle the theme in the first book of these inimitable commentaries of his: "Even the disabilities that the wife lies under are for the most part intended for her protection and benefit — so great a favourite is the female sex with the laws of England."

One of the earliest achievements of English feminists was the elimination of the common law rules as to married women's property and the institution of "separation of property,"[15] whereby each spouse in the marriage is treated as an individual owner of all property acquired before or during the marriage.

Grounds for divorce. Until 1925 in Canada, a husband could obtain divorce on the simple ground of the wife's adultery, while wives had to prove adultery plus cruelty; moreover, wives would be disentitled to maintenance if they had committed uncondoned adultery.[16] The current Divorce Act is the culmination of a trend toward elimination of "fault" as the basis for divorce, a trend which some feminists at earlier stages encouraged, given the way in which "fault" operated against women.

Analytical Framework for this Approach

The basic premise is that "women are people too" — and therefore should be assimilated under the legal principles governing people in general. Under this approach it is unnecessary to question the legal principles governing "people" in general or what is meant by "people." The goal is simply to have the same rules apply to everyone, and to have the rules enforced the same way for everyone. This is the approach consistent with classical liberalism. It seeks to maximize the opportunity for individual choice for all human beings.

Analogies between sexism and racism are strong in this class of cases, since arguments about racist legislation have often begun from a similar premise, such as "Chinese immigrants are people too." Exclusion from the franchise or the professions may seem equally invidious whether based upon sex, race, or religion. The anti-slavery movement in Britain and the United States, and later the Civil Rights movement in the United States, provided models which were often drawn upon by early feminists in formulating arguments and rhetoric. The Equal Protection Clause of the Fourteenth Amendment to the Constitution of the United States took racial discrimination as its paradigmatic case. The meaning of "equality" in American constitutional law has been clearly influenced by the necessities of dealing with racial discrimination (MacKinnon 1979: 127-8; Smith 1986: 363-6.)

Research Methodology for this Approach

The research methodology could be roughly described as follows:
1. Identify areas in which women are treated differently from men before or under the law.[17] Pinpoint the differences.
2. Consider whether the law or the manner of enforcement of the law could be rendered gender neutral.

Effectiveness of this Approach

There is no doubt that much of what was accomplished through the use of this approach (the electoral franchise, entry to the professions, separation of property in marriage, equal guardianship of children, identical minimum wages, and so on) was necessary and provided a base for what followed. However, it now seems that some of the gains were illusory, and that many of the real problems remain untouched or even worsened by gender-neutral solutions. The legal system has a spongy way of yielding in one area and creating new obstacles in another (for a discussion of an example of this in the area of wife battering, see Smart 1986).

To review the examples discussed above: first, there is now a large-scale presence of women in the junior levels of the legal and medical professions. However, this highly visible phenomenon has not eliminated the overall concentration of women in the workforce in jobs with low salaries and low prestige (Abella 1985: 62-74), yet it provides a focus for those who wish to say that problems for women in employment have been eliminated. Further, it has come at the same time as overcrowding in both the medical and legal professions, and much poorer job opportunities (as well as signs of lessening prestige).

Second, the Criminal Code section allowing for punishment of female prostitutes who were on the streets and unable to give a good account of themselves was repealed in 1972 and replaced by an apparently neutral soliciting offense, which in turn has been replaced by the current Criminal Code provisions, again gender neutral. Boyle and Noonan (1986: 248) review the history of prostitution laws against the background of the economic inequalities of men and women, and express doubt that the double standard for male and female conduct in this area has been eradicated. Even if it has, they say:

> the eradication of the double standard (should that happen) does not address the question of what standard to apply to the law in asking if it displays equal respect for women and men in the circumstances in which they have to live, earn their living and express their sexuality (1986: 248).

For example, there have been injunctions sought in two cities,[18] Vancouver and Halifax, against individual prostitutes (all or almost all female) to prohibit them from creating a nuisance in public places in connection with carrying on their business. As the Fraser Committee Report on Pornography and Prostitution pointed out (525-54), given that prostitution is to be a legal activity in Canada, the laws should make it possible for that activity to be carried out with some measure of safety and dignity for those who are the prostitutes. A gender-neutral approach that deals with male and female prostitutes the same way, and even makes the consumers and providers of the services equally responsible for creating a nuisance, does not deal successfully with that problem.[19]

Third, separation of property proved unhelpful to most women, who had no property to speak of when they married and failed to acquire any thereafter due to working in the home. When cases such as *Murdoch v. Murdoch*[20] came along, graphically illustrating the inequities consistent with gender neutrality in this area, a popular outcry ensued. Legislation followed in all common law provinces permitting, in varying circumstances, division of some of the property of a couple upon the breakdown of the marriage, under what have been described as "deferred discretionary community regimes" (McClean 1981: 361.) These are improvements over the two previous models (married women's loss of property, and separation of property) but have proved problematical in both their content and their interpretation by the courts (Steel 1985; Weitzman 1985).

Fourth, the quest for gender-neutral divorce rules has resulted in the achievement of "no-fault" divorce, allowing marriages to be ended much more easily. This has created a large group of divorced single-parent families headed by women, with inadequate maintenance awards for the children inadequately enforceable through the legal system and often short-term "rehabilitative" maintenance awards for the women themselves (this has been called "equality with a vengeance"). (See Mossman and Maclean 1986; Ehrenreich 1983; Weitzman 1985; Bruch and Wikler 1985; Scutt 1983).

With respect to the problem set out above, concerning pregnancy discrimination as sex discrimination, this analytical framework results in the conclusion that it is a non-issue. Pregnancy is something that happens to women, not to "people" in general, and therefore no argument can be made for assimilating women to the general rule. There is no general rule. (Alternatively, as the Court did in *Bliss*, the issue can be analyzed in a way which ignores that pregnancy happens only to women, so that a rule which treats all "pregnant persons" alike is acceptable.)

Second Phase of Feminist Legal Research

Explanation of Approach

This approach involves identifying areas in which the law has particularly important implications for women, whether or not the legal rules in those areas are gender neutral, and assessing whether there are some analogous circumstances in which the law would treat men better, or mustering arguments justifying special treatment for women.

Examples

Some of the areas in which laws have a most crucial role to play in women's lives are the treatment of victims of sexual offenses; provisions for maternity benefits and maternity leave, and safety legislation restricting the right to work in particular areas during pregnancy; regulation of spousal relationships during and after marriage, including protection against battering, and division of matrimonial property and maintenance; and protection against discrimination in employment with respect to wages and other terms of employment.

There is not space to do justice to all of these issues. I will use the treatment of victims of sexual offenses as my chief example.

Analytical Framework for this Approach

Under this approach, rules or systems which have the effect of keeping women in a particular role or of denying them physical protection may be questioned. Nevertheless, there is still a basic acceptance of the "general principles" of the legal system despite a concern that some of those principles do not adequately account for women's experience or treat them fairly. Alternatively, there may be full acceptance of the "general principles" of the legal system along with a view that "special treatment" is necessary for women in order for them to be able to reach a position where they can participate fully (have as many choices as men) in the society.

This could be called an extension of liberalism — there is often an emphasis on equal opportunity to make choices, but an expanded definition of what equal opportunity really means. The extension may be accompanied by a concern about state activity designed to bring about substantive equality. The concern might be either that such activity may result in imposing a particular model on all women (for example, that provision of universal daycare amounts to endorsement of women working outside the home, as opposed to working in the home — see Kirp and Yudof 1986), or that attempts such as affirmative action programs are theoretically dubious as amounting to state-imposed discrimination (likely to be a non-issue in Canadian courts, in the light of the Supreme Court of Canada decision in *Action Travail des Femmes v. Canadian National Railway Company*).[21]

On the other hand, this extension of liberalism is also consistent with support for affirmative action programs and other measures designed to remedy particular problems experienced by women. What distinguishes this approach from the "third phase" which I will describe is its continuing acceptance of the existing legal system as a framework within which equality for women can be accomplished.

The fundamental premises of this approach could be said to be "Women are people too" along with "The law can disadvantage women just as much by ignoring their situation and treating them the same way as men where that is inappropriate, as by setting up express rules which differentiate them, when *that* is inappropriate."

Research Methodology for this Approach

The methodology may be described as follows:

1. Identify legal issues which affect women's lives, whether or not they also affect men's lives. These may arise where the law expressly differentiates women or where seemingly neutral rules have a differential impact on women.

2. Find analogous legal problems involving men, or men and women. Look at the ways in which other legal systems have dealt with similar problems.

3. Ask whether the legal solutions to those problems could be applied to the one involving women. Ask whether the methods used by other legal systems could be adapted.

Effectiveness of this Approach

I will begin by discussing the example of the treatment of victims of sexual offenses. The feminist analysis of rape shows a progression through the first two phases of research I have described. Initially, rape was seen as a "women's issue" but not necessarily an "equality issue" because there is no analogous phenomenon in men's lives and no equivalent body of law and practice dealing (or failing to deal) with it. It is interesting to note that the Royal Commission on the Status of Women in 1970 limited its recommendations in the area of sex offenses to those areas in which there were departures from gender-neutrality on the face of the law, such as the "statutory rape" offenses, which protected only young girls and not young boys from sexual abuse, or blatant archaisms such as the references to "previous chaste character" in the definition of victims of certain offenses (*Report of the Royal Commission on the Status of Women*: 372-5.) The evidentiary rules in sexual offense cases, the definition of consent in rape and the entitlement of a husband to rape his wife (the crime was defined in terms of non-consensual intercourse by a male with a female who was not his wife)[22] escaped the operative definition of women's equality issues used by that Commission.

Subsequently, beginning in the early 1970s, feminists formulated a critique of the treatment of sexual offense cases. Comparisons were made between the reporting rates, prosecution rates, and conviction rates for rape and indecent assault as opposed to ordinary assault, assault causing bodily harm, and other crimes involving physical aggression. As well, arguments were made that the rules of evidence should be the same in sexual offense cases as in all others (Clark and Lewis 1977).[23]

Feminist attacks on the former rape laws were successful in bringing about some changes.[24] The prevalent feminist theory[25] was that rape is essentially an act of violence—it is not about sex, but about aggression. Therefore, sexual offenses should be seen in this way, and treated similarly to other acts of violence. Thus, the 1983 legislation (Bill C-127)[26] changed the definition of the relevant offenses and made them gender-neutral. The crimes of rape and indecent assault no longer exist. Now there is sexual assault,[27] sexual assault with a weapon, threats to a third party or causing bodily harm,[28] and aggravated sexual assault.[29] Spouses are no longer immune from charges under the sections. The corroboration[30] and recent complaint[31] requirements have been removed, as has the unrestricted right to cross-examine on previous sexual history[32] and the right to lead evidence or cross-examine about a complainant's sexual reputation.[33] An important aspect of the law which remains unchanged is that lack of consent is part of the definition of the offense, and must be proved by the Crown beyond a reasonable doubt. A full description of the new sexual assault provisions and their potential impact may be found in Boyle (1984).

Some of the problems which have already arisen with these amendments are instructive. The *Chase* case[34] brings out one of them—an attempt to find a gender-neutral definition of "sexual assault" led a court to the conclusion that since it is not sexual assault to touch a man's beard without his consent, it cannot be sexual assault to touch a woman's breast without her consent. Both are secondary sexual characteristics, and must be treated equally.

The *LeGallant* case[35] shows another problem. At the trial level, the Court analogized between cross-examination of a complainant on previous sexual conduct in a sexual assault case, and cross-examination of a complainant on previous violent conduct in an ordinary assault case involving a fight. The Court said that since the latter is permitted when relevant, so should be the former. But upon closer inspection, there are some real difficulties with the analogy. The complainant in a case of ordinary assault may have previously been involved in other fights. What he was involved in in the case in question was also a fight, and the issue may be who started it. With sexual assault, however, the complainant is cross-examined about whether she has taken part in activity which is totally different from sexual assault, namely consensual sexual activity, and the issue to be determined in the case is whether sexual activity on that occasion was consensual or not. The true analogy with the fight cases would be cross-examination of a complainant about previous non-consensual sexual activity, and it is difficult to see how that would be relevant.[36]

One other example arises under section 442 of the Criminal Code, which provides that judges must make order prohibiting the publication of the name or identifying characteristics of the complainant in sexual assault cases if the prosecutor or the complainant requests it. Not only has this section been challenged by the press (*Canadian Newspapers Co. Ltd. v. A.G. Can.*),[37] but one lower court has held that it means that the accused should equally be entitled to a non-publication order in such cases.[38]

At a fundamental level, some feminist writers such as Estrich (1986) and Boyle (1984) have questioned the consent element of the definition of sexual offenses, on the basis that it is derivative of the male, rather than the female, perspective. Estrich says (1986: 1182):

> In a better world, I believe that men and women would not presume either consent or nonconsent. They would ask, and be certain. There is nothing unromantic about showing the kind of respect for another person that demands that you know for sure before engaging in intimate contact. In a better world, women who said yes would be saying so from a position of equality, or at least sufficient power to say no. In a better world, fewer women would bargain with sex because they had nothing else to bargain with; they would be in at least as good a position to reject demands for sexual access as men are to reject demands for money.

> If we are not at the point where it is appropriate for the law to presume nonconsent from silence, and the reactions I have received to this Article suggest that we are not, then at least we should be at the point where it is legitimate to punish the man who ignores a woman's explicit words of protestations. I am quite certain that many women who say yes—whether on dates or on the job—would say no if they could; I have no doubt that women's silence is sometimes the product not of passion and desire but of pressure and pain. But at the very least the criminal law ought to say clearly that women who actually say no must be respected as meaning it; that nonconsent means saying no; that men who

proceed nonetheless, claiming that they thought no meant yes, have acted unreasonably and unlawfully.

Estrich goes on to say (1986: 1183):

> In a very real sense, what does make rape different from other crimes, at every level of the offense, is that rape is about sex and sexual violation. Were the essence of the crime the use of the gun or the knife or the threat, we wouldn't need—and wouldn't have—a separate crime.

The difference in approach from earlier attempts to force analogies between rape and other crimes (out of a felt necessity to assimilate rape cases to the "general rules") is apparent, and, in my view, shows the effects of what I will call the "third phase" of feminist research, which involves questioning the most fundamental premises of the legal system and addressing legal issues in what has been called "women's voice."

We can see other examples of situations in which research and analysis to date do not appear to have been satisfactory in defining women's problems and formulating solutions. Wives subject to mental or physical abuse during marriage[39] are a central concern for feminist researchers. The thinking about this problem over the years has gone through an evolution similar to the thinking about rape. Initially, there was an emphasis on assimilating the battering problem into the existing criminal law model—getting the cases heard in criminal court, not family court, having the sentences consistent with those for stranger assault, having the police attend domestic disputes and press charges in the same circumstances in which they would press charges in cases of stranger assault (United Way Task Force on Family Violence). Some of these changes have been implemented in places and may have had a salutary effect. However, they have not put an end to wife battering and do not seem reasonably likely to do so in the foreseeable future. More recently, analysis has focused on the features about wife battering which differentiate it from assault on strangers, recognizing that battering is a form of control exercised, not only over individual women, but also over women as a group.

The wife battering example serves to explain a criticism of the first two phases of feminist research: that they leave unquestioned the presumptive division into "public" and "private" spheres which characterizes traditional views of the law (as well as political and economic theory). Because women have been relegated to the "private" sphere (O'Donovan 1985), much of what keeps women in their place has not been required to "get itself up in law" (MacKinnon 1986: 42.) There are basic common law principles which help to maintain the line between "public" and "private" in a way that does not work to the advantage of those largely governed by the "private." For example, the principles that what is not forbidden is permitted, that legislation will not be construed as interfering with common law rights in the absence of express language, that "a man's home is his castle" (meaning that agents of the state must not enter there without a proper warrant or reasonable cause to believe a felony is being committed), and that the "liberty of the subject" is a fundamental value, again not to be interfered with unless justifiably so. As O'Donovan explains, putting together respect for the liberty of the subject and the sanctity of the home with a recognition of a family structure in which the male was the head of the household and entitled to govern household members, leads to physical oppression of women without legal remedy.[40]

In the context of the *Canadian Charter of Rights and Freedoms*,[41] the recent decision of the Supreme Court of Canada in *Dolphin Delivery*[42] leaves some disquieting questions, since it indicates that the *Charter* will be taken only to apply to legislative activity and to that portion of the common law relating to governments. This leaves immune from Charter review many of the common law rules which assume traditional models of the family and the extra-legality of activities in the "private" sphere[43] (Frost 1987).

A related issue arises in connection with the attacks by men on the parts of the law which are advantageous to women,[44] using equality provisions such as those in section 15 of the *Charter*.[45] Because these parts are almost always recent and legislatively created, they stand out like lone trees on an otherwise flat plain of the male-oriented common law and statutory system, and they make easy targets for an attack based on the principle of gender neutrality.

An overall assessment of the effectiveness of this second approach is difficult, because we are more or less in the middle of it. By and large, those who have thought about women's equality issues have come at least to the conclusion that identical treatment for women and men will not always achieve the kind of equality they have in mind. See, for example, the *Report of the Royal Commission on Equality in Employment*, although in some instances (such as the franchise) identical treatment is the only acceptable possibility. Much of the development of equality theory in the past few decades has been in the employment field, and consequently there has been considerable elaboration on the meaning of equality of opportunity, such that it can mean not only the opportunity to be considered on individual merits but also the opportunity to benefit from affirmative action programs designed to remedy past discrimination.

The theory behind the second phase of feminist research has been argued to contain inherent contradictions. If it springs from the same initial premise as the first approach, that "women are people too" and should therefore be treated the same way as other "people" under the law, it proves unable to deal with the problems which men do not have and which the law has reached no general (male) solution for (such as the research question above — the treatment of pregnancy). On the other hand, if the critique springs from the premise that women are different in some relevant ways and that sometimes you have to treat women differently in order to treat them equally, it proves unable (without incorporating further premises) to define when the differences should "count" and when they should not.

MacKinnon has made the point (1979, 1986) that both the "sameness" approach (women should be treated the same as men so long as they act the same as men) and the "differences" approach (women should be treated in a way which takes account of their differences from men) invoke a male standard. Under the "sameness" approach (gender neutrality), issues such as the treatment of rape victims, wife battering, and pornography are silenced out of the definition of equality problems because they involve "real" differences. That they happen mostly to women is seen as an unfortunate reflection of the different cards which fortune has dealt to the two different sexes. Under the "differences" approach (special treatment), there is the need to justify and explain the need to deviate from the norm, which has been developed to meet male conditions. An example of this is the attempt to cope with battered women who have murdered their husbands after years of abuse, yet whose actions do not fit neatly within the criminal law concept of "self defence" (Rosen 1986; Ewing 1987).

There is the further very important problem, the frequent need to fend off special treatment which is not to women's advantage (Williams 1982.) Whether views about the necessity for special treatment for women are held in good faith or in bad faith, the effect of disadvantaging special treatment is the same, and some feminists, for that reason, argue against concessions that special treatment may be necessary.[46]

In summary, some important features of women's legal inequality do not seem to yield understanding through research into how the treatment of women is different from that of men (the first phase), or even through research into laws which particularly affect women's lives (the second phase). Without deeper questioning, many things can seem inevitable, or at least impossible to change in the world as we know it.

To address the research question set out above, regarding dismissal for pregnancy, this approach would look for analogous circumstances in which men were treated better. This could mean comparisons between pregnancy and illness or disability. However, those comparisons are not especially close; moreover, they can be seen to devalue the reproductive function and emphasize the physical vulnerability of pregnant women. Alternatively, this approach might result in emphasizing the uniqueness of pregnancy and the consequential need of pregnant women for "special treatment." Again, a request for special treatment is an unfortunate way to begin a quest for equality.

Third Phase of Feminist Legal Research

Description of the Approach

I will begin this description by saying that it is incomplete. A proper description, let alone a critique, of recent trends in feminist legal theory is beyond the scope of this paper, which concentrates on describing how the research methodologies consistent with various theories have developed. Important writers and theories have been left out of this account. As well, I have not attempted to compare the feminist critique of the legal system with that of the Critical Legal Studies Movement, although they share important common features such as the denial of the neutrality, objectivity, and universalizability of the present legal system.

This approach begins with a radical skepticism about the neutrality and universalizability of the existing legal system. It questions our laws and practices in fundamental ways, as well as the reasoning process by which we understand and apply them (Scales 1986). It does so from the beginning premise that the existing system does not embody women's perspective. MacKinnon (1983: 638) expresses it this way in a now-classic passage:

> This defines our task not only because male dominance is perhaps the most pervasive and tenacious system of power in history, but because it is metaphysically nearly perfect. Its point of view is the standard for point-of-viewlessness, its particularity the meaning of universality. Its force is exercised as consent, its authority as participation, its supremacy as the paradigm of order, its control as the definition of legitimacy.

In a recent article, Miles (1985) reviews the history of the strands of feminist theory and practice to date. It may be seen roughly in terms of the three phases I have described—promoting identical treatment of the sexes, promoting the need for differential treatment in order to recognize women's specificity, and, at present, attempting to integrate the two through an attack on the neutrality and universalizability of the legal system and a reconstruction of it. She discusses legal reform, and concludes that it is necessary to break with the male norm in conceiving legislative reform (1985: 66-7):

> However, if they are not to reinforce the differences and disadvantages that they purport to redress, these laws must also radically revalue female activities and concerns as they break with the male as norm. In order to alleviate women's subordination, legal reform which recognizes women's special role in reproduction must also recognize the enormous economic contribution of this work and the social imperative of restructuring society and redistributing social resources to meet human needs more successfully than has been the case. This would be to make women's human-centered activities—which are often burdensome yet unrewarded—a central social priority and responsibility. It would necessarily involve both redistribution of social resources to women and redistribution of social and individual responsibility and labour to men. It would thus have to be framed in such a way as not to entrench reproduction and support activity as female, but to break down sexual divisions.

> This requires a revolutionary shift of perspective which is still in the process of being articulated and which will require a long term struggle and major social restructuring to achieve. But it is essential. For without a conscious alternative value framework/perspective to shape the feminist articulation of issues, piecemeal changes may very well reinforce rather than redress inequalities.

> In the struggle for legal reform, as elsewhere, a synthesis of the principles of equality and specificity is thus essential to feminist politics. An effective struggle for equality requires a break with the notion of male as norm—a break which can only be achieved if female specificity is recognized and revalued. Surpassing the male norm in turn makes it possible to take women's struggle for legal reform and equality beyond the strategy of assimilation to reflect alternative human values and affirm a new society.

In practical terms, an essential element of the legal research in this phase consists of developing arguments to show why women are not "trying to have it both ways" when they argue for identical treatment under the law in some cases and differential treatment in other cases.[47] One possible line of argument could go as follows.

Only from the perspective that sameness/difference with respect to males is the crucial and determinative issue, does the concern about "trying to have it both ways" ever arise. If women had been the dominant force in the creation of our society, including our legal system, and our legal system had considered women's needs as human needs, with men as necessary appendages to "human" (women's) lives, it would doubtless look very different from the present model. The legal system would not have developed a great many of the features that have been referred to in this paper. It might have developed features which did the same things to men which our present system does to women, through ignoring their perspective in some important ways.[48] Under that hypothetical system, it would be absurd to speak of women "trying to have it both ways" through accepting the benefits of the system: "both ways" would have no reference point. It is the same as, at the present, the lack of reference point for the notion of men "trying to have it both ways." It is not necessary for men to make any such attempt, because the system was designed with their needs wholly in mind in the first place.

The difficulties inherent in this third approach are discussed by Scales (1986: 1376):

> A new jurisprudence emerges as we cease to conduct the debate in prescribed legalistic terms. The equal/special rights debate, for example, reflects the circularity of liberal legal thinking. The rights formula, described in terms of constitutional fit, presumes a fixed reality of gender to which the law must conform. The problem of sexual inequality, however, when understood as systematic domination, is not susceptible to that view. Our past reliance on rights/rule structuring has been disappointing, because we have been unable to see the solipsism of the male norm. Our tendency as lawyers to seek comprehensive rules in accordance with that norm is a dangerous learned reflex which defeats feminism's critique of objectification.

Analytical Framework for this Approach

One such framework is suggested by MacKinnon (1986: 40) who says:

> The fundamental issue of equality is not whether one is the same or different. It is not the gender difference, it is the difference gender makes. In this perspective, equality is not exclusively or

even primarily an issue of irrational differentiation. To be on the bottom of a hierarchy is certainly different from being on the top of one, but it is not simply differences that most distinguishes them. It is, in fact, the lesser access to resources, privileges, credibility, legitimacy, authority, pay, bodily integrity, security, and protection that is effective for you: *less* of all of what is valued in society. The issue here is not entirely how to make access to those things non-arbitrary, because the situation we are confronting is anything but arbitrary. It is an issue of systematic male supremacy and how it shall be ended. Confronting this problem leads to a much more substantive approach to the notion of equality. It leads to the principle that to be equal is to be non-subordinate: not to be subordinated. This principle is not voided by difference; it is only voided by parity. If systematic relegation to inferiority is what is wrong with inequality, we are not going to be spending the rest of our jurisprudence looking for conditions under which inequality can be justified.

There is an emphasis in this approach, as there has always been in feminist legal scholarship, on concrete changes in existing institutions which will bring about improvements in the position of women.[49] But the improvements are to be measured not in terms of the extent to which women gain acceptance into the social/economic world as it now is, but rather in terms of the extent to which subordination of women is ended and substantive equality between the sexes is achieved. This means revaluation of women's work, and rather profound changes in human sexuality as we now understand it, among other things. The program cannot be described as unambitious.

"Consciousness-raising" and the belief that "the personal is the political" are seen as essential tools in this approach. Scales says (1986: 1401):

Feminist method proceeds through consciousness raising. The results of consciousness raising cannot be verified by traditional methods, nor need they be. We are therefore operating from within an epistemological framework which denies our power to know. This is an inherently transformative process: it validates the experience of women, the major content of which has been invalidation.

The discussion of personal experiences of women leads to the insights about the existing state of the law which underlie the analysis. The incorporation of personal experience into the critique is a refutation of the male hegemony on appropriate reasoning processes in the law. A recent example is provided by Estrich's scholarly article on "Rape" in the *Yale Law Journal*, which begins with this passage:

> Eleven years ago, a man held an ice pick to my throat and said: "Push over, shut up, or I'll kill you." I did what he said, but I couldn't stop crying. A hundred years later, I jumped out of my car as he drove away.

> I ended up in the back seat of a police car. I told the two officers I had been raped by a man who came up to the car door as I was getting out in my own parking lot (and trying to balance two bags of groceries and kick the car door open). He took the car, too (1986: 1087).

Estrich's detailed analysis of United States laws regarding rape is informed by her experience and by this perception which she explains in her account of that experience (1986: 1088):

> I learned, much later, that I had "really" been raped. Unlike, say, the woman who claimed she'd been raped by a man she actually knew, and was with voluntarily. Unlike, say, women who are "asking for it", and get what they deserve. I would listen as seemingly intelligent people explained these distinctions to me, and marvel; later I read about them in books, court opinions, and empirical studies. It is bad enough to be a "real" rape victim. How terrible to be — what to call it — a "not real" rape victim.

Research Methodology for this Approach

One of the characteristics of this approach to feminist legal research is that it tends to be interdisciplinary. Researchers spend relatively less time in hunting the latest word from the courts and the legislatures (although that is essential information) than in exploring other academic fields, including the social sciences, legal history, psychoanalysis, psychology, and philosophy. A possible explanation for this is the search for an "Archimedean point" outside the existing legal system upon which one can stand and apply leverage to move it.

A second characteristic is that it examines areas of the law which most feminists have previously been content to accept as neutral and therefore uninteresting, such as taxation, damages for personal injuries, general criminal law principles, "legal reasoning" and "rights theory."

Often this approach leads to insights into the way in which the privatization of women has combined with an individualistic approach to equality, to women's detriment. The economics of marriage breakdown have attracted substantial recent attention (Weitzman 1985; Scutt 1983;

Abella 1981; Mossman and Maclean 1986). Mossman and Maclean argue (1986: 108):

> Along with the development of no-fault divorce has developed an assumption of a partnership and concurrently an assumption of equality. The result is that alimony is based on need, child support has become a shared responsibility, and marital property is divided equally. As previously mentioned, however, the difficulty with the legislation is that sexual equality is stated as an accomplished fact. As another writer has suggested this may be because there is confusion as to the meaning of equality; does it mean equality of opportunity or of result? In our current legislation, family members are "judicially equal." Yet, as has been suggested [by Olsen 1984: 10-11]:

> This view treats women's subordination as though it occurred by chance. That men happen to earn almost twice as much as women, and that this affects the social relations between the sexes is, according to this view, not the state's concern. Similarly, that children are economically dependent upon their parents and that parents sometimes use this dependence to dominate or exploit their children, is likewise not the state's concern. Rather, the mistreatment of wives and children is simply a series of unfortunate individual occurrences.

Similarly, the liberal definition of "freedom of expression" and its significance in the contest of pornography has been examined by feminists from varying perspectives (Lahey 1986).

Effectiveness of this Approach

It is impossible to say how effective this approach will be, since it has so recently begun to be attempted, and it makes such fundamental challenges to the status quo. One problem is its indeterminateness: it is very difficult to derive and articulate "tests" which will neatly solve legal problems. It seems fairly common for discussions of the findings of feminist researchers in this phase to end with a statement that they are offering no solutions, but attempting a new definition of the problems.[50]

There is also the difficulty in reconciling the view of the public/private dichotomy as mistaken and productive of non-protection for women, with a view also held by some feminists that intrusion by a male-dominated state is not necessarily going to be an improvement. Recent incidents in which pregnant women have found themselves to be the containers of foetuses which have been "apprehended" under child protection legislation illustrate this problem.[51]

A third problem is the potential for this approach to become focused on biological males rather than "malestream" reasoning and institutions.

Finally, it must be recognized that interdisciplinarity has its risks: "insights" transported carelessly or without sufficient contextual understanding from one discipline into another can prove seriously misleading.

Nevertheless, the analysis yielded in this third stage is exciting and productive. The sexual harassment remedy, for example, was the first legal remedy fashioned by women out of the process of taking seriously women's perspective about an issue. To paraphrase MacKinnon, in this particular context there has come to be a measure of acceptance that what men perceive as pornography women experience as degradation, what men perceive as humor women experience as insult, and what men perceive as sex women experience as rape: that the male view (often embodied in the law) is not the objective one.

On a practical level, in some court cases women are attempting to put forward arguments in "women's voice": to speak about particular events or larger issues in the way in which women understand them, rather than automatically translating the concepts into the language traditionally used in courts and developed from a male perspective.[52]

To return to our research problem arising from the woman dismissed due to her pregnancy, let us consider what the third phase of research might entail. First, one might look into the empirical evidence about pregnant women's abilities during pregnancy, and the social sciences literature about pregnancy as a social phenomenon. One would look at protection against pregnancy discrimination in other jurisdictions to see if any good working models are available, and at the economics of pregnancy from the pregnant woman's point of view as well as from the employer's. One might even look at psychoanalytic material to learn something about our unconscious reactions to pregnancy.

In formulating arguments in the case, the analysis would begin with the premise that the male worker should not be taken as the norm: taking the female worker as the norm is the only way to produce substantive equality. Taking the female worker as the norm would mean assuming that almost all workers are susceptible, at some stage of their lives, to becoming pregnant. It would also mean disabusing ourselves of the mistaken view that pregnancy is a voluntary condition. Pregnancy may well be voluntary for some women at some times. It is not a voluntary condition for women as a group, unless we are willing to contemplate the end of the human race. As well, the assumption would have to be that persons in the work force have a strong interest in continued employment with the same employer. The question then becomes whether employers should be able to dismiss employees when they become pregnant, assuming that virtually all employees are susceptible to that risk, and that pregnancy is a condition which must be assumed by some employees in order to continue the human race. Posing the question that way seems to dictate an answer that dismissal would not be permitted. By contrast, posing the question on the assumption of a male norm may dictate the opposite, since the female worker who becomes pregnant is acting in an anomalous way which the system should not have to accommodate. If the way the questions are posed does make the difference, what justification is there for using the first question rather than the second? In my view, the justification stems from the normative statement that the question must be posed that way in order for women to achieve equality.

Scales summarizes her views about the present stage of feminist jurisprudence this way (1986: 1400-1):

Feminism now faces the charge leveled at Realism, that it destroys the citadel of objectivity and leaves nothing to legitimate the law. Our response to this state of affairs begins with an insight not exclusive to feminist thought: The law must finally enter the twentieth century. The business of living and progressing within our disciplines requires that we give up on "objective" verification at various critical moments, such as when we rely upon gravity, or upon the existence of others, or upon the principle of verification itself. Feminism insists upon epistemological and psychological sophistication in law: Jurisprudence will forever be stuck in a post-realist battle of subjectivities, with all the discomfort that has represented, until we confront the distinction between knowing subject and known object.

Conclusion

The three phases of feminist legal research correspond with different approaches to feminist legal theory. To some extent, as far as research methodology goes, all of them are inclusive of the standard approach to legal research, the difference being that they do not accept the answers it produces as the final ones.

For practical legal research, to a large extent, they are cumulative of one another, and those who are working in the third phase must encompass consideration of everything involved in the first and second phases. To some extent, however, this is not the case: if the test is, does this rule or practice produce substantive equality for women, and the answer is no, it is not necessary to consider whether there are analogous provisions in other areas of the law in order to decide that it needs changing. However, the development of arguments in court to produce such change may still largely depend upon analogizing and, where possible, pointing out express differentiation in the law. If the research is to enter the third phase, the trap to avoid is the conclusion that the research should stop when the search for analogies or express differentiation is unsuccessful. Rather, the question should then be asked whether the problem has been defined in a way which assumes a male norm, and, if so, how it could be redefined in a way which leads to a solution.

As for theoretical work, the third phase of feminist research amounts to a radical transformation of not only the research agenda, but the scope and methods of research. The gap between the theoretical work and what is argued (or arguable) in courtrooms is obviously very wide, but not unbridgeable. The historical tendency of feminists interested in the law to work on concrete problems has continued, and should mean that feminist thinking will continue to have an impact on legal change.

Endnotes

1. The notion of a remedy for sexual harassment was initiated in the United States, but has become relatively well accepted in Canada. Numerous Human Rights tribunals and some court decisions have recognized it as warranted in the context of protection against sex discrimination. However, recently the Manitoba Court of Appeal has held that legislation prohibiting sex discrimination cannot be taken to prohibit sexual harassment: see *Janzen and Goverau v. Pharos Restaurant and Grammas* (1987) 43 Man. R. (2d) 293, leave to appeal to the Supreme Court of Canada granted June 25, 1987.

2. I am using the term "legal research" in its broadest sense, to include conventional (doctrinal), theoretical, law reform, and fundamental research, in the terminology used in *Law and Learning (1983: 65-66)*.

3. These facts are similar, but not identical, to those at issue in a case decided by the British Columbia Human Rights Council: *Davies v. Century Oils Inc. and Production Supply Company Ltd.* (1986) 8 C.H.R.R. D/3770 (James R. Edgett, Member Designate). The case, at the time of writing, has been partially heard on an application for judicial review in the British Columbia Supreme Court.

4. The "golden rule" requires that, where a statute is ambiguous, the grammatical or ordinary sense of the words be applied, unless that leads to some absurdity or inconsistency with the rest of the statute. If there would be an absurdity or inconsistency, then it may be avoided through modifying the ordinary meaning of the words.

5. Under the "mischief rule," the court must consider, when interpreting an ambiguous statute, what problem or "mischief" the legislature was attempting to remedy in enacting the legislation, and what remedy for the mischief was chosen. The statute should then be construed in a manner which would suppress the mischief and advance the remedy.

6. The rules requiring adherence to rulings in cases previously decided by superior courts.

7. *Bliss v. A.G. Canada* [1979] 1 S.C.R. 183, [1978] 6 W.W.R. 711, 78 C.L.L.C. 14, 175, 23 N.R. 527, 92 D.L.R. (3d) 417. The specific legislation at issue in *Bliss* has since been amended. For a discussion of *Bliss* in the context of its political consequences, see Pal and Morton 1986.

8. The *Canadian Bill of Rights*, S.C. 1960, c. 44 (R.S.C. 1970, App. III), was enacted under the Diefenbaker government. It applies only to the federal government, and protects certain fundamental rights and freedoms, including "equality before the law." For various reasons, including the fact that it is not constitutionally entrenched, the *Canadian Bill of Rights* has been given a very narrow interpretation by the Supreme Court of Canada.

9. *Wong v. Hughes Petroleum Ltd.*, (1983) 4 C.H.R.R. D/1488 (Alberta Queen's Bench); *Brooks et al. v. Canada Safeway Ltd.*, (1985) 7 C.H.R.R. D/3185 (Manitoba Queen's Bench.)

10. *Magnussen v. Winestock and Merlon Management Ltd.*, (1986) 8 C.H.R.R. D/3641 (A.G. Agnew, Sask. Board of Inquiry); *Stefanshyn v. Four Seasons Management Ltd. (Four Seasons Racquet Club)*, (1986) 8 C.H.R.R. D/3934 (John I.D. Joe, Member Designate, B.C. Human Rights Council); *Pattison v. Fort Frances Commissioners of Police*, (1987) 8 C.H.R.R. D/3884 (Daniel Jay Baum, Ontario Board of Inquiry); *Holloway v. Clair McDonald and Clairco Foods Ltd.*, (1983) 4 C.H.R.R. D/1454 (William Black, B.C. Board of Inquiry); *Tellier-Cohen v. Treasury Board*, (1982) 3 C.H.R.R. D/792 (Fed. Trib.), 4 C.H.R.R. D/1169 (Fed. Rev. Trib.)

11. A Manitoba Court of Appeal case on pregnancy discrimination is on its way to the Supreme Court of Canada, and the issue is likely to be determined in that case: *Brooks, Allen and Dixon et al. v. Canada Safeway Ltd.* (1987) 42 Man. R. (2d) 27.

12. Quebec was the last province to admit women; Ontario the first.

13. It was parallel reasoning which brought the famous "Persons Case" to the Supreme Court of Canada and then to the Judicial Committee of the Privy Council (*Edwards v. A.G. Canada* [1930] A.C. 124.) The issue was whether women were qualified to be Senators under the British North America Act of 1867, which said of a senator that "He shall be of the full age of Thirty Years..." (s. 23(a)). The difference in the approach taken by the Privy Council in that case from the one taken by courts in the admission to the practice of law cases is shown in Lord Sankey's metaphor

for a constitution which is flexible and capable of progressive interpretation (at A.C. 136):

> The British North American Act planted in Canada
> a living tree capable of growth and expansion within
> its natural limits.

This was in contradistinction to the view of the Supreme Court of Canada of the day, which had been that since women senators could not have been contemplated in 1867, the Constitution should be so interpreted for all time.

14. She was called to the Bar of Ontario in 1897.

15. Through statutes such as the *Married Women's Property Act*, R.S.B.C. 1979, c. 252, repealed S.B.C. 1985 c. 68, s. 84 effective April 17, 1985 and replaced with *Law and Equity Act*, R.S.B.C. 1979, c. 224, s. 55. See, in general, McCaughan 1977, Chapter 1.

16. For example, the *Wives and Children's Maintenance Act*, R.S.B.C. 1960, chap. 93, s. 9(1) and (2); repealed and replaced with the *Family Relations Act*, 1972. It must be added that men could not obtain alimony at all. This likely reflected two things: the assumption that men would be income earners and supporters, and the fact that men had been entitled to their wives' property during marriage during early stages of the development of the laws relating to alimony.

17. "Before or under the law" is the phrase used in section 15(1) of the *Canadian Charter of Rights and Freedoms*, and invokes the notion that it is not only that all persons must be amenable to the law, but also that the content of the law must not differentiate improperly.

18. Granted in Vancouver (*Attorney-General for British Columbia v. Couillard et al.*, (1984), 11 D.L.R. (4th) 567, 14 C.C.C. (3d) 169 (B.C.S.C.)); denied in Halifax (*Attorney-General for Nova Scotia v. Beaver et al.*, (1985), 66 N.S.R. (2d) 419 (N.S.S.C.), affirmed (1985), 67 N.S.R. (2d) 281 (N.S.C.A.)). For a discussion of these cases, see Cassels.

19. This is not to suggest that the Fraser Committee recommendations necessarily achieve that goal either. I agree with what I take Boyle and Noonan to be saying: there are no good answers at the present time to the question about a feminist approach to prostitution. Most feminists would probably be of the view that prostitution would not exist in the ideal world, and feel

great dissonance in the context of discussions about how to make it more palatable as a career choice. Yet the paternalism inherent in saying that women should be deterred for their own good from prostitution is problematical as well.

20. [1975] S.C.R. 423, [1974] 1 W.W.R. 361, 41 D.L.R. (3d) 367. This was a Supreme Court of Canada decision in a case in which an Alberta woman was denied a share in the family ranch, held in her husband's name alone, despite her extraordinary labors over the years. Her efforts were described as those to be expected of a ranch wife. For a description of the impact of this case on the efforts to obtain matrimonial property legislation, see Atcheson *et al.* 1984.

21. Unreported, June 25, 1987. The Supreme Court of Canada, in a unanimous decision, discussed the problem of systemic discrimination in employment and the reasons for which affirmative action programs are necessary. It expressed no concern whatsoever about "reverse discrimination."

22. Criminal Code of Canada, R.S.C. 1970, chap. C-34, section 143.

23. The rules of evidence were very different for complainants in sexual offense cases than they were for other witnesses in other cases. There were three main differences: the complainant's evidence had to be corroborated in a material particular, the complainant could be cross-examined about her previous sexual conduct with other men either on the theory that this was relevant to whether she had consented to intercourse with the accused, or on the theory that this would go to her credibility as a witness, and the complainant was expected to have made a "prompt complaint" — a relic of the medieval expectation that the victim of a felony would raise hue and cry.

24. The changes were the result of a ten-year lobbying effort by women's groups (and perhaps the imminent proclamation of the Canadian Charter of Rights and Freedoms) and went through several stages. After the creation of the first rape crisis centres in the early 1970s, and the publication of works such as the Clark and Lewis book (1977), a consensus emerged among feminists that the criminal law system was not affording adequate protection for women's physical autonomy. Several years of work resulted in some early changes to the Criminal Code — the 1976 removal of the corroboration requirement along with an attempt to protect complainants from irrelevant questioning about

previous sexual conduct. Unfortunately, because of the way in which the courts interpreted the new provision (then s. 142), complainants were put in a worse position than they had been previously, since defendants were now able to call evidence to contradict them in what they had said about previous sexual conduct in those cases where the questioning was still permitted. Lobbying and studies continued, and many organizations became involved, including the Law Reform Commission of Canada. In 1982, more sweeping changes were made. These included changing the names and definitions of the crimes formerly known as rape and indecent assault.

25.   Shared by the writer at the time, although my views have now changed.

26.   S.C. 1980-81-82, c. 125.

27.   Criminal Code, s. 246.1.

28.   Criminal Code, s. 246.2.

29.   Criminal Code, s. 246.3.

30.   Judges are now prohibited from warning the jury that it is unsafe to convict in the absence of corroboration of the complainant's testimony with respect to the sexual assault charges as well as incest and gross indecency: Criminal Code, s. 246.4.

31.   Criminal Code, s. 244(4).

32.   The exceptions still allow for cross-examination in rebuttal, on identity, and in cases involving group sex: see Criminal Code, s. 246.6. The legislation has been challenged, with varying results. See *R. v. Le Gallant* (1986), 29 C.C.C. (3d) 29133 D.L.R. (4th) 444 (B.C.C.A.) (upholding the legislation) and *R. v. Seaboyer; R. v. Gayme* (Ontario C.A., August, 1987, *The Lawyer's Weekly*, August 28, 1987, p. 1).

33.   Criminal Code, section 246.7.

34.   (1984), 13 C.C.C. (2d) 187, 40 C.R. (3d) 282, leave to appeal to the Supreme Court of Canada granted October 1, 1984. At the time of writing, the appeal has been heard but no decision has yet been announced. Other courts at the appellate level have taken different views about this point: see *R. v. Alderton* [1985] O.R.

(2d) 257, 17 C.C.C. (3d) 204 (Ont. C.A.); *R. v. Cook* (1985), 20 C.C.C. (3d) 18 (B.C.C.A.); *R. v. Taylor* (1985), 19 C.C.C. (3d) 156 (Alta. C.A.)

35.   (1985), 6 B.C.L.R. (2d) 105 (S.C.), reversed on appeal [1986] 6 W.W.R. 372, 6 B.C.L.R. (2d) 105, 54 C.R. (3d) 46, 29 C.C.C. (3d) 291 (C.A.)

36.   I acknowledge my debt to Megan Ellis for this argument, and for other parts of this discussion about the new sexual offense provisions.

37.   (1985), 17 C.C.C. (3d) 385, 44 C.R. (3d) 97 (Ont. C.A.), leave to appeal to S.C.C. granted C.C.C. loc cit.)

38.   *Regina v. R.* (1986), 28 C.C.C. (3d) 188 (Ont. H.Ct.)

39.   Recently estimated at one out of eight Canadian women in a report prepared for the Canadian Advisory Council on the Status of Women: Macleod 1987.

40.   It must be recalled that until quite recently wives could not sue their husbands for personal injuries, even when intentionally inflicted. That rule has now been changed in several provinces.

41.   *Constitution Act, 1982*, enacted by the *Canada Act, 1982* (U.K.), c. 11, Schedule B, Part I.

42.   [1987] 1 W.W.R. 577; 33 D.L.R. (4th) 174.

43.   On the other hand, feminists (such as the writer) who are also civil libertarians feel a significant level of discomfort about inviting the state into many spheres of activity traditionally immune from intrusion. The answer may be to recognize that "privacy" refers to a number of rather distinct interests. The interest of a family member in being able to prevent legal authorities from interfering with abuse of another family member, when such interference is requested or clearly needed, seems very different from, for example, the interest of an unmarried mother in refraining from naming the father of her child. Women have used the privacy interest to their own ends in some cases. The use of the "privacy" interest to protect a woman's right to choose abortion during the first two trimesters of pregnancy in the United States Supreme Court provides a case in point: see *Roe v. Wade*, 410 U.S. 113 (1973).

44.   Recent examples are *Re MacVicar and Superintendant of Family &
        Child Services et al.*, December 24, 1986, B.C.S.C. (unreported), in
        which section 8(1)(b) of the *Adoption Act*, which authorizes an
        adoption order to be made with the consent only of the child's
        mother where the mother and father have never been married,
        was held unconstitutional because of the denial of equality to
        men; *Regina v. Howell* (1986), 26 C.C.C. (3d) 104 (Nfld. Dist. Ct.)
        where section 153 of the *Criminal Code*, which prohibits sexual
        intercourse between male persons and their stepdaughters, foster
        daughters or female wards was struck down because females are
        immune from being charged with an offense for similar activity;
        Reference re Family Benefits Act, (1986), 75 N.S.R. (2d) and 186
        A.P.R. 338 (N.S.S.C., App. Div.), in which social assistance
        provisions for needy single mothers of dependent children were
        struck down as unconstitutional because of the failure to provide
        similar benefits for needy single fathers of dependent children.

45.   Section 15 of the *Charter* reads:
        > 15(1) Every individual is equal before and under the
        > law and has the right to the equal protection and
        > equal benefit of the law without discrimination and,
        > in particular, without discrimination based on race,
        > national or ethnic origin, colour, religion, sex, age or
        > mental or physical disability.
        >
        > (2) Subsection (1) does not preclude any law,
        > program or activity that has has its object the
        > amelioration of conditions of disadvantaged
        > individuals or groups including those that are
        > disadvantaged because of race, national or ethnic
        > origin, colour, religion, sex, age or mental or
        > physical disability.

46.   Note that several large women's groups recently argued in the
        United States Supreme Court, in *California Federal Savings and
        Lan Association et al. v. Guerra et al.*, against the constitutionality
        of state legislation providing female employees with four months
        unpaid maternity leave and guaranteed job protection upon their
        return, on the theory that this amounted to a return to "special
        treatment" inconsistent with equality for women. The decision of
        the Supreme Court was handed down on January 13, 1987,
        upholding the legislation.

47.   In very practical terms, as Kenney points out, sometimes
        arguments can be made in analogical terms where that works.
        The danger, obviously, is that the thought patterns of the decision-

maker become geared to finding justification for measures eliminating inequality only when arguments by analogy can be made.

48. For example, it does not seem overly far-fetched to imagine that such a legal system might attach various economic and social consequences to child-rearing or assistance in child-rearing, such that participation in the society was contingent upon successful raising of children, an activity from which men, "not through legislation but nature," were precluded.

49. These include, in MacKinnon's case, the remedy for sexual harassment and the attempt to create a civil remedy against pornography: see MacKinnon 1984. A civic anti-pornography ordinance along the lines suggested by MacKinnon was struck down as unconstitutional by the United States Supreme Court: *American Booksellers Assoc. v. Hudnu*, 771 F. 2d 323 (7th Cir. 1985), affirmed 106 S. Ct. 1172 (1986). However, subject to revision by a newly-constituted Supreme Court, remedies for sex harassment as sex discrimination have been recognized: see *Meritor Savings Bank, FSB v. Vinson*, 106 S. Ct. 2399.

50. As Hanen (1987) points out, however, this is consistent with a change in perspective as fundamental as the one which is being described.

51. See In the Matter of the Family and Child Service Act and In the Matter of Baby Boy "R", British Columbia Provincial Court, September 3, 1987, Vancouver Reg. no. 876215.

52. A recent example has been the formulation of the Ontario Women Teachers Federation response to the challenge to its continued separate existence.

References

_____.
1970 *Report of the Royal Commission on the Status of Women in Canada*. Ottawa, Information Canada. (Florence Bird, Chairman).

_____.
1979 *Family Violence: Report of the Task Force on Family Violence*, United Way Task Force on Family Violence. Vancouver (unpublished).

_____.
1983 *Law and Learning: Report to the Social Sciences and Humanities Research Council of Canada by the Consultative Group on Research and education in Law*, Ottawa: Information Division of The Social Sciences and Humanities Research Council of Canada (Harry Arthurs, Chairman).

_____.
1985 *Pornography and Prostitution in Canada: Report of the Special Committee on Pornography and Prostitution*. Ottawa: Minister of Supply and Services, Canada (Paul Fraser, Chairman).

Abella, Rosalie.
1981 Family Law in Ontario: Changing Assumptions. 13 *Ottawa Law Review* 1.

1985 *Report of the Royal Commission on Equality in Employment*. Ottawa: Supply and Services Canada.

Atcheson, M. Elizabeth; Eberts, Mary; and Symes, Beth; with Stoddart, Jennifer.
1984 *Women and Legal Action: Precedents, Resources, and Strategies for the Future*. Ottawa: Canadian Advisory Council on the Status of Women.

Backhouse, Constance.
1985 "To Open the Way for Others of my Sex"; Clara Brett Martin's Career as Canada's First Woman Lawyer. *Canadian Journal of Women and the Law* 1: 1 ff.

Backhouse, Constance, and Schoenroth, Lorna.
　　1983　A Comparative Survey of Canadian and American Rape Law. *Canada-United States Law Journal* 6: 48-88.

Banks, Margaret.
　　1985　*Using a Law Library: A Guide for Students and Lawyers in the Common Law Provinces of Canada.* Toronto: Carswell.

Boyle, Christine.
　　1984　*Sexual Assault.* Toronto: Carswell.

Boyle, Christine, and Noonan, Sheila.
　　1986　Prostitution and Pornography: Beyond Formal Equality. *Dalhousie Law Journal* 10: 225-65.

Bruch, Carol S., and Wikler, Norma J.
　　1985　The Economic Consequences *Juvenile and Family Court Journal* Fall: 5-26.

Cassels, Jamie.
　　1985　Prostitution and Public Nuisance: Desperate Measures and the Limits of Civil Adjudication. *Canadian Bar Review* 63: 764-804.

Clark, Lorenne M.G., and Lewis, Deborah J.
　　1977　*Rape: The Price of Coercive Sexuality.* Toronto: The Women's Press.

DuBois, Ellen C.; Dunlap, Mary C.; Gilligan, Carol J.; MacKinnon, Catharine A.; and Menkel-Meadow, Carrie J.
　　1985　Feminist Discourse, Moral Values, and the Law—a Conversation. *Buffalo Law Review* 34: 11-87.

Ehrenreich, Barbara
　　1983　*The Hearts of Men: American Dreams and the Flight from Commitment.* Garden City, N.Y.: Anchor.

Ellis, Megan.
　　1986　Judicial Interpretation of the New Sexual Offences in Light of the Charter of Rights and Freedoms: An Examination of Gender-Neutrality, Discrimination and Inequality. (unpublished paper).

Estrich, Susan.
    1986   Rape. *Yale Law Journal* 95: 1087-208.

Ewing, Charles Patrick.
    1987   *Battered Women Who Kill: Psychological Self-Defense as Legal Justification*. Lexington and Toronto: Lexington Books.

Frost, Susanne.
    1987   Prosecutorial Discretion, Wife Battery and Patriarchy. *Canadian Journal of Women and the Law* (forthcoming).

Goodman, Jill Laurie.
    1981   Sexual Harassment: Some Observations on the Distance Travelled and the Distance Yet to Go. *Capital University Law Review* 10: 445-69.

Hanen, Marsha.
    1987   Feminism, Reason, and Philosophical Method. (Included in this anthology.)

Kenney, S.J.
    1986   Reproductive Hazards in the Workplace: the Law and Sexual Difference. *International Journal of the Sociology of Law* 14: 393-414.

Kirp, David L., and Yudof, Mark G.
    1986   *Gender Justice*. Chicago: University of Chicago.

Lahey, Kathleen A.
    1986   The Charter and Pornography: Toward a Restricted Theory of Constitutionally Protected Expression. In *Litigating the Values of a Nation: The Canadian Charter of Rights and Freedoms*, eds. J. Weiler and R. Elliot. Toronto: Carswell.

MacEllven, Douglas T.
    1983   *Legal Research Handbook*. Toronto: Butterworths.

MacKinnon, Catharine A.
    1979   *Sexual Harassment of Working Women: A Case Study of Discrimination*. New Haven: Yale University.

1983 Feminism, Marxism, Method, and the State: Toward Feminist Jurisprudence. *Signs: Journal of Women in Culture and Society* 8: 635-58.

1986 Making Sex Equality Real. Pp. 37-43 in *Righting the Balance: Canada's New Equality Rights*, eds. Lynn Smith, Gisele Cote-Harper, Robin Elliot, and Magda Seydegart. Saskatoon: Canadian Human Rights Reporter.

Macleod, Linda.
1987 *Battered but not Beaten: Preventing Wife Battering in Canada*. Ottawa: Canadian Advisory Council on the Status of Women.

McCaughan, Margaret M.
1977 *Legal Status of Married Women in Canada*. Toronto: Carswell.

McClean, A.J.
1981 Matrimonial Property—Canadian Common Law Style. *University of Toronto Law Journal* 31: 361-435.

Miles, Angela R.
1985 Feminism, Equality and Liberation. *Canadian Journal of Women and the Law* 1: 42-70.

Mossman, Mary Jane, and Maclean, Morag.
1986 Family Law and Social Welfare: Toward a New Equality? *Canadian Journal of Family Law* 5: 79-110.

O'Donovan, Katherine.
1985 *Sexual Divisions in the Law*. London: Weidenfeld and Nicolson.

Olsen, F.E.
1984 The Politics of Family Law. *Law and Inequality* 2: 1-19.

Pal, Leslie A., and Morton, F.L.
1986 *Bliss v. Attorney-General of Canada*: from Legal Defeat to Political Victory. 24 *Osgoode Hall Law Journal* 141.

Rosen, Cathryn Jo.
1986 The Excuse of Self-Defense: Correcting a Historical Accident on Behalf of Battered Women Who Kill. *American University Law Review* 36: 11-56.

Sachs, Albie, and Wilson, Joan.
　　1978　*Sexism and the Law*. Oxford: Martin Robertson Co. Ltd.

Scales, Ann C.
　　1986　The Emergence of Feminist Jurisprudence:　An Essay.
　　　　　Yale Law Journal 95: 1373-403.

Scutt, Jocelynne A.
　　1983　Principle v. Practice:　Defining 'Equality' in Family
　　　　　Property Division on Divorce.　*Australian Law Journal*
　　　　　March: 143-60.

Smart, Carol.
　　1986　Feminism and Law:　Some Problems of Analysis and
　　　　　Strategy. *International Journal of the Sociology of Law* 14:
　　　　　109-23.

Smith, J.C., and Weisstub, David N.
　　1983　*The Western Idea of Law*. Toronto: Butterworths.

Smith, Lynn.
　　1971　Case Comment:　R. v. Lavoie.　*University of British
　　　　　Columbia Law Review* 6: 442-49.

　　1986　A New Paradigm for Equality Rights.　Pp. 353-407 in
　　　　　Righting the Balance: Canada's New Equality Rights, eds.
　　　　　Lynn Smith, Gisele Cote-Harper, Robin Elliot, Magda
　　　　　Seydegart. Saskatoon: Canadian Human Rights Reporter.

Smith, Lynn; Stephenson, Marylee; and Quijano, Gina.
　　1973　The Legal Profession and Women:　Finding Articles in
　　　　　British Columbia.　*University of British Columbia Law
　　　　　Review* 8. 137-75.

Steel, Freda.
　　1985　The Ideal Marital Property Regime.　Pp. 127-68 in *Family
　　　　　Law in Canada:　New Directions*, ed. Elizabeth Sloss.
　　　　　Ottawa:　Canadian Advisory Council on the Status of
　　　　　Women.

Weitzmann, Lenore.
　　1985　*The Divorce Revolution: the Unexpected Social Economic
　　　　　Consequences for Women and Children in America*. New
　　　　　York: The Free Press.

Williams, Wendy W.
    1982   The Equality Crisis: Some Reflections on Culture, Courts, and Feminism. *Women's Rights Law Reporter* 7: 175-200.

Yogis, John A., and Christie, Innis M.
    1974   *Legal Writing and Research Manual.*   Toronto: Butterworths.

Chapter 5

THE INFLUENCE OF FEMINIST PERSPECTIVES ON HISTORICAL RESEARCH METHODOLOGY

Micheline Dumont*

The practice of women's history first appeared in major Western countries sometime between 1965 and 1970 and this "birth" was evidently linked with the awakening of the feminist movement. All major feminist writings from the early 1970s revealed important historical developments: one tends to think of Susan Brownmiller's book on rape, *Against Our Will*, of books by Shulamith Firestone, or by Kate Millett, which, also, raised an increasing number of historical questions. In fact, the relation between the feminist perspective and the history of women did not need to be demonstrated: it compelled recognition as an established fact.

Preparing this paper, I have found more than ten different ways of looking at women's history. Unable to decide which one was the best, I chose to present yet another one: my own.

Various types of methodological reflections

This new field of study, just getting off the ground, produced many types of reflections which might be interesting to recall briefly. First of all, the absence of the reality of women, resulting from a purely masculine definition of the domain of history, in contemporary historical production and in historiography was measured.[1] The simple observation "Women have a history; women are in history" had the importance of a manifesto, as Gerda Lerner explained (1979: xx,169). Secondly, many historiographical accounts (descriptive, analytical, or critical) were regularly published. These became precious tools when it came time to undertake new studies, to confirm the questions raised by these studies, and to compare the research findings with the tendencies in other major countries.[2] We are now in the "second wave," reassessing the findings of the early seventies.

---

*Translation by Carol Cochrane

Thirdly, many methodological texts were also published to examine the ways of countering the absence of women in the archives; to explore the possibilities of contributions from other social sciences; to investigate differently the periodization; to reveal the real facts behind normative discourses which condition the lives of women; to establish archives specifically for women; to decode contemporary historiographical production differently.[3] It seems, however, that these methodological adjustments barely influenced historians as a whole, for they simply reintegrated these particulars into their own frames of reference.

The most striking of all the reflections, however, was the fourth type which was comprised of theoretical, even epistemological, writings. They were lucid writings that stated fundamental problems which had to be resolved if the history of women was to achieve its scientific credibility with respect to the corporation of historians and if the studies carried out were to be clearly situated with respect to theoretical assumptions, traditional definitions, and the most often used concepts.[4] Both originated in the androcentric perspective which has always characterized historical studies. When Joan Kelly published "The Social Relations of the Sexes: Methodological Implications of Women's History," (Kelly-Gadol 1983), many feminist historians stressed the relevance of this proposal which could form the basis for a "paradigm shift" to enable the re-evaluation of all human experience. Too often identified with natural phenomena, the differences between the sexes had to be introduced into the domain of history. It is quite certain that traditional, historical discourse obscured social relations between the sexes and did not recognize that sexual roles constituted evolving phenomena. You remember at school, and even at university, you learned about the fur-trade, the colonial wars, the stages of the Canadian Constitution, the West, the railroads, the political parties, the Canadian identity, etc. There was no place in this scenario for a theme as outlandish as the social relationship between the sexes.

From another point of view, if this historical analysis of men/women relations were undertaken, it would have to go beyond simple description. While revealing the destiny of women, their ambivalence, their exploitation, their inequality and especially the repetition, under different forms, of a condition or a role which seemed natural, it would be necessary that the history of women not reinforce the collective image that women had of themselves. It is not enough to explain, and even denounce, that collective image if the research results in reinforcing traditional definitions of power and social order.[5] Only a feminist analysis can change the focus. In fact, the thinking on a theoretical level about women's history favored the feminist analysis, thus often freeing it from the pitfalls of a whig (liberal) interpretation or those of a Marxist analysis. These two analyses, indeed, even in the field of the history of women, have not greatly altered our conception of history. In fact, it is by means of theoretical analysis that the influence of women's history on the whole of historical production can be measured.

The fundamental question is as follows: on what basis do women share an historical existence? Evidently, sexual identity is not enough. In women's history, even though it is relatively easy to establish a new periodization, to propose feminine or feminist interpretations of past phenomena, to base the history of women on the history of unknown persons, and on the actions taken by women according to the social roles which have been culturally assigned to them, it is more difficult to act in such a way that this new history is incorporated into the old. It is always found, after all, to one side, on the inside, in a hollow, in black, in white, in pink, gathered in special chapters, squeezed into an index between "West" and "Work" and, as Arlette Farge (1983), a French historian says, in an assigned, therefore controlled, place. Sandra Harding asks:

> How then are we to construct adequate feminist theory, or even *theories*...? Where are we to find the analytical concepts and categories for the absent, the invisible, the silenced that do not simply replicate in mirror-image fashion the distorting and mystifying categories and projects of the dominant discourses? (Harding 1986: 648).

Let us look at three of the many concepts which have been used in women's history: equality, difference, and oppression (subordination). We shall thereby describe the impact of feminist thinking on historical research.

Equality

The concept of equality suggests theoretical frames which are less and less operational.[6] Basically, there is conviction that the reform of democratic institutions ensures social progress for all individuals. All histories of feminism and so-called "reformist" feminist theories present this problem. This analysis uses the masculine model as a basic standard and corresponds almost intrinsically to the strategies adopted by men to provoke the desired change. More and more, feminist historians think it is perhaps the opposite that can be said. By revealing women's history, "we are in a position to demonstrate that a problem other than evolution exists, a future for women who question the very concepts of social change, determinism and historical progress."[7] In the nineteenth century, Suzanne Voilquien, one of the first French feminists, a disciple of Saint-Simon, thought that the equality of the sexes, by feminizing the society, would release the unknown. Today, the principle is accepted, but the unknown is still there, oh! just around the corner, on the threshold between the visible and the invisible. It seems that all hope for equality will remain an illusion as long as the rules (or the laws)? determining so-called "traditional" social roles are strictly maintained.

Most historiographical interpretations would like to keep to the equality frame of reference for their analysis but its validity is increasingly disputed by feminist historians. In fact, it is the egalitarian perspective which the history books most voluntarily incorporate because it does not disturb traditional interpretations.

Difference

The problem of difference first created much enthusiasm with some of the nineteenth-century feminists who wished to regenerate society: we claim our rights in order to better perform our roles as wives and mothers. This form of feminism has been rightly called "maternal feminism." However, the concept of difference also inspired the newer feminists of the 1970s, even those labelled "radicals." As opposed to the male standards, they offered another model: the feminine model, because they exalted "la féminitude" (womankind?). Consequently, feminist historians identified the difference in the physical body as the specific source of the oppression of women, thus specifying new areas for research: fertility, health, domestic sphere, autonomy, violence, family, feminine-oriented discourse.

Whatever the case may be, it is well-known that feminist historians produced an increasing number of studies about the woman's body (sexuality, fertility, maternity, physiology, health, professions close to the "feminine nature"). Likewise, they also increasingly studied normative discourse even though such studies did not always take into account the social practices and the means of resisting this type of discourse. Among male historians, there were many who entered this field of research and many took pleasure in researching the stages and the aberrations in discourse against women, and it is not clear whether their insistence was not a way of displaying their hate for women while disguising it in denunciation. Male studies on sexual conduct, prostitution, and pornography often produce such perverse effects.[8] To be sure, they analyze the issues with a masculine bias.

The best example is Family History. In 1980, leading scholars gathered in Bellagio, Italy, to discuss the current practices and trends in various fields of research. Speaking about Family History, Lawrence Stone pointed out the enormous production pouring out of England, France, and the United States. More than 800 books and scholarly articles had been published between 1972 and 1976 and the trend is now accelerating. Reading everything that is being published in Family History is now a full time job. Stone's panorama suggests however that theoretical frames adopted by male historians (that of Shorter, Degler, Duby, etc.) have been more often publicized and that feminist views on Family History are more likely to be marginalized or obliterated.[9]

In addition, male and female historians have documented *ad nauseam* the segregation of the sexes, the confinement of women, the poor performance by women in the different spheres of artistic and scientific creation, and the concealment of feminine accomplishments. Basically, the difference between the sexes as a framework for analysis has, on the whole, hardly shaken our overall knowledge of the history of humanity.

The concept of difference seems full of pitfalls which are difficult to avoid. It is important to be aware of the paradox of a concept which, at the same time, denounces and exalts maternity, fertility, femininity, etc. The eternal conflict between nature and culture is the basis of this paradox. The truth of the following statement is inevitable: "Historians must accept the gender identities and roles that different societies assign to males and females as historical facts that require historical analysis" (Fox-Genonese 1982). Joan Kelly was right: It is the relation between the sexes which must be studied historically, rather than the difference between the sexes. This affirmation is found in the most important theoretical statements of feminist historians.

Natalie Davis (1975) claims the aim is:

to understand the significance of the sexes, of gender groups in the historical past. Our goal is to discover the range in sex roles and in sexual symbolism in different societies and periods, to find out what meaning they had and how they functioned to maintain the social order or to promote its change.

Joan Wallach Scott (1983: 153) states:

The point is to examine social definitions of gender as they are developed by men and women, constructed in and affected by economic and political institutions expressive of a range of relationships which include not only sex but class and power.

Pauline Schmitt-Pantel (1984, my translation) declares:

Take into account within an equal treatment, masculine and feminine in every historical analysis and think that the relations between the sexes might be the motor of history.

Michelle Perrot (1984b: 15, my translation) concludes:

As we see, the question is not to constitute a new territory that would be "women's history," a quiet land where they could work at ease, far from any contradiction; but much more to change the direction of the historical look, asking the very central question: what are the relations between the sexes? Women's history shall be possible only at that price.

From the difference between the sexes
to the relation between the sexes

A cultural approach seems most appropriate in considering this question. It must be immediately added that the issue of belonging to one sex or the other is different from such issues as beliefs, attitudes, and codes in a given society. It also can be stated that the issue of belonging to one sex or the other distinguishes one society from another. Owing to this parameter, new fields of research, with exciting findings, have opened up in the unlimited area of social history within "la nouvelle histoire."

Thus, a disturbing observation must be made. It is difficult to focus the lens of our research instruments on the relation between the sexes.

Let us give an easily identifiable example. A number of studies, especially in France, have recorded the kinds of male and of female social interaction, as well as the places where this socializing occurred. The studies show places of male socializing, varying in time, such as 'abbayes de jeunesse', hunting parties, army barracks, taverns, cafés, smoking rooms, clubs. The places for women were le 'lavoir,' the open oven, the fountain, the market, the home. In earlier societies men and women rarely met. Even in church, they sat on opposite sides of the aisle. And that is not all! You must surely have noticed that most of the places of socializing for men have been places of leisure and that the places for women have been places of work (Annales, E.S.C. 1986: 274)! From this evidence of inequality it is possible to state that the analysis of cultural models raises the problem of the relationship between these models and the exercise of power. Do women have powers? Do they have power? The distinction is important and is conducive to new thinking in regard to the other series of concepts used in women's history; namely, those concepts subsumed under the pair of notions "male domination/female oppression," including subordination, power, liberation, etc.

Subordination and Oppression

Fifteen years ago, this dialectic of "male domination/female oppression" occupied the whole field. Frequent and complex systems of cultural variations and even forms of power exclusive to women were often neglected in order to document better and denounce the millennial oppression of women. This omission justifiably drew criticism of those early "denunciations" by feminist historians. More recent studies have attempted to document the positive aspects of the universe of women. At that point, a new interpretation emerged. If women have their version of a social sense, if they have the use of practices destined to help the entire community to cross from life to death, it becomes evident that they do have power (or powers?). Besides, studies have shown that to conserve these powers, in certain societies or social groups, the women themselves have contributed to the perpetuation of the models of male domination and those of female subordination.[10]

The intensive practice of cultural history (in the anthropological sense) in France opened the way to numerous studies, as many by women as by men, which thus reoriented the overall analysis of reality. Other concepts have been specified as well: male authority versus the powers of women (in the family, in birth rituals, in domestic production, in symbolism, etc.). But we must not be fooled. The updating of the "feminine powers" during historical periods carries the risk of disguising, in the name of complementarity of powers, the inequality of the relation between the sexes. Often, this complementarity is one of subordination; in addition, values and symbols attached to each function must be studied. Often the modalities of feminine contestation are overlooked and there is an attempt to neutralize such neglect by using the concept of marginality as a cover. The functional aspect of complementarity should therefore not hide the precarious balance, real or symbolic, between the masculine and feminine universes.

The methodological practice for the last twenty years of referring to different temporal levels; "la longue durée, le temps conjoncturel, le temps court," has resulted in never placing the feminine "facts" on the same tempo as the masculine "facts." For the history of women there is the "longue durée," that of the attitudes, mentalities, norms, rituals, etc.; and for traditional history, conjunctural time or "le temps court," that of wars, politics, revolutions, business, etc. Thus, the objects of "longue durée" (the family, the couple, love, domestic work, etc.) are those which most frequently set forth the difference between the sexes and most of all the social relation of the sexes; and in doing so, exclude them from historical studies centered on "le temps court" (Perrot 1986: 278).

The areas of tension between the sexes are therefore excluded from the investigations of political history or of economic history, which conduct their studies with the good conscience that "la longue durée" facts which belong to women's history do not directly interfere with their perspective. In light of this marginalization, the history of the relationship between the sexes cannot succeed in breaking out of private life: it therefore cannot influence the methodology of history on most of the themes.

There is, however, an example which includes possible relations between the history of feminism and political history. The liberal tradition has a custom of associating primitive feminism with a demonstration of the reformist movement, which seemed to disappear as the winds of conservatism started to blow after 1918. Elise Boulding writes in her book *The Underside of History* (1976: 620-21):

> More and more it was middle- and upper-class women who were realizing the larger picture. They were developing new approaches to the problems of urban poverty. For the first time middle-class women were in a position to make the kinds of judgments possible earlier only for royal women, and this produced tensions. On the one hand, the women were developing their analytic capacities and developing confidence in their own abilities as they got reality-feedback from their efforts. On the other hand, they were repeatedly confronted with absurdities: the absurdity of the conventional limitations on their role, the absurdity that men controlled the resources with which women needed to do their work, and the absurdity that these same men held a definition of women which implied that women could not possibly understand the issues they were dealing with.

> In the end, women found that task-orientated cooperative relationships with men in social welfare work could not be carried out as women and men were not equal partners in political decision making. The detour which women took on behalf of women's suffrage was not at first primarily a consciousness-raising

phenomenon. The consciousness raising came as a consequence of the violence of the reactions of the men to the very pragmatic course the women chose. Neither was there any grand theory of history involved, only a simple conviction that the rights of man were also the rights of woman.

Therefore, at the intersection of reformism and the industrial revolution may be situated an area of friction between the sexes which has escaped traditional political history (feminism was only a marginal chapter in the history of reformism) and even the history of feminism, which neglected the private and domestic aspects of the early feminist struggles. It therefore is not enough to restore discourse and knowledge peculiar to women, nor even to attribute forgotten powers to them. One must try to understand how a feminine culture is created inside a system of unequal relationships; how its attributes are disqualified; how the mechanisms of exclusion are constituted and maintained; how texts justifying the difference between the sexes are modified; how the examples of feminine resistance are erased from the collective memory. Thus, the accent placed on the importance of women's roles at certain levels of social life should not suppress the main problem of male domination. It seems that all groups have a tendency to hide the conflicts and contradictions which taint the beautiful, complementary portraits of private life which historians have begun to paint.[11]

In short, within the two theoretical frames of equality and difference, any feminist perspective has been dissolved. It has been relegated to a simple chapter on the history of democracy or used as a way of sampling the eternity of differences. Family History is the best example of that fate.

On the other hand, the dialectic "male domination/female oppression" has often been neutralized under the cover of "new" theoretical frames: that of complementarity, that of female powers, that of marginality, that of class stratification, and so on.

Since the end of the second World War, history has moved from the avenues of politics, diplomacy, and war to the vast and yet unexplored fields of social, economic, and cultural history. At the same time, the discipline has accomplished a radical shift in methodology. Once a narrative subject (history/story), it is more and more organized within a theoretical frame similar to the model of the social sciences. Above all, the practitioners abandoned the assumption that history was mainly concerned with what had happened only once and initiated the theory that if it is history it should concentrate on recurrent phenomena. This three-level mutation could have been particularly favorable to the joining of history with women's history. As we have seen, however, the theoretical frame most frequently adopted by feminists has not modified the lenses by which historians look at the past. Women's history is still relegated to the periphery of history.

I could have presented you with different analyses. Women's history, written by women from a feminist perspective, considers women as *subjects of history*. Here, I think, is a fundamental break. It is not a coincidence that women's history is mainly undertaken by women. By doing so, female historians have entered the "territory of the male historian" and are occupying a very disquieting position there. For they investigate social practices, discourses, images, and the dichotomies of nature/culture and private/public in a different way. I could well have presented an analysis on the number of feminist historians in the various departments. There are only a few. Each department, however, has at least one feminist. They all, in turn, have been feared, excluded, tolerated, sought after (to ease conscience) and their importance is, even at this moment, being minimized under the false pretext that the history of women has been recognized. It seems to me that their situation is very close to that of a token female historian in the eyes of their colleagues.

The same analysis holds for the *object of history*. In consulting scholarly journals, I could have counted the number of articles, book reviews, questions debated, and could have repeated the exercise for scientific conferences. I would have gathered a meager 10% at best to confirm that the sector exists, that it is even brilliant, stimulating, innovative, etc.[12]

But articles are pouring out on so many "new" themes. In France, one speaks of "l'histoire totale," an explosion of themes which do not actually alter the traditional view of the past. And, here in Canada, *The Dictionary of Canadian Biography*, in spite of intense research, is unable to offer more than 3% of its biographies about women in each of its volumes. And most historians think that women's history should remain where it belongs, in a "special" chapter of social history.

It is certain that adding women to history is not the same as adding women's history. "In spite of the path-breaking monographs, however, it is still rare to find histories which include women and women's activities as an integral part of the narrative," says Patricia Hilden, commenting on the second wave of women's history in a recent issue of *The Historical Journal* (1982: 510):

> Most historians continue to write as though women were absent from history altogether. Those who recognize the presence of women tend to assign them a separate (and rarely equal) place.

More and more historical monographs feature a chapter called "Women."

The brief analysis by Sylvia Van Kirk (1984) shows that the accumulation of knowledge in Canada about the history of Canadian women has barely influenced the usual practice of history. Certainly, in Quebec, in any case, books of syntheses with chapters on women are now being published. In addition to the fact that the chapters are few in number, analysis shows that they do not take into account research conducted by feminist historians or that they have obliterated the very interpretation which rendered them more or less subversive.

These mediocre accounts seem only to be the consequence of the preceding theoretical analysis. The investigation of feminist analysis in history has not yet succeeded in making a dent in the certainties of traditional historical knowledge. Ten years later, Gerda Lerner's statement is still very accurate:

What is needed is a new universal history, a holistic history which will be a synthesis of traditional history and women's history. It will be based on close comparative study of given periods in which the historical experiences of men are compared with those of women, their interactions being as much the subject of study as their differences and tensions. Only after a series of such detailed studies has been done and their concepts have entered into the general culture can we hope to find the parameters by which to define the new universal history. But this much can be said already: Only a history based on the recognition that women have always been essential to the making of history and that men and women are the measure of significance, will be truly a universal history (1979: 180).

Endnotes

1. One of the first examples is D.B. Schmidt and E.R. Schmidt (1976). The essay was written in 1971 and was succeeded by numerous articles of the same type.

2. It is impossible to present an accurate list of that kind of historiographical account, as many journals publish "review essays" and most collective books are prefaced by such chapters. Here is a list of a few "classics" from which articles on specific topics (e.g., education, birth control, work, etc.) have been omitted. Margaret Andrews (1977); Nathalie A. Davis (1975); Richard J. Evans (1982); Nadia Fahmy-Eid et M. Dumont (1983); Arlette Farge (1983); Elizabeth Fox-Genonese (1982); Patricia Hilden (1982); Alwen Hufton (1983); M. Lavigne et Y. Pinard (1983); Carolyn C. Lougee (1977); Michelle Perrot (1981); Ruth Pierson (1977); Alison Prentice (1978); Joan W. Scott (1981; 1983); Barbara Sicherman (1975); B. Sicherman *et al.* (1980); Carol Smith-Rosenberg (1975).

3. Here is a sample of recent publications on more technical aspects of methodology in women's history: Deirdre Beddoe (1982); Joyce D. Falk (1983); Arlette Farge (1984); Susan N.G. Geiger (1986); Ann P. Gordon, Mari-Jo Buble, and Nancy Schrom-Dye (1976); Sheila R. Johansson (1976); Christiane Klapish-Zuber (1984); Yvonne Knibiehler (1984); Marie Lavigne (1976); Elizabeth K. Minnich (1985); Darlene R. Roth (1983); Hilda Smith (1976); Susan M. Trofimenkoff (1985: 1-9); Syvie Van de Casteele-Schweitzer et Danielle Voldman (1984: 59-71).

4. From memory, here is an obviously incomplete list: Berenice Carroll (1976); Joan Kelly (1984); Gerda Lerner (1979); J. Newton *et al.* (1983); Michelle Perrot (1984).

5. There is a striking example of that situation in the trial EEOC v. Sears, Roebuck, and Co. where two feminist scholars testify in two different interpretations about history of women's work in the United States. Cf. Women's History Goes to Trial. *Signs* 11, 4 (Summer 1986): 751-79.

6. Many aspects (philosophical, legal, sociological, historical) are discussed in *Egalité et différence des sexes*, Actes du colloque international sur la situation de la femme. Ville Colloque

interdisciplinaire de la Société de philosophie du Québec, Montréal, Cahiers de l'ACFAS, no. 44, 1986.

7.   Marie-Jo Bonnet (1984: 371, my translation).

8.   See the chapters written by Richard Poulin in R. Poulin and C. Coderre (1986).

9.   Lawrence Stone (1982: 52). His statements should be compared to those of Rapp, Ross, and Bridenthal, Examining Family History. Pp. 232-58 in *Sex and Class in Women's History*, ed. J. Newton *et al.* (1983).

10.   See, among others, C. Lacoste-Dujardin (1985) and M.E. Handman (1983).

11.   Currently published in France, a prestigious collection, *Histoire de la vie privée*, under the direction of Philippe Ariès and Georges Duby. (The collection will be eventually published in English.)

12.   Large bibliographies published regularly prove, at least, that women are now in history.

References

_____.
1979   *L'histoire sans qualité*. Paris: Galilée.

_____.
1984   *Strategies de femmes*. Paris: Tiercé.

_____.
1986   Culture et pouvoir des femmes: essai d'historiographie.
       Dans *Annales ESC* (mars-avril).

_____.
1986   *Égalité et différence des sexes*. Montréal: Cahiers de
       l'ACFAS 44. Ville Colloque interdiciplinaire de la Société
       de philosophie du Québec.

Andrews, Margaret.
1977   Attitudes in Canadian Women's History: 1945-1975.
       Journal of Canadian Studies. Revue d'études canadiennes
       12: 69-78.

Beddoe, Deirdre.
1982   *Discovering Women's History: A Practical Manual*.
       London: Pandora.

Bonnet, Marie-Jo.
1984   Adieux à l'histoire: Pp. 363-72 dans *Stratégies des femmes*.
       Paris: Tiercé.

Boulding, Elise.
1976   *The Underside of History: A View of Women Through Time*.
       Boulder: Westview.

Carroll, Berenice A. (ed.).
1976   *Liberating Women's History: Theoretical and Critical
       Essays*. Chicago: University of Illinois.

Davis, Nathalie A.
1975   Women's History in Transition: The European Case.
       Feminist Studies 3: 83-103.

Evans, Richard J.
>   1982   The History of European Women: A Critical Survey of Recent Research. *Journal of Modern History* 52: 656-75.

Fahmy-Eid, Nadia, et Dumont, M.
>   1983   Les rapports femmes famille éducation au Québec: bilan de la recherche. Pp. 5-46 dans *Maîtresses de maison, maîtresses d'école*. Montréal: Boréal Express.

Falk, Joyce D.
>   1983   The New Technology for Research in European Women's History: Outline Bibliography. *Signs* 9: 120-33.

Farge, Arlette.
>   1983   Dix ans d'histoire des femmes en France. *Le Débat* 23: 161-69.

>   1984   Pratique et effets de l'histoire des femmes. Pp. 18-35 dans *Une histoire des femmes est-elle possible?*, ed. Michelle Perrot. Paris: Rivages.

Fox-Genonese, Elizabeth.
>   1982   Placing Women's History in History. *New Left Review* 133: 5-29.

Geiger, Susan N.G.
>   1986   Women's Life Histories: Method and Context. *Signs* 11: 334-51.

Gordon, Ann P.; Buble, Mari-Jo; and Schrom-Dye, Nancy.
>   1976   The Problem of Women's History. Pp. 75-93 in *Liberating Women's History: Theoretical and Critical Essays*, ed. Berenice A. Carroll. Chicago: University of Illinois.

Handman, M.E.
>   1983   La violence et la ruse: Hommes et femmes dans un village grec. Aix-en-Provence: Edisud.

Harding, Sandra.
>   1986   The Instability of the Analytical Categories of Feminist Theory. *Signs* 11: 645-64.

Hilden, Patricia.
>   1982   Women's History: The Second Wave. *The Historical Journal* 25: 501-12.

Hufton, Alwen.
1983 Women in History: Early Modern Europe. *Past and Present* 101: 125-40.

Johansson, Sheila R.
1976 Herstory as History: A New Field or Another Fad? Pp. 400-30 in *Liberating Women's History: Theoretical and Critical Essays*, ed. Berenice A. Carroll. Chicago: University of Illinois.

Kelly, Joan.
1984 *Women, History and Theory*: Chicago: University of Chicago.

Kelly-Gadol, Joan.
1983 The Social Relations of the Sexes: Methodological Implications of Women's History. Pp. 11-25 in *The Signs Reader: Women, Gender and Scholarship*. Chicago: University of Chicago. (Reprint of an article of 1976.)

Klapish-Zuber, Christiane.
1984 Le médiéviste, la femme et le sériel. Pp. 37-49 dans *Une histoire des femmes est-elle possible?*, ed. Michelle Perrot. Paris: Rivages.

Knibiehler, Yvonne.
1984 Chronologie et histoire des femmes. Pp. 49-59 dans *Une historie des femmes est-elle possible?* ed. Michelle Perrot. Paris: Rivages.

Lacoste-Dujardin, C.
1985 Dès mères contre les femmes; maternité et patriarcat au Maghreb. La Découverte.

Lavigne, Marie.
1976 L'histoire de quelles femmes? *Sciences sociales au Canada* 4: 1-2.

Lavigne, M., et Pinard, Y.
1983 Travail et mouvement des femmes: une histoire visible, bilan historiographique. Pp. 7-61 dans *Travailleuse et féministe, les femmes dans la societé québécoise*. Montreal: Boréal Express.

Lerner, Gerda.
    1979   *The Majority Finds its Past: Placing Women in History.*
            Oxford: Oxford University.

Lougee, Carolyn C.
    1977   Modern European History. *Signs* 2: 628-50.

Minnich, Elizabeth K.
    1985   Friendship between Women: The Act of Feminist
            Biography. *Feminist Studies* 11: 287-305.

Newton, J. *et al.*
    1983   *Sex and Class in Women's History.* London: Routledge and
            Kegan Paul.

Perrot, Michelle.
    1981   Sur l'histoire des femmes en France. *La revue de nord*
            LXIII: 569-79.

Perrot, Michelle (ed.).
    1984   *Une histoire des femmes est-elle possible?* Paris: Rivages.

Pierson, Ruth.
    1977   Women's History: The State of Art in Atlantic Canada.
            Acadiensis 7: 121-31.

Poulin, R. and Coderre, C.
    1986   La violence pornographique. Hull: Asticon Editions.

Prentice, Alison.
    1978   Writing Women into History: The History of Women's
            Work in Canada. *Atlantis* 3: 72-83.

Roth, Darlene R.
    1983   Growing Like Topsy: Research Guides to Women's
            History. *Journal of American History* 70: 95-100.

Schmidt, D.B., and Schmidt, E.T.
    1976   The Invisible Woman: The Historian as Professional
            Magician. Pp. 42-54 in *Liberating Women's History:
            Theoretical and Critical Essays*, ed. Bernice A. Carroll.
            Chicago: University of Illinois.

Schmitt-Pantel, Pauline.
  1984   La différence des sexes, histoire, anthropologie et cité
         grecque. Pp. 97-120 dans *Une histoire des femmes est-elle
         possible?*, ed. Michelle Perrot. Paris: Rivages.

Scott, Joan W.
  1981   Dix ans d'histoire des femmes aux Etats-Unis. *Le débat* 7:
         127-32.

  1983   Women in History: The Modern Period. *Past and Present*
         101 (November).

Sicherman, Barbara.
  1975   American History. *Signs* 1: 461-85.

Sicherman, Barbara *et al*.
  1980   *Recent United States Scholarship in The History of Women.*
         Washington: American Historical Association.

Smith, Hilda.
  1976   Feminism and the Methodology of Women's History. Pp.
         369-85 in *Liberating Women's History: Theoretical and
         Critical Essays*, ed. Berenice A. Carroll. Chicago:
         University of Illinois.

Smith-Rosenberg, Carol.
  1975   The New Woman and the New History. *Feminist Studies* 3:
         185-98.

Stone, Lawrence.
  1982   Family History: Future Trends. Pp. 51-87 in *The New
         History. The 1980s and Beyond: Studies in Interdisciplinary
         History*. Princeton: Princeton University.

Trofimenkoff, Susan M.
  1985   Feminist Biography. *Atlantis* 10: 1-9.

Van de Casteele-Schweitzer, Syvie, et Voldman, Danielle.
  1984   Les sources orales pour l'histoire des femmes. Pp. 59-71
         dans *Une histoire des femmes est-elle possible?*, ed.
         Michelle Perrot. Paris: Rivages.

Van Kirk, Sylvia.
　　1984　What has the Feminist Perspective done for Canadian History? Pp. 43-58 in *Knowledge Reconsidered: A Feminist Overview/Le savoir en question: vue d'ensemble féministe.* Ottawa: ICREF/CRIAW.

Chapter 6

FEMINIST REVISIONS TO THE LITERARY CANON: AN OVERVIEW OF THE METHODOLOGICAL DEBATE

Pamela McCallum

What would the traditional introductory English Literature course, usually entitled "English Literature from Chaucer to the Present," be like if it contained the work of women writers? Alongside Chaucer, we could study Christine de Pisan and Margery Kempe. With the Renaissance and Baroque lyrics of Shakespeare, Jonson, and Donne, we could read Mary Sidney Herbert, Anne Bradstreet, and Mary Cavendish. With the heroic couplets of Dryden and Pope, we might study Aphra Behn and Anne Finch. As we reach the later eighteenth century the names of women writers become more familiar, but it is worthwhile reminding ourselves that Fanny Burney's novel *Cecilia* was arguably as influential as Richardson's canonized *Clarissa*. Together with Jane Austen, the Brontes, and George Eliot in the nineteenth century are the prose writings of Mary Shelley, Margaret Fuller, and Maria Edgeworth; together with Virginia Woolf in the twentieth century we find Dorothy Richardson, Gertrude Stein, Marianne Moore, and Zora Neale Hurston. The list could go on and on. What I would like to note is that the very fact that we can put together such a list is the result of the research of feminist scholars in recent decades who have set out to discover and recover the work of women writers. Such work varies from the pioneering mapping in a book like Ellen Moers' *Literary Women* to the innovative re-readings in Mary Poovey's *The Proper Lady and the Woman Writer*. Indeed, the publishing projects of the *Norton Anthology of Literature by Women* and the Virago reprints of novels by women make it possible to construct an alternative "canon" by women writers — an issue to which I shall return later.

The project motivating this body of research would seem to be the creation of a "canon" of women's literature, either conceived as an alternative to the established canon or as an addition to be integrated into it. At certain times the canon of English literature has proved to be open and flexible, incorporating whole groups of previously neglected works (the metaphysical poets) or the rediscovered writings of individuals (Gerard Manley Hopkins). Indeed, in "Tradition and the Individual Talent," T.S. Eliot envisioned a body of literary tradition which was always engaged in a process of modification, assimilating the new work into itself at the same time the canon itself was altered by its very encounter with the new work. He describes this effect in a famous passage:

> The existing monuments form an ideal order among themselves, which is modified by the introduction of the new (the really new) work of art among them. The existing order is complete before the new work arrives; for the order to persist after the supervention of novelty, the whole existing order must be, if ever so slightly, altered; and so the relations, proportions, values of each work of art toward the whole are readjusted (1950: 5).

Such a formulation would appear to invite, even to welcome, the transformation offered by the innovative text. It is possible, however, to trace a somewhat different tendency in canon formation, especially in the institutionalization of modernism within the universities. In his prestigious and influential book, *The Well Wrought Urn*, Cleanth Brooks proposes that modernist poetry and metaphysical poetry provide the basis for strategies of reading and textual decipherment which can be extended throughout the whole of English literature. In his words, "One was to attempt to see, in terms of this approach, what the masterpieces had in common rather than to see how the poems of different historical periods differed—and in particular to see whether they had anything in common with the 'metaphysicals' and with the moderns" (1947: 193). Clearly what Brooks proposes here is that the characteristic features of modernist and metaphysical poetry—an oblique paradoxical structure, a dense texture of imagery—are able to furnish a methodological perspective by which to approach five centuries of English poetry. Moreover in the writings of Brooks and others this interpretive strategy could be extended to drama and the novel: *The Well Wrought Urn* contained a chapter dealing with a passage from *Macbeth* and, to note another example, the chapters on *Middlemarch* in F. R. Leavis' *The Great Tradition* initially appeared in *Scrutiny* with the subtitle "the novel as dramatic poem." The overall effect of such critical presuppositions was to construct the canon around a conception of literature drawn from poetry and to exclude or marginalize texts which failed to conform to this conception. Thus, little by little the canon shifted from being inclusive and potentially expansive to being exclusive and organized around one genre.

Against this tradition the very task of constructing a canon of women writers offers a significant challenge to the traditional conceptions of genre. Whereas the canon centered around male writers foregrounds poetry, a canon of women writers would foreground prose. This is not to slight the significant achievements of women poets from Sappho to the present. Rather, it is to point out that the writer whose voice is marginalized is unlikely to have access to the classical education which provided the knowledge and tools to write sonnets, couplets, and so on. The writer who begins to speak from the periphery of the literary tradition will likely begin to speak prose. It comes as no surprise that it is in the tradition of the nineteenth-century novel where the most canonized women writers are to be found. But there are further considerations: how is one to classify a text such as Agnes Smedley's *Daughter of Earth*? Is it an autobiography, a novel, a political history of the American west? Or, again, can we specify a genre to which Linda Brent's accounts of slave life in the South, and Catherine Parr Trail's narratives of early Upper Canada would belong? The point here is not the construction of some more global classifying genre, but the way in which these texts provoke an interrogation and rethinking of the category of genre itself.

Yet the most significant question raised by the new approaches to women's writing is the issue of methodology. I would like to open up some of the themes and motifs raised by feminist critics as they begin to theorize women's writing. My focus will be, first, to examine the interpretive models and codes suggested in the work of Elaine Showalter, Sandra Gilbert and Susan Gubar, and the "new French feminists" Luce Irigaray and Hélène Cixous; second, to encapsulate briefly the critique of these critics elaborated in the work of Toril Moi; third, to sketch out some of the methodological questions which confront the feminist critic.

In her pioneering book *A Literature of Their Own* and in subsequent work, Elaine Showalter sketches out a master narrative of the development of women's literature (1977; 1979: 22-41). Drawing on the initial outline suggested by Virginia Woolf in *A Room of One's Own*, Showalter constructs a "history" of women's writing that proceeds through three stages. The first, which she calls the "feminine," designates the moment when women writers strive to discover their own voices, only to find that they must speak within a language which is already dominated and structured by male writers. This gives rise, according to Showalter, to two divergent responses. Women writers either strive to deny their feminine identity, taking up the guise of masculine pseudonyms (think of Currer and Ellis Bell, or George Eliot), and attempt to create a literature acceptable to the (male-defined) literature. Or, in an opposite strategy, they accentuate their "femininity" by adopting conventional stereotyped images of woman (the American novelists Grace Greenwood and Holme Lee are her examples). The second phase, the "feminist," Showalter locates near the end of the nineteenth century and in the initial decades of the twentieth. At this point, women writers turn away from the realist narratives of the earlier stage and produce frankly oppositional utopian visions of a world built around female principles. Her example is Charlotte Perkins Gilman's *Herland*, a novel which revives and restructures the adventure novel to tell the story of a society of women in a forgotten African canyon, a society which, not surprisingly, offers ingenious "solutions" to the problems confronting early twentieth-century America. In this phase, then, women writers try to detach themselves from the weight of the male-dominated canon, to seek out new worlds in which their voices can find expression. Showalter's third stage, the "female," is conceived as taking shape in the work of such women modernists as Virginia Woolf and Gertrude Stein. Here the woman writer neither seeks to negotiate a literary world dominated by male writers, nor to distance herself from that world in a separatist gesture. She is, rather, able to take steps towards a confident articulation and representation of her own voice. Showalter sees this moment continuing into the present as women writers are able increasingly to constitute and express their own storytelling forms.

One is tempted to see Sandra Gilbert and Susan Gubar's *The Madwoman in the Attic* as an extended exploration of the woman writer caught up in Showalter's first stage. Gilbert and Gubar draw out what they see to be the predicament of the woman writer in chapters on Mary Shelley, Jane Austen, Emily and Charlotte Bronte, Emily Dickinson, and George Eliot. For Gilbert and Gubar not only the tradition of writing but also the very conventions and technique — the active stylus which in marking the passive, virginal paper confers identity on the author, father of the text — are unavoidably enmeshed and caught up in a set of assumptions which situate the writer in a male subject position. How, then, is the woman writer to speak from such a site? The answer suggested by Gilbert and Gubar involves a twofold process. First of all she can attempt to reappropriate and redefine the formal linguistic and discursive conventions available to express what she wishes to say. Thus in *Jane Eyre*, to take one example, Charlotte Bronte retrieves and refashions the language of spiritual development, the religious conventions of the soul's path to salvation, most notably codified in Bunyan's *Pilgrim's Progress*. She redeploys this narrative in the form of Jane's secular search for identity in the world, the story of a propertyless woman who must construct her own identity within a hostile society. Yet the very duplicity underpinning such a way of speaking gives rise to the second characteristic of women's writing. Because she must speak in the language and conventions of another she develops a demonic *alter ego*, a repressed rage which desires to shriek out her anger at the intricate process of negotiation which she must conduct with male dominated traditions. Consequently, in Bronte's text the madwoman in the attic (Bertha Mason, Rochester's first wife) represents, not Jane's rival, but her other self, her repressed anger at the institutions of property and marriage which deny her desire. Bertha does what Jane wishes to do but cannot: she sets fire to Rochester's bed; she rips the bridal veil; she burns down Thornfield. Such a double-voiced narrative admits no easy closure, and Gilbert and Gubar's reading goes a long way to explaining the curiously artificial ending of *Jane Eyre* (1979: 336-71). Although their readings are focused on nineteenth-century texts, the tensions and contradictions they ascribe to the situation of the woman writer do not appear to issue easily into the confident freedom of Showalter's "female" stage.

If *The Madwoman in the Attic* can be read as an exploration of the woman writer in Showalter's "feminine" stage, it is possible to grasp the work of the new French feminists as an attempt to sketch out the details of her third stage. Luce Irigaray, Hélène Cixous, Marguerite Duras, and others have all, in various ways, taken up the question of what "woman's writing" or *écriture féminine* might be.[1] Each of these writers draws on the critique of the Western rationalist tradition elaborated by poststructuralist thinkers such as Jacques Derrida. Cixous argues that the binary oppositions around which Western rationalism constructs its paradigms — active/passive, subject/object, nature/culture — are all sanctioned by one master paradigm, male/female. The privileged masculine term then depends on the marginalized feminine one to reflect its mirror image: by looking at her (what he is not), he confirms what he is. The task which the woman writer must take up is the struggle to break through the prison of such oppositions, to speak with her own voice, without definition by the male term. In a similar manner, Irigaray sees woman caught up within 'phallogocentrism'; a word which expresses both the 'phallocentrism' of patriarchal social relations and the 'logocentrism' of the Western philosophical tradition. Again, the question Irigaray poses concerns the means by which woman can subvert the confining pressures of such a weighty system.

It is when they begin to suggest their answers that the work of the new French feminists turns decisively away from the analyses of Gilbert and Gubar. For, whereas the woman writer in *The Madwoman in the*

Attic cannot escape the tension between her desire to speak and her repressed rage, Irigaray and Cixous celebrate a new *écriture féminine* whose disruptive, multiple voices exceed and overwhelm the confines of masculine, rationalist discourse. Irigaray's strategy of "stealing" and "flying away" with language preserves more of a notion of struggle than does Cixous' axiom, "Write your self. Your body must be heard. Only then will the immense resources of the unconscious spring forth" (Marks and de Courtivron: 250). Yet it is clear that both Cixous and Irigaray envision a joyously celebratory *écriture féminine* which bursts through the strictures of patriarchal discourse.

Recently the methodological assumptions of all these approaches have been examined in a careful and searching critique by the Norwegian feminist critic Toril Moi in her provocative book *Sexual/Textual Politics*.[2] Moi begins by emphasizing that an empirically-minded methodology has stood in the way of a more complex and self-reflexive theoretical discourse in Anglo-American feminist criticism. Ample confirmation of this is to be found in Moers' *Literary Women* whose organizational framework does not go beyond the usual boundaries of Anglo-American empiricism. A similar difficulty occurs in Showalter's *A Literature of Their Own* which privileges a 'realistic' mimesis over Virginia Woolf's modernism. In *The Madwoman in the Attic* Gilbert and Gubar reintroduce a slightly modified empiricist position in the form of an unselfconscious 'genetic' historicism. Their nostalgia for origins and preference for narrative homogeneity turns out to be symptomatic of "the desire to write the narrative of a mighty 'Ur-woman' " (Moi 1985: 67). Of course, Moi sees the solid and important accomplishments of Anglo-American feminist texts. But at the same time she wishes to reproblematize the unacknowledged empiricist assumptions that are built into them.

What basically distinguishes new French feminism for Moi is that it is based on a theoretical discourse. Like poststructuralist thinkers (Lacan, Derrida, Barthes, *et al.*) Hélène Cixous, Luce Irigaray, and Julia Kristeva conceive of the literary work of art as textuality or *écriture* and not as a simple organic unity. The theoretical awareness of the French feminists, however, does not blind Moi to the shortcomings of their writings — on the contrary, she aims at a critical re-evaluation of their texts in the light of a more committed sexual/textual politics. Cixous' euphoric desire to exalt woman's writing as an exercise in sensory intensities and unbounded flux culminates in a return to an 'original' primordial mother. Such mythological and elementary archetypes ultimately reduce the heterogeneity of her utopian texts to the bad immediacy of the Imaginary. Much the same elimination of disturbing rifts and discontinuities is to be detected in other 'new French feminist' texts. While Irigaray is able to show that the specular structure of patriarchal discourse systematically downplays woman's voice, she makes "power . . . a question of philosophy alone" and patriarchy "a univocal, non-contradictory force" (Moi 1985: 147). This metaphysical essentialism according to Moi turns away from a materialist analysis of power; it also turns away from a concrete historical/political analysis of patriarchal authority.

What Moi's critique makes clear is the underlying assumption of a centered self or personality substance in all of these theoretical perspectives: it is there in the quest for an authentic female voice in *A Literature of Their Own*; in the search for a unified and undivided psyche in *The Madwoman in the Attic*; in the plenitude of the female body/text in *New French Feminisms*. It would, therefore, appear that feminist methodology had inadvertently incorporated into its own strategies the presupposition of an authentic authorial voice from which the classics of literature are generated. For it is in the metonymic shift from text to author that the canon reveals its genuine principle of coherence. It is organized around the individual human subject constituted, as poststructuralism has pointed out, as white, male, and usually middle class. But a further question immediately presents itself: is the critique of such a centered, individual subject to be applied to the marginalized voices of women, or, we might add, to the doubly marginalized voices, of non-white, working class, lesbian writers? What is the strategy which might be taken by the feminist critic who wishes to take up the poststructuralist critique of the centered subject but also wants to insist on the value of texts marginalized from the canon? Is she caught in an intractable dilemma?

It is clear that these questions take on a special force when the situation of women writers outside the Anglo-American and Western European traditions are considered. For such women writers must attempt to speak in a tradition which is alien not only because it is dominated by the voices of men but also because it is the culture of the colonial power. If the literary critic—however sympathetic she may be—sets out to 'canonize' these texts, she may inevitably fashion and distort their textual practice to incorporate them within the very tradition they hope to interrogate. To cite only one example here: When *The Collector of Treasures*, a book of stories by the African writer, Bessie Head, is placed alongside the stylistic audacities of modernist and postmodernist texts, its recovery and reincorporation of the tribal storytelling forms may appear to lack the densely textured patterns of Western literature. Therefore, to integrate the book into curriculum and teaching may inevitably alter its discursive practice; at the same time, to refuse to integrate such writing condemns it to the margins of literature. In this context, Gayatri Spivak has urged a careful and self-reflexive situating of texts by non-Western European women writers; she insists on grasping the text firmly within the layered traditions of language and culture in which it speaks.[3]

It would seem, ultimately, that feminist criticism would have little to gain by an alternative canon of women writers. If canonization implies the construction of a fixed and stable body of writers organized around a principle of identity which functions to exclude difference, then any notion of canonization would reinstate many of the assumptions feminist methodologies have sought to challenge. And if the various efforts to define women's writing or *écriture féminine* were to issue into a prescriptive codification of invariant qualities, then women's literature would begin to reproduce the homogeneous, exclusive canon which feminist scholars set out to subvert. The issues that the new feminist methodologies have posed — whatever contradictions any particular theory may contain — put into question the very conception of a literary canon. This is not to suggest that we would cease to read the works of canonized authors or leave behind the 'great tradition' of English literature. Rather, it is to suggest that new strategies of reading might be devised to put into play a dialogue among texts, both 'canonized' and peripheral. This is not the place to elaborate a full and developed theory; however, I would like to conclude with one observation. We might begin to negotiate this issue if we were to see the texts we study as the praxis projects of writers intervening in a specific context. Thus we might see, for instance, Christa Wolf's novel, *Cassandra*, not as yet another use of that fountainhead of the literary canon, Homer, but rather as a strategy — a political and textual strategy — to rewrite Homer as a specific intervention in her own socio-historical context. We might see Ntozake Shange's *For colored girls* not as a literary use of black street slang to establish her authentic voice, but as a tactical juxtaposition of languages which throws into question the domination of one over the other. This perspective, the situated political site of feminism, would release us from the frozen stasis of the canon into an intertextual dialogue which is without center and periphery, multiple and heterogeneous, but which also reminds us that the literary text is, above all, a gesture of critical and political practice.

Endnotes

1.   A general introduction to their work can be found in Marks and de Courtivron (1980).

2.   I am drawing here on my review of *Sexual/Textual Politics* in *Signs* (Summer 1987).

3.   See her Introduction to the Bengali writer, Mahasveta Devi, in Abel (1982: 261-72).

References

Abel, Elizabeth (ed.).
　　1982　*Writing and Sexual Difference*. Chicago: University of Chicago Press.

Bronte, Charlotte.
　　1975　*Jane Eyre*. London: Oxford University Press.

Brooks, Cleanth.
　　1947　*The Well Wrought Urn*. New York: Harcout Brace.

Bunyan, John.
　　1966　*Pilgrim's Progress*. London: Oxford University Press.

Burney, Fanny.
　　1820　*Cecilia*. 3 vols. London: Rivington.

Eliot, T. S.
　　1950　*Selected Essays*. New York: Harcourt Brace.

Gilbert, Sandra, and Gubar, Susan.
　　1979　*The Madwoman in the Attic*. New Haven: Yale University Press.

Gilman, Charlotte Perkins.
　　1979　*Herland*. New York: Pantheon.

Head, Bessie.
　　1977　*The Collector of Treasures*. London: Heineman.

Jacobus, Mary (ed.).
　　1979　*Women Writing and Writing About Women*. London: Croom Helm.

Leavis, F.R.
　　1948　*The Great Tradition*. London: Chatto and Windus.

Marks, Elaine, and de Courtivron, Isabelle (eds.).
　　1980　*New French Feminisms*. Amherst: University of Massachusetts Press.

McCallum, Pamela.
  1987 Review of *Sexual/Textual Politics* by Toril Moi in *Signs* 12: 822-23.

Moers, Ellen.
  1976 *Literary Women*. New York: Doubleday.

Moi, Toril.
  1985 *Sexual/Textual Politics*. London: Methuen.

Poovey, Mary.
  1984 *The Proper Lady and the Woman Writer*. Chicago: University of Chicago Press.

Richardson, Samuel.
  1968 *Clarissa*. 4 vols. London: Dent.

Shange, Ntozake.
  1977 *For colored girls who have considered suicide when the rainbow is enuf*. New York: Macmillan.

Showalter, Elaine.
  1977 *A Literature of Their Own*. Princeton: Princeton University.

  1979 Towards a Feminist Poetics. Pp. 22-41 in *Women Writing and Writing About Women*, ed. Mary Jacobus. London: Croom Helm.

Smedley, Agnes.
  1973 *Daughter of Earth*. New York: The Feminist Press.

Spivak, Gayatri.
  1982 "Draupadi" by Mahasveti Devi. Pp. 261-72 in *Writing and Sexual Difference*, ed. Elizabeth Abel. Chicago: University of Chicago Press.

Wolf, Christa.
  1984 *Cassandra*. New York: Farrar, Straus, Giroux.

Woolf, Virginia.
  1977 *A Room of One's Own*. London: Granada.

Chapter 7

"ON THE FAR SIDE OF LANGUAGE": FINDING THE WOMAN IN CLASSICS

Rosemary M. Nielsen and E. D. Blodgett*

> Let us agree, then, that a paper read by a woman to women should end with something particularly disagreeable.
>
> (Woolf 1977: 105)[1]

The American classicist and feminist, Marilyn Skinner (1985: 8), has criticized classics in women's studies for producing "bland" scholarship. She also complains that, although both disciplines *should* achieve an area for dispute and confrontation between the traditionalist male establishment in classics and "the new wave of female scholars," there has been neither dialogue nor debate. The approaches and methods of women's studies, she admits, have generally been used to reproduce faithful catalogues of "historical and literary realities" (1985: 9). And these new accounts never "proceed beyond the facile recognition of sexist bias in our primary sources to inquire whether similar enticing biases may not have crept into our secondary sources as well..." (1985: 9). Skinner is being blunt. For her, the main distinction between conventional research and an ideal women's studies research in classics is the proposition (which she apparently accepts) that sexist bias automatically exists in primary texts and commentary written by men. To say as much implies that the feminist in classics can do nothing but adopt a negative posture; for, with the rarest of exceptions, all classical texts and commentaries are men's writing. This is a crucial point, one that is basic to a woman's understanding of an act of reading, and one which will be discussed more fully later in the paper.

The severity of Skinner's criticism that women's studies in classics has failed to address gender bias in commentaries, and its timeliness for Canadians, are intensified when one realizes that her remarks were delivered at a 1984 national conference in the United States designed explicitly to promote an even stronger alliance between the two

---

*This paper is dedicated to Professor Robert J. Buck in gratitude for his encouragement and support.

disciplines of classics and women's studies. Skinner, one must emphasize, is raising a vital question for the female researcher in classics: how is she to express her creative and imaginative autonomy within a field where few women have *ever* had a voice?

This paper continues Skinner's radical critique of feminist research in classics. It proceeds in two stages: first, to an examination of Judith Hallett's response to Skinner, which will lead to a consideration of the problem posed by the classical languages and the character of the woman they inscribe; and second, to a discussion of the necessity for the woman classicist to "read as a woman." This latter section outlines four types of approaches developed by scholars outside classics that offer help to such a woman classicist. Finally, it will become clear that the approaches of women's studies as they are now employed by classicists are not adequate for interpreting Greek and Latin literature, especially poetry, in female terms.

I. The Ancient "Rules" of Language

There were other sources of enlightenment. Thoby returned home from his first school—Evelyns—and in an odd shy way—walking up and down stairs as he talked—told Virginia about the Greeks, about Troy and Hector and a whole new world which captured her imagination. Perhaps it was then that she decided that one day, like Thoby, she would learn Greek; and perhaps it was then that she realized that the Greeks belonged to Thoby in a way that they didn't belong to her, that they formed a part of the great male province of education... from which she...[was] to be excluded (Bell 1976: 27).

Much of Hallett's reply to Skinner turns upon an issue of central importance to the woman classicist: how to urge her colleagues to redesign the territory. In particular, Hallett says, she must discourage not only the entrenched possession of areas of specialization, but also the zealous guarding of the classical languages by those "who adhere closely to philological, linguistically-focussed approaches [of analysis] as proof of their own superiority" (1985: 32). It is precisely at this point, according to Hallett, that the woman classicist can effect changes. Both Skinner and Hallett recognize that the question of what we achieve as feminist classicists is inextricably linked to the question of how access to Latin and Greek is regarded. Skinner does not wish to exclude "all non-specialists" from examining the written traditions of the field, feeling that to do so would be to reaffirm the elitist Victorian image of classics as the prerogative of the best-educated men in society.[2] But, equivocally, she adds that "the more we retreat behind the barrier of our precious languages. . .the more we compel *amateurs* to attempt to satisfy a genuine psychological hunger for knowledge by *expropriating* aspects of antiquity only *superficially* understood" (Skinner 1985: 11, emphasis added). Skinner's argument about the barrier allows her to have it both ways — to be a feminist while totally surrendering, in this statement, to the traditional (and masculinist) attitude toward the classical languages: they are, for her, still the center and central tool of research in classics, a tool that remains inaccessible to all but the privileged few at the heart of an androcentric discipline. Skinner's metaphor of the barrier implies that only the feminist critic versed in Greek and Latin is fit to engage in the interpretative (and creative) process of reading ancient woman in the male text. Skinner, and any woman who would follow her prescription, is both elitist and non-elitist, in an apparent contradiction. Such a defensive attitude from a feminist about language scholarship relegates many female researchers and female students in classics to a subordinate position. It is ironic that this role exactly parallels the *literary* construct of ancient woman. Just as her image is isolated behind the barrier of the men's language of classical texts, so, too, many modern women without Greek or Latin, but drawn to the text of the woman, stand in front of the barrier and feel unable, because of their ignorance of these languages, to decode and liberate the meaning of the image of literary women. They will stand outside the privileged circle so long as studying the languages means merely repeating male-derived definitions for words, phrases, or lines of literary texts.

Judith Hallett does not connect the study of Greek and Latin with the metaphor of the barrier, nor with any notions of female alienation, nor with any diminution of authority for women classicists. For her, the concept of a barrier is irrelevant because academics outside classics look upon the field as a "parody" (1985: 28) of its former self. Classics is a fallen giant, a corpse, which, for many, forms simply "background" to English studies. Hallett, paradoxically, draws consolation from this attitude. She declares, ". . .I view the marginality of classics positively, as a source of professional vitality and as a development which has not only facilitated the survival but also fueled the transformation of our field. . .during the past three decades" (1985: 29). Any woman, then, who teaches or does research on the literary images of women in antiquity, as a feminist or as a conventional scholar (or even as a non-specialist), is necessarily at the "cutting-edge" of her discipline. In addition, Hallett argues that the major task for the woman researcher is to make the

field of classics "more accessible to the non-initiate" (1985: 29).
Therefore, one of the most important means of reaching a wider
audience, we believe, would be the development of feminist theories of
translation that would attempt to release the woman in the text.[3] In this
way, the privileged circle (dare we say classical sorority?) would be
opened. Women who are aware of aspects of the languages which
remain uncultivated by male interpreters and translators would be able
to share these aspects through translations, critical articles, and
conferences with their sisters who do not study Greek and Latin.

When approving the marginal character of classics, Hallett
neglects, however, to indicate how to find the woman within the literary
text. That woman is lost in a house built by men with no opening for
women. Nor is it opened by studies of women in their historical context.
Although for non-classical feminists the new center is at the classical
margin, Hallett's definition of classical margin is inhibiting for the woman
classicist. It invites her to avoid any examination of her own perspective
on the logocentric tradition of male-dominated literature and language,
and of male-dominated modes of literary criticism. Sucn an examination
must be part of the self-scrutiny Hallett urges upon us. Hallett's
awareness of her own female autonomy, of not feeling locked in or
constrained to write like a male classicist, is refreshing. But it is merely a
reaction, with no basis in a fully expressed and developed feminist literary
theory.[4] Furthermore, when she describes how, for her, women's studies
have invigorated classics, she forgets that such studies have, for the most
part, simply enlarged the zone of enquiry. They merely collect
knowledge hitherto ignored by male critical theory and practice in
classics. Although the literary figure of ancient woman is the center of
some women's research, the gain is minimal if a conventional method of
enquiry simply "adds" women to the list of classical themes or *topoi*.[5]
Moreover, the ease with which this information is assimilated by current
routine research in classics belies Hallett's praise of women's studies as
necessarily encouraging in women a rigorous new self-evaluation. Nor
does it, as she claims, work at any feminist margin.

For lesbian feminists, one must remember, the term "margin" has
a special denotation. It refers to the "politics of separation," by which
they mean "women creating a new consciousness of and with each other"
(Zimmerman 1985: 204). Lesbian feminists "see [themselves] as prime,
find [their] centers inside of [themselves]" (1985: 204). In literary terms,
lesbian feminist theory offers a strategy of reading that would locate the
woman classicist on the boundaries, the margins, of male texts and
accounts of patriarchal languages and literatures. A "lesbian" literary

scholar in classics would emphasize gender difference as a major constituent of women's readings (Kennard 1986: 77) and consequently look for a woman's self-definition as she reads. She would place the act of reading rather than the text at the margin.

The truly marginalist enterprise of reading is revisionist and one potentially exciting for the future of classics, but at present it is not happening in the field. Just as philosophy was considered to be the *ancilla* (handmaiden) of theology during the Middle Ages, so, too, the "women-added" approach as practiced by many in classics is now performing the same feminine supportive service for the traditional and received canon of the ancient literatures. Such a misunderstanding of the possibilities of women's studies in classics makes the woman who pursues it the handmaiden of the brotherhood of classical studies. To search in literature for a single, universal image of ancient woman is fruitless work; and to research without any theoretical basis (developed through debate) in feminist literary methodologies is merely, like the proverbial upstairs maid (*ancilla*), to sweep out the closets and attics of classical tradition on behalf of men.

Such an apparent feminism is justly stigmatized by Skinner for its blandness. The theme of compartmentalization that has been emphasized in this section, and the metaphors of a barrier or a territory that accompany it, are intentional. For, while this is a central issue in feminist discussions about the accessibility of the classical literatures, it is an argument that we do not share. The ancient male artist in classics, it could be said, has created an edifice and the female critic, whether she knows the classical languages or not, is one who should move freely across boundaries and through zones while trying to understand what he has done with woman. This view of the dynamic possibilities of the interaction of the male artist and female critic can be feminist. The female critic, reading the work of the ancient male artist, can confront and re-examine the aesthetic implications of sexual difference in the representation of women in classical literature.

II. Giving the Greek "Quite a Contrary Turn"[6]

Let us turn over the pages, and I will add, for your amusement, a comment in the margin (Woolf 1986: 161).

What keeps the literary figure of ancient woman obscured and her voice unheard is *not* the languages describing her nature in classical writing, but the masculinized interpretations, in English and other languages, which have become permanent and have been transmitted through the ages as if the Greek and Latin words spoke with one voice. Nor is the time-worn assumption, most succinctly phrased by Gerard Manley Hopkins, that "the male quality is the creative gift" the major difficulty (Gilbert and Gubar 1979: 3).[7] The major difficulty to overcome is the reluctance of the contemporary female classicist to "read as a woman" (Culler 1982: 42).[8] By reading as a woman, however, we need not follow what Elaine Fantham (1986: 22-23) has proposed:

> Until then [a time of dispassionate scholarship] it will require all the advocacy of committed *feminists* with expertise and eloquence to persuade our students...that Women in Antiquity is a substantial part of Classical Scholarship with lessons for women's history. *It can and should be pursued with all the tools and techniques traditionally used in His-story and His-literature* (emphasis added).

Not only is this a retrograde position, but it also blurs the distinction between studies of women and feminist-oriented research. This misuse of the term "feminist" is all too common in modern classical scholarship. For example, Fantham's recent critical summary of classical scholarship in women's studies is a catalogue of work done on ancient women, most of it in sociological, anthropological, historical, and demographic discourses. Fantham's discussion of ancient woman in this scholarship suggests that the figure of literary woman is most relevant when it reflects women's historical life.[9] Adding women to history is paramount. Our task, however, should be to distinguish between historical women and women as literary constructs in classical studies, and to recognize the values of the woman in literature. To accomplish this last aim, we need to do more than bring conventional research methodologies to the study of women; we need instead to ask specifically feminist questions about gender representation in the text and the role of gender in our reading.

In order to read as a woman, the woman in classics must first determine how she understands the woman in classical literature. For the latter is undeniably a male creation. Is she, therefore, only an artifice of language, an illusion of the feminine fashioned from literary conventions, structures, and rhetoric? This question raises another: how can the literary figure of woman inscribed in male texts be said to speak both "in the name of" and "to" women? Such a question should alert the feminist reader to a sense of her sisterhood with the classical heroine. Both are constrained by having to use the male *logos*. Both women must communicate themselves, that is, engage in a re-vision of stories of their powers, desires, and limitations, in male tongues—the one modern, the other ancient. As Shoshana Felman (1975: 4) observes, "Is [this] not a precise repetition of the oppressive gesture of *representation*, by means of which, throughout the history of *logos*, man has reduced the woman to the status of a silent and subordinate object, to something inherently spoken for?" These are questions of fundamental importance if the classicist is to discover the woman in the literary text. They must be raised if she is to discern how subtly drawn and complex the female image is in male-authored discourse.

Virginia Woolf, herself an astute reader of classical poetry, once cast doubt upon the authenticity of heroines created by the male artist (Barrett 1979: 65):

> Some are plainly men in disguise; others represent what men would like to be, or are conscious of not being; or again they embody that dissatisfaction and despair which afflict most people when they reflect upon the sorry condition of the human race. To cast out and incorporate in a person of the opposite sex all that we miss in ourselves and desire in the universe and detest in humanity is a deep and universal instinct on the part both of men and of women. But though it affords relief, it does not lead to understanding.

But Woolf came to think differently about this problem of sexuality and textuality. She modifies her opinion in a rarely-quoted passage:

> Indeed, if woman has no existence save in the fiction written by men, one would imagine her a person of the utmost importance; very various; heroic and mean; splendid and sordid, infinitely beautiful and hideous in the extreme; as great as a man, some think even greater. But this is woman in fiction (1977: 42-43).

Even if one allows Woolf her customary playful ambiguity,[10] she implies that in very gifted male authors the female character has access to more far-ranging patterns of thought and action than does the real historical woman. Recently, Hélène Cixous (1983: 283) has said much the same thing, pointing out the gifted male poet's desire to "break the codes that negate" the literary figure of woman precisely because he is a man "capable of imagining the woman who would hold out against oppression and constitutes [her] as a superb, equal, hence 'impossible' subject, untenable in a real social framework." In spite of the skepticism of some critics, even feminist critics, the literary figure of woman as shaped by a man can serve and has served as a series of dynamic exemplars for women readers in classics. Nor is the plurality of the feminine image necessarily pejorative. If Cixous' ideas are combined with Woolf's theory about women writers (and researchers) "thinking back" (1977: 72) through their "mothers," the heroines of Greek epic and tragic poetry provide a variety of maternal voices, albeit voices heard through the father-poet.

It is possible for the woman classicist to draw an analogy between the significance to Woolf of Judith Shakespeare in *A Room of One's Own* and of Clytemnestra, Antigone, and other such imposing female figures to Greek classical poets. Both Judith and Clytemnestra are female precursors of mythic proportions in literary works of art, who fulfill a poetic need and transcend the text. The text may bear the signs of the sexual difference of its author, but the characters are not confined by their creators. Without the presence of Judith, the poet "who never wrote a word" (1977: 107), there would be for Woolf no woman's voice. Judith as the silent talent shows the consequences for future generations of women of burying our voices and talents in silence and acquiescence. Woolf sees the role of the woman writer as, in part, rehabilitative; each time she writes something "however vast however trivial" (1977: 103), she brings Judith back to life and reaffirms Judith's influence as a "great poet"; "but I maintain that she would come *if we worked for her*," Woolf argues, "and that so to work, even in poverty and obscurity, is worth while" (1977: 108, emphasis added). Similarly, the "silent poets" Clytemnestra, Antigone, and the other women of Greek literature depend upon the woman classicist for their rebirth. Her sensitivity in recognizing and responding to the transcendent voice of Judith assists her to hear the women in Greek poetry. In reminding us of our ancient mothers, then, Judith Shakespeare summons us to read and write with a "gift for poetry" (1977: 48).

Judith and Clytemnestra are not only mothers of a feminine creativity, they are also agents of the feminine in their authors. Such an agent is not to be understood as a Muse in Hesiod's sense, associated in his *Theogony* with his own negative image of woman as goddess, whose power to control Zeus' *logos* remains indeterminate in the text. Hesiod's Muses boast of being able to "utter lies that look just like the truth" (1970: 27, our translation), thus proclaiming how their female language can delude the unwary reader. Hesiod fears these Muses, that is, the feminine in himself, for they embody in their ambiguous gift of song all the difficulties *men* face with knowledge and self-government in the chaotic world-view of his epic. The Judiths and Clytemnestras, by contrast, are inspirers and *daimons*, numinous powers who mediate aspects of the feminine condition through the vessel of the artist. And their stories of woman, even when she is superhuman, subhuman, or simply human,[11] triumphant or frustrated, offer meaningful paradigms for posterity. These female *daimons* address, as Virginia Woolf insists the best fiction must always address, "the common life which is the real life and not the little separate lives which [women] live as individuals. . ." (1977: 108). Under these conditions of story-telling, it would be rash to agree, for example, with the feminist classicist Froma Zeitlin (1978: 171), who reads Clytemnestra's placement in Aeschylus' *Oresteia* trilogy within a system of binary oppositions as an indictment of her femininity and an indication of the poet's misogynistic use of myth and mythmaking. If, as Woolf maintains, "the truer the facts the better the fiction" (1977: 17), we can read Aeschylus as borrowing traditional stories, that is, myths about woman as the irrational, woman as the dark and demonic, and woman as the Opposite, so as to be able to turn them around, to portray how women really suffer in masculine culture. Close examination of the trilogy's structure and rhetoric reveals how Aeschylus undermines the ideal of civilization and shows the destructive and enervating results of androcentric values for the autonomy of both the family and the individual. Aeschylus plays a language that is unremittingly binary against clusters of ambiguous images. Tension created at this primary level thwarts any easy picture of woman as the Other. Clytemnestra perishes, her legitimate plea for an old-fashioned retributive justice enforced by the female Furies overridden by the advent of a new male social code. Nonetheless, after-images of her struggle, both in action and through language, to gain ascendancy over patriarchy haunt the feminist reader, making Clytemnestra one of Woolf's "great poets" and one of the continuing female presences in Western art.

Encouraging an independent and aesthetically coherent response in the woman classicist, like discovering the woman in the classical text, is a challenge. The woman researcher must *not* be dispassionate, but must engage in "passionate scholarship." Barbara Du Bois (1981: 18) defines this kind of research as involving "necessary heresy" because, for the literary researcher, it means continuous, disruptive, and radical re-readings of her father's texts. The techniques of this research—which avoids looking for simply one meaning in texts, that is, for closure, and looks beyond the stereotypical, the literal, and the historical images of ancient woman—will necessarily put the woman classicist into conflict within the "house" of classics. Nevertheless, "poetry," Woolf asserts, "depends upon intellectual freedom" (1977: 103), and if the woman classicist fails to find a voice, a feminine voice, she risks reading "as a man"—the subtlest form of censorship. This means that she will be unable, as Jonathan Culler (1982: 54) puts it, "to identify the special defenses and distortions of male readings [or writings] and provide corrections."

There are four kinds of feminist approaches outside the field of classics that might enrich future revisionist work on gender and literary forms in our field. The first two assist the classicist as writer, the second pair the classicist as reader.

1. S/he should be conversant with the implications of French psychoanalytical feminisms that endeavor to counteract the power of a domineering father-artist upon a daughter-critic. See, for example, Gallop (1982).

2. S/he should know how Gilbert and Gubar (1979) uncover the many signs in a woman's writing of her fear of taking up the pen and entering her self in the story of woman.

3. S/he should see the application of Cixous' theories (1983), which emphasize woman's cultural and libidinal difference from man. Cixous' approaches are analytical devices to understand the often repressive self-definitions offered by a Phaedra, Electra, and Antigone of their self-hatred, shame, and obsessions.

4. S/he should study feminist theories of reader-response criticism, such as those outlined by Schweickart (1986), which arm the woman reader against becoming an agent of her own disempowerment when reading male texts.

In other words, examining new strategies of reading will not only give us access to innovative ways of recuperating the literary figure of woman, but also help us to survive in the male-dominated house of classics. We cannot any longer place ourselves out of account in comparison to women scholars in other fields, who are defending our intellectual and psychological right to explore our differences as human beings and our right to differ in our writing. We can no longer exclude ourselves from dialogue with women in our field, like Hallett and Skinner,[12] who are seeking to interrupt the monologue of our masculinist fellow classicists. We, as women classicists, will not be recorded in future texts the way that Virginia Woolf remembers Jane Harrison in *A Room of One's Own*. Jane Harrison, the mother of our half of classical scholarship this century, is to Virginia Woolf (1977: 18) merely a "phantom," "half guessed, half seen," a "bent figure" of a woman hurrying across a darkened campus scene.

Endnotes

1. All citations to *A Room of One's Own* are from the 1977 Granada edition and occur parenthetically in the second section of the paper. The quoted phrase in the paper's title belongs to Virginia Woolf, and describes the rich ambiguity she finds in Aeschylus' metaphorical language in the *Oresteia* trilogy. Furthermore, in Greek tragedy Woolf discovers not only "types of the original man or woman," but also "the stable, the permanent" (1984: 27).

2. A good example of how Greek was used to define Victorian societal ideals is found in J.K. Steven's important 1891 article "The Living Languages. A Defence of the Compulsory Study of Greek at Cambridge." In his view, Greek is one means of ensuring the "non-survival of the unfittest" and the dominion of "an intellectual aristocracy" in England. For him, Greek was a test of a young *man's* right to maintain authority granted to him by his birth in an advantaged society when the worth of a *man* might derive from the rewards of "industry, rapacity, or [the] good luck of an ancestor, immediate or remote" as much as from natural achievement. Quotations cited by Marcus (1983: 96).

3. The need for a woman to develop a uniquely female re-reading of Greek and Latin was recognized by Woolf in her own classical studies: "I should be at Aeschylus, for I am making a complete edition, text, translation, & notes of my own — mostly copied from Verrall; but carefully gone into by me" (Bell 1981: 215). For an example of the effects of gender difference in translation, see Page Du Bois' study of Richmond Lattimore's version of Sappho's Helen Poem. She argues that Lattimore's male point of view "makes the poem exclusively a love poem" whereas Sappho attempts "to universalize her insight, to move toward logical thought. She is defining desire *with the vocabulary at hand*," in "Sappho and Helen" (1984: 97, emphasis added).

4. The "women-added" approach, e.g., of Lefkowitz' (1983: 50-52) study of *Antigone*, can be feminized by posing such essential questions as:

    (1) What assumptions about woman underlie Sophocles' juxtaposition of images of death to those of dutiful women; and

(2)   What in Greek society encourages the addition of male rhetoric and dramatic stature to the character of Antigone in order to grant heroic focus?

Antigone herself demands that the woman reader, at least, encounter such questions.

5.   Although Hallett's critical approach in "The Role of Women in Roman Elegy" (1973) is feminist, her metacritical statements in *Helios* (1985) do not directly address the function of feminist literary theory and its usefulness in women's reappropriation of classical texts.

6.   The title of this section is borrowed from Charlotte Bronte's Caroline Helstone, who says, "and besides, I dare say, if I could read the original Greek, I should find that many of the words have been wrongly translated, perhaps misapprehended altogether. It would be possible, I doubt not, with a little ingenuity to give the passage quite a contrary turn" (1968: 260).

7.   Gilbert and Gubar also examine connections between masculine sexuality and literary creativity, and conclude: "Underneath all these [ideas of authorship] is the imagery of succession, of paternity, of hierarchy" (1979: 5).

8.   Jonathan Culler uses the expression to focus a discussion based on the following premise: "If the experience of literature depends upon the qualities of a reading self, one can ask what difference it would make to the experience of literature and thus to the meaning of literature if this self were. . .female rather than male" (1982: 42).   Other citations from this text are included parenthetically in the text.

9.   In an earlier study of women in New Comedy, Fantham proposes:

> to test and use the evidence of Menandrian comedy in order to present an account of social roles available to different categories of women in the everyday world of around 300 B.C. . . .Hence the plot-structures of Greek comedy can be assumed to represent society in their treatment of the civil status, eligibility for marriage, liability to divorce, etc., of the female roles. . . (1975: 44-45).

10.   See Patrocinio P. Schweickart, however, who believes that Woolf's statement indicates that "male poets cannot be relied on for the truth about women" (1986: 34). Yet, both the context of Woolf's

statement and her expressed admiration for poets and poetic
fiction in the essay suggest the contrary. In fact, Woolf implies
that the conditions in which historical woman lived—in
intellectual and physical poverty—are the reasons why no woman
has ever written "a word of that extraordinary literature" (1977:
41).

11. In borrowing these three terms from Judith Fetterley (1977: ix),
    the authors propose that traditional and superficially negative
    images of women need not necessarily be antifeminine in function
    or ones that estrange the woman reader from her own female
    experience.

12. See, for example, Skinner's feminist reading of Cicero's derisive
    treatment in oratory of the historical figure Clodia Metelli. The
    representation of the fictional Clodia, Skinner argues, is a
    rhetorical flight, a lawyer's case to win: "There is a good *prima
    facie* case, then, for regarding the 'Clodia' of the *pro Caelio* as a
    literary construct similar to [Catullus'] 'Lesbia,' a fiction designed
    to conform to cultural expectations and play upon standard
    prejudices" (1983: 275-276).

References

Barrett, Michèle.
>   1979   *Virginia Woolf. Women and Writing.* London: The Women's Press.

Bell, Anne D. (ed.).
>   1981   *The Diary of Virginia Woolf. Vol. II. 1920-24.* Great Britain: Penguin Books.

Bell, Quentin.
>   1976   *Virginia Woolf. A Biography, Vol. I. 1881-1912.* London: Triad/Granada.

Brontë, Charlotte.
>   1968   *Shirley.* New York: Everyman's Library.

Cixous, Hélène.
>   1983   The Laugh of the Medusa. Pp. 279-97 in *The Signs Reader: Women, Gender, & Scholarship,* ed. Elizabeth Abel and Emily K. Abel. Chicago: The University of Chicago.

Culler, Jonathan.
>   1982   *On Destruction: Theory and Criticism after Structuralism.* Ithaca: Cornell University.

Du Bois, Barbara.
>   1981   Passionate Scholarship. Pp. 11-24 in *Theories of Women's Studies II,* ed. G. Bowles and R. Duelli-Klein. Berkeley: University of California.

Du Bois, Page.
>   1984   *Women in the Ancient World: The Arethusa Papers.* New York: State University of New York.

Fantham, Elaine.
>   1975   Sex, Status, and Survival in Hellenistic Athens: A Study of Women in New Comedy. *Phoenix* I: 44-74.

>   1986   Women in Antiquity: A Selective (and Subjective) Survey 1979-84. *Classical Views* 5: 1-24.

Felman, Shoshana.
　　1975　Women and Madness: The Critical Phallacy. *Diacritics* 4:
　　　　　2-10.

Fetterley, Judith.
　　1978　*The Resisting Reader: A Feminist Approach to American
　　　　　Fiction*. Bloomington: Indiana University.

Flynn, Elizabeth A., and Schweickart, P. P. (eds.).
　　1986　*Gender and Reading*. Baltimore: Johns Hopkins
　　　　　University.

Gallop, Jane.
　　1982　*The Daughter's Seduction: Feminism in Psychoanalysis*.
　　　　　Ithaca: Cornell University.

Gilbert, Sandra M., and Gubar, Susan.
　　1979　*The Madwoman in the Attic: The Woman Writer and the
　　　　　Nineteenth-Century Literary Imagination*. New Haven:
　　　　　Yale University.

Hallett, Judith P.
　　1973　The Role of Women in Roman Elegy. *Arethusa* I: 103-24.

　　1985　Response II: Buzzing of a Confirmed Gadfly. *Helios* 2:
　　　　　23-37.

Heilbrun, Carolyn G., and Higonnet, Margaret R. (eds.).
　　1983　*The Representation of Women in Fiction*. Baltimore: Johns
　　　　　Hopkins University.

Hesiod
　　1970　*Theogonia Opera et Dies*. Oxford: Oxford University.

Kennard, Jean E.
　　1986　Ourself behind Ourself: A Theory for Lesbian Readers.
　　　　　Pp. 63-80 in *Gender and Reading: Essays on Readers, Texts,
　　　　　and Contexts*, ed. Elizabeth A. Flynn and Patrocinio P.P.
　　　　　Schweickart. Baltimore: Johns Hopkins University.

Lefkowitz, Mary R.
　　1983　Influential Women. Pp. 49-64 in *Images of Women in
　　　　　Antiquity*, ed. Averil Cameron and Amélie Kuhrt.
　　　　　Australia: Croom Helm Ltd.

Marcus, Jane.
    1983   Liberty, Sorority, Misogyny. Pp. 60-97 in *The Representation of Women in Fiction*, ed. Carolyn G. Heilbrun and Margaret Higonnet. Baltimore: Johns Hopkins University.

Schweickart, Patrocinio P.
    1986   Toward a Feminist Theory of Reading. Pp. 31-62 in *Gender and Reading*, ed. Elizabeth A. Flynn and P. P. Schweickart. Baltimore: Johns Hopkins University.

Skinner, Marilyn.
    1983   Clodia Metelli. *Transactions of the American Philological Association* 113: 273-87.

    1985   Classical Studies vs. Women's Studies: *Duo Moi Ta Noêmmata*. *Helios* 12:3-16.

Steven, James K.
    1891   *The Living Languages: A Defense of the Compulsory Study of Greek at Cambridge.* Cambridge: Macmillan and Bowes.

Woolf, Virginia.
    1977   *A Room of One's Own.* Great Britain: Granada.

    1984   On Not Knowing Greek. Pp. 23-38 in *The Common Reader First Series*. London: The Hogarth Press.

    1986   *The Waves.* London: Triad Grafton.

Zeitlin, Froma I.
    The Dynamics of Misogyny: Myth and Mythmaking in the Oresteia. *Arethusa* 2: 149-84.

Zimmerman, Bonnie.
    1985   What Has Never Been. An Overview of Lesbian Feminist Literary Criticism. Pp. 200-24 in *The New Feminist Criticism*, ed. Elaine Showalter. New York: Pantheon Books.

Chapter 8

A FEMINIST PERSPECTIVE IN LITERATURE

Jeanne Lapointe*

Female historians complain, and rightfully so, about the absence of women in historical documents written by men. Literary works, however, are riddled with far too many male fantasies about women, who are generally presented as male-dominated objects. Whenever a woman does appear as the subject and controlling force, she is usually a criminal or a depraved character who will be punished at the end of the narrative.

Despite an often stronger female enrollment in French-speaking universities today in literature courses, this discipline continues to be taught by a large majority of male professors, that is, in a masculine perspective. Some of them utilize a sociological approach giving significant weight to statistical data, which is merely a passive recognition of the content of literary works, with no regard to any perspective as to their socio-historical role. A number of studies centered on themes concerning women simply provide a tautological description of the same stereotypes advanced by literary works; and these, in turn, reflect the social roles and stereotypes extant on the subject of women and the male/female relationship. As Barthes (1957) has indicated, the mythologies and ideologies proposed by the press and by literature merely justify and render commonplace, natural, even plausible the power structure which supports society. Marxist thinkers, such as Althusser (1970), also point to the conservatism of the "State's ideological apparatus"; these are the education systems, the mass media, as well as religious, cultural, and even sports institutions. Literature plays an active, determining part in consolidating power structures as concerns the male/female relationship. Any changes in these perspectives are usually instigated by women.

These notes on the feminist movement's contribution to literature will set aside a major part of university-level women's studies which focuses on the works written by women. Such teaching and research are indispensable and have tried to return women's works to the rightful place usually denied them by literary history. For example, George Sand would have long been recognized as one of the greatest writers of the

---

*Translation by Mary Brennan

nineteenth century had she been a man. Recognizing the value of women's works in literary history, shedding light on their originality and value are all in line with the intention of male historians to achieve a so-called pure objectivity.

Over the past few years, I have centered my research and teaching on analyzing how cultural ideologies and the male imagination function as concerns women in literature. This multidisciplinary work has historical, sociological, geographical, linguistic, and psychoanalytical dimensions. For example, a study of the Quebec agriculturalist novel (Poulin 1986) reveals that the return-to-the-land movements, which were started even before 1900 and were instigated to fight an economic slump and resulting unemployment, took some inspiration from the political and religious discourse of these decades. Such discourse praised the submissive, strong and healthy woman, who was respectful of traditions and who would repulse like sin the temptation of city life. The mentality with regard to women, as evidenced by various thinkers — including Bourassa — and prelates of that era, sheds much light on the relationship between ideology and literature. In the novel, such a mentality led to many simplistic, sanctimonious works but also a masterpiece, *Maria Chapdelaine* (Hémon 1913), whose literary worth hides its unconscious ideological function. And today, while pornography holds sway in the Western world, talented writers such as Robbe-Grillet, Klossowski, and a few others in Quebec reproduce, in novels they no doubt view as being inventive, the most pathetic, hackneyed series of masculine fantasies on the subject of male/female domination.

As a rule, literature is believed to be avant-garde, premonitory, and innovative; yet, it is ultra-conservative in the view of the male/female relationship. Neither Mallarmé, nor Beckett, nor Joyce — all of whom created new literary forms — proposed the slightest change-for-the-better in the male/female relationship. Veiled beneath the charm, the pomp, and the literary daring of their works appears an intolerable, often degrading perception of human relations which women now reject when they come to recognize it.

Marxism provided the working-class with a theory of social structures and with strategies to correct the oppression which was crushing them; yet it avoided giving women similar tools although Engels (1884) had recognized them as proletarians of the working class.

Several methods are practical for analyzing how a mentality geared to dominating women functions as represented in patriarchal-type literature, usually written by men, and sometimes by women. I shall mention six methods — no doubt there are many others — which are useful when adapted to this specific analytical objective, and when employed as methods and instruments of work and not as theories and methods for the sake of theory and methods.

The first and easiest method is to establish, then analyze a comparative list of nouns, adjectives, and action verbs which are used to depict women and men in a given novel. This vocabulary usually illustrates in a striking fashion the stereotypes about women and men offered by the dominant social imagination. Attempts are now being made to rid school books of these clichés. Since they cannot be expunged from literature, they must at least be recognized.

A second, elucidative method is the grid for semiological analysis developed by Greimas (1966); this method may be focused on the male/female relationship which is often central to the novel—although secondary in other works but always highly insignifcant. We see this at work when the masculine hero nurtures ambitions of social, political, or metaphysical nature, as in the novels of Malraux and Saint-Exupéry. To begin, Greimas reduces the whole narrative framework to a single sentence. Take *Wuthering Heights* (Brontë 1847) for example: Catherine is deeply in love with Heathcliff, her childhood companion, a crude and violent character; however, she finally marries Linton, a courtly young gentleman from a neighboring bourgeois family. In the preceding sentence, we now look for the coveting Subject, the mainspring of the action, and also for the Object of her (his) desire (who wants what?). Here, Catherine is the Subject and Heathcliff the Object of this quest. Who are the acolytes and who the adversaries? The principal acolyte is Catherine's maidservant and confidante; the adversaries are the social customs and the theme of the bourgeois matrimony; the latter triumph in the end. This could be a feminist novel only to the extent that Catherine is the Subject of the action, the central character, and also because her love for Heathcliff is evoked with great force and recounted with even more complicity by the author. But here, as in *Maria Chapdelaine*, the women's personal values are sacrificed to value scales and standards which have never taken the identity and the will of women into consideration.

This use of Greimas' outline of the forces at work in the narrative framework indicate that when a woman is the Subject of the action, there are three possible consequences if she fails to reflect the image of submission and gentleness proposed as a model for all women. Either she gives in to social or other forces as in *Wuthering Heights* and *Maria Chapdelaine*, or she is depicted as dangerous, a criminal, or depraved, like Lady Macbeth (Shakespeare 1605). Or she is ridiculed—*the Taming of the Shrew* (*La mégère apprivoisée*) (Shakespeare 1593). Racine's choice of female characters such as Athalie (1691) from the Bible or Agrippine (1669) from Roman history, both of whom exemplify feminine power and subsequent punishment, was no accident. An author's perception of women and their role is determined by the stereotypes current during his era. Greimas' outline seeks to prove that a particular determinism conditions the narrational logic and that every situation is governed by the same forces of action.

If we attempt to examine the system underlying the fiction, what interests me as a feminist researcher is to show that beneath this determinism exists an even more significant determinism conditioned by the ideology of male/female domination. In short, the way in which the social mores handed down from generation to generation by the parental Superego, as Freud explains the phenomenon, eventually constitute a false "good conscience" in regard to the powers that be. This conformism, this conservatism, quite often unconscious, is thwarting all the attempts made by women to help society's evolution towards a more reasonable equality, in line with the democratic principles proclaimed by all. Since Greimas's grid is tautological in regard to the forces of actions present in the novel, it can only emphasize the novel's role as being itself a mirror of society.

I would suggest, to the feminist researchers who might be interested, that they utilize Greimas' outline to establish, just as Propp (1970) did for the Russian short story, a repertory of all the situations extant in the male/female relationship, taking as a corpus one hundred of the best French, English, or world novels. Shades of meaning are varied and often misleading. In certain novels, where the woman appears to control the action by intellectual or strategical means, she is, in fact, doing so simply to serve a man. Mme de Merteuil in *Les Liaisons dangereuses* (Laclos 1782) is a good example; she has the role of go-between, one that is often allotted to certain feminine characters in the literary pornographic novel.

Along with the study of the vocabulary of the male/female stereotypes, and Greimas' initial semiotic approach, a third method for analyzing the male/female relationship in the narrative—a method also derived from Greimas' semiotic grid—has already given interesting results in a thesis at Laval University (Beauregard 1983). It consists in looking for the semiotic square or the logical outcome of the narrative's underlying structures as evidenced by recurring words and networks of images and symbols. The semiotic square is based on certain antithetic terms upon which the narrative reposes. The details of this method

(Hénault 1979) are too involved to explain here; however, I would suggest using the contradictory terms woman/man and their opposites: non-woman/non-man as the key to apprehend the ultimate meaning of the action, the word, and images recurring. Such refocusing of Greimas' logical binary system on a binary system based on the difference in the sexes gives enlightening results in Micheline Beauregard's (1983) thesis on Michel Tournier's novel, *Vendredi ou les Limbes du Pacifique* (1967). The domination of women—here represented by the island to be domesticated or tamed—and the ambiguous sexuality of the character Robinson Crusoe, exercising his narcissistic authority over his companion and slave, Vendredi, are clearly visible in the text's inherent logic at every level: semantic, semiotic, and narrational. In the end, we see illustrated the desire for domination proposed as the stereotypical model for the male in our societies.

Pierre Guiraud (1978a and 1978b) and Marina Yaguello (1978) have indicated that the French vocabulary, and in all likelihood that of most languages, is constructed so as to valorize the phallus-penis and to devalue women. Women are reduced to two roles—the comforting mother, or the woman as the Other, different and anguishing, the figure upon whom the male projects his own sexuality and distress; and, according to the period in history, he calls her witch, "personne du sexe," or whore.

Male narcissism, and its counterbalancing distress, is one of the themes central to male imagination. Macbeth (Shakespeare 1603) wants to conquer the King's scepter-phallus just as Lady Chatterley's lover (Lawrence 1928) seeks to bring Lady Chatterley back to life with a magic wand, the phallus-king, whose beauty and glory they both extol with lyrical effusion. Here, pleasure for the male derives not so much from the sexual act as from that narcissistic exaltation. The same is true in the pornographic novel where the man seeks to control and dominate the woman much more than to make love to her.

The aforementioned methods allow us to gauge with a degree of precision just how mentalities function in regard to women in the works under scrutiny. I would now propose a fourth implement, also adaptable to our specific aim, namely psychocriticism (Mauron 1957). As in Greimas, this method reduces the narrative framework to a single sentence. Then, all the works of a given author are superimposed, having first been reduced to their essentials, whence may be observed a certain recurrence of themes, in paternal-type characters (kings or others), maternal-types, and male and female lovers—the three figures of Oedipus, as well as the acolytes and adversaries who surround them.

That which Greimas calls the Subject or driving force of the action is labelled the Ego of the work, according to psychocriticism. The other characters represent as many aspects of that Ego which are more or less repressed by or confronted with the Ego. They may in fact, represent the Id, i.e., desire, as well as the Superego. Examined in that light, Catherine, of *Wuthering Heights*, represses in herself all the savage and passionate elements incarnated in Heathcliff, namely her unavowed desire. In the end she conforms to the values of the familial and social Superego and to the bourgeois standards Linton incarnates. Psychocriticsm, inspired by psychoanalysis, proceeds with a psychic analysis of the images and symbols which constitute the texture and literary characteristics over the schematic structure: Ego, Superego, and Id. Psychocriticsm can be adapted to feminist research on the ideology relating to women when we consider that in so many masculine novels the object of the quest, both pursued and feared, is the woman. She is the sexual Other who is perceived with all the ambivalence that may exist between sexual desire and socio-familial standards. At times, the Ego projects on the Other certain psychic elements one refuses to accept within oneself. We see Catherine doing this in *Wuthering Heights*. We would likely discover equivalent forces of action in novels evoking homosexual relationships; with this difference: the social standard is placed in opposition to the sexual desire rather than in an ambivalent position or in union with it.

The use of any or all these methods will often help researchers see that what differentiates one work from another may be the personal slant taken by a particular fantasy, the quality or the images employed, or narrative inventiveness; whereas the dominating/ dominated relationship between these fictional men and women is always the same. The Harlequin series offers a fine example of such narrative variations and pirouettes on a single theme. The social inequality between men and women which this commercial enterprise consolidates and renders commonplace, according to Barthe's expression in his analysis of ideologies, justifiably concerns feminists. No feminist critic would be satisfied with merely collecting data, establishing sales statistics, or simply listing the cast of characters—efforts which could only lead to passive, even complacent observations. Rather, she would attempt to analyze the ideological functioning of a phenomenon, so as to help cultural attitudes progress.

The last two methods I shall speak about are inspired by two female theoreticians. The research and work of Mieke Bal (1985) deals with subjectivity in regard to women in certain Biblical passages; this subjectivity is masculine and unconscious. Mieke Bal integrates within a single unified outline such notions as point of view, focuser, and the temporal aspects which Genette (1972) presents as distinct separate notions. In this synthesis the narrative, and comments within a narrative, derive their full subjective value and tone. Certain silences and omissions about women in the passages concerning them are quite often as revealing as all the disparaging and idealizing remarks made about them. If we combine these narrative signs with the subjectivist linguistic signs proposed by Benveniste (1966; 1970), and we also add the interventions of authors in the form of valorizing or devalorizing adverbs and adjectives, we can perceive certain aspects of the author's extra-linguistic and extra-narrative subjectivity and mentality.

Is it possible to see this subjectivity as masculine or feminine? This question interests me at present. A few authors, Balzac for one, who address their "dear reader" when they speak as writers qualify themselves as masculine. These rare instances of the author's sexualization inside the narration are functions of the French rules of gender. Beyond such explicit linguistic signs, what could enable us to distinguish a male from a female novelist? In my opinion, the answer may be discovered only at the ideological level. When Mauriac (1927: 43), who sympathizes with the heroine Thérèse Desqueyroux, has her recount her own story in the form of a long inner monologue, he identifies in a way with her. But, when the same Mauriac lets slide a cliché like "Le caquetage des dames" (the women's prattle), we see a word that would never even enter the mind of any woman with a feminist awareness. As a rule, women today know exactly where to situate "prattle" when the choice lies between women who are perhaps talking about their children and men who may be discussing football or hockey.

In a novel written by a woman, the main character is almost always a woman, and with male authors it is a man. Yet, several works defy this majority, such as *Thérèse Desqueyroux* or *Les Fous de Bassan* (Hébert 1982). In the latter novel, an inner monologue is attributed to a male character although the central monologue belongs to a woman, Olivia.

Would *Thérèse Desqueyroux'* inner monologue have been different had it been written by a woman? We could ask the same question about Molly Bloom's monologue in *Ulysses* (Joyce 1922) or about many other monologues or reflections attributed to women in masculine works. With a clever author, the question of plausibility never arises. However, if we consider the ideological differences between authors, let us compare two novels in which a woman murders her husband. Thérèse Desqueyroux is presented as a depressed, apathetic individual who kills almost mechanically as a result of a long and gradual poisoning. Mauriac himself assumes his character's guilt in a curious preface where he entrusts her soul to God's mercy. In the novel *Kamouraska* (Hébert 1970), the heroine, Elisabeth, is level-headed and determined; she organizes her husband's assassination with great lucidity, almost joyfully; afterwards, she will regret only her lost passion and her lover who has fled.

The main masculine characters Gabrielle Roy evokes in *Alexandre Chenevert* (1964) and *La montagne secrète* (1974) represent the metaphysical or aesthetic preoccupations usually attributed to men. She thus conforms to the stereotype, whereas in *Bonheur d'occasion* (Roy 1947), a woman shoulders her family's poverty and all their other problems.

Signs which identify the sex of the author are rare in the novel and difficult to detect, as they are usually found at the ideological level, which is determined by one's history. For, transposing Simone de Beauvoir's turn of phrase, one is not born a man, ideologically, but school, the family, and society condition a man, gradually force him to resemble the masculine stereotype — a rather artificial creature, mistakenly sure of himself and of his pseudo-superiority over women. He perceives women as conforming to the stereotype imposed upon them: submissive, always gentle creatures. Today, men and women are well aware that these models and roles are simply delusions. The day is at hand when such delusions will abate and eventually disappear. Society will be more egalitarian, less aggressive, less belligerent, even in games and sports which by their very nature are imbued with a spirit of fun and fair play.

One last implement might enable us to discover the author's value system which is projected more or less consciously on the characters. Marisa Zavalloni and Christiane Louis-Guérin (1984), using questionnaires and analytical grids, investigate how one identifies with the norms of the different social groups to which one belongs (nations, institutions, religions, sex, etc.). It is always difficult to apply to fictional characters methods for analyzing the psyche of real human beings. The psychocritic faces the same difficulty. This particular analytical instrument, however, has the advantage of being situated at a preconscious level which neither the psychoanalyst nor the psychocritic have attempted systematically to understand. Therein lies an area of investigation which could well open new and promising avenues for literary analysis.

In closing, I would like to mention that these six methods, still at the experimental stage in the field of feminist studies at my university, will most probably contribute to advancing research on how mentalities and ideologies function in regard to women in literary works. In certain instances, they have already produced substantial results.

References

Althusser, Louis.
1970   L'Idéologie et les appareils idéologiques d'Etat. *La Pensée* 151: 3-39.

Bal, Mieke.
1985   *Femmes imaginaires*. Montreal: Hurtubise HMH.

Barthes, Roland.
1957   *Mythologies*. Paris: Editions du Seuil.

Beauregard, Micheline.
1983   *L'image de la femme dans un roman de Michel Tournier: Vendredi ou les Limbes du Pacifique*. Thèse de maîtrise, Université Laval.

1985   *Tournier ou l'art d'invalider la femme*. Ottawa, The CRIAW Papers/Les documents de l'ICREF, no. 8. (This is a summary of Beauregard's thesis 1983.)

Benveniste, Emile.
1966   *Problèmes de linguistique générale*, 1. Paris: Gallimard.

1970   *Problèmes de linguistique générale*, 2. Paris: Gallimard.

Brontë, Emily.
1847   *Wuthering Heights*. Trad. *Les Hauts de Hurle-vent*. Paris: Payot [1984].

Engels, Friedrich.
1884   *Les origines de la famille, de la propriété privée et de l'Etat*. Paris: Editions sociales [1983].

Genette, Gérard.
1972   *Figures II*. Paris: Editions du Seuil.

Greimas, A.J.
1966   *Sémantique structurale*. Paris: Editions du Seuil.

Guiraud, Pierre.
1978a   *Sémiologie de la sexualité*. Paris: Payot.

1978b   *Dictionnaire érotique*. Paris: Payot.

Hébert, Anne.
   1970   *Kamouraska*. Paris: Editions du Seuil.

   1982   *Les Fous de Bassan*. Paris: Editions du Seuil.

Hémon, Louis.
   1913   *Maria Chapdelaine*.   Montréal, Editions Fides, Collection Le Nénuphar [1946].

Hénault, Anne.
   1979   *Les enjeux de la sémiotique*. Paris: PUF.

Joyce, James.
   1922   *Ulysses*. London, The Bodley Head [1952].

Laclos, Pierre Choderlos de.
   1782   *Les liaisons dangereuses*.

Lawrence, D.H.
   1928   *Lady Chatterley's Lover*.   Trad. *L'amant de Lady Chatterley*. Paris: Gallimard [1932].

Mauriac, François.
   1927   *Thérèse Desqueyroux*. Paris: Grasset, Livre de poche.

Mauron, Charles.
   1957   *L'inconscient dans l'oeuvre et dans la vie de Jean Racine*. Aix-en-Provence, Editions Ophrys.

Poulin, Louise.
   1987   *L'image de la femme dans le roman agriculturiste québécois*.   Thèse de maîtrise, Département des littératures, Université Laval.

Propp, Vladimir.
   1970   *Morphologie du conte*. Paris: Editions du Seuil.

Racine, Jean.
   1669   *Britannicus*. Paris: Garnier [1986].

   1691   *Athalie*. Paris: Garnier [1986].

Roy, Gabrielle.
1947   *Bonheur d'occasion*. Paris: Flammarion.

1964   *Alexandre Chenevert*. Montréal: Beauchemin.

1974   *La montagne secrète*. Montréal: Beauchemin.

Shakespeare, William.
1593   *The Taming of the Shrew*. Trad. *La mégère apprivoisée*.
            Oxford University [1971].

1603   *Macbeth*. Oxford University [1971].

Théry, Chantal.
1987   *Lettres québécoises*. La droite amoureuse rallume ses
            brasiers 44: 69-70, 86-87.

Tournier, Michel.
1967   *Vendredi ou les Limbes du Pacifique*. Paris: Gallimard.

Yaguello, Marina.
1978   *Les mots et les femmes*. Paris: Payot.

Zavalloni, Marisa, et Louis-Guérin, Christiane.
1984   *Identité sociale et conscience*. Montréal: PUM et
            Toulouse, Privat.

Chapter 9

DUALISM AND DANCE

Anne Flynn

At the risk of stereotyping myself as a dancer and therefore – as everyone knows – as someone highly emotional and dangerously introspective, I will begin by saying that I was very happy to be part of the conference from which this anthology emerged. To my knowledge, this is the first time in Canada that dance has been represented at a conference dealing with feminist issues as they apply to the scholarly enterprise. I congratulate the conference organizers for the twofold statement they have made by including dance. First, they have recognized dance as an academic discipline, which, as we shall see later, is not insignificant, and second, they have suggested that dance is relevant to a larger feminist agenda.

With regard to the second point, I offer the following observation. There are many parallels which can be drawn between the development of women's studies programs and the development of dance programs in higher education. They have both had to, and in many places continue to, struggle against the power of a largely male academic community for acceptance as legitimate areas of study. They have to face the challenge of developing research strategies appropriate for interpreting data which have previously been ignored or viewed as unimportant. And, perhaps most importantly, the work in both women's studies and in dance is conducted predominantly by women. Although this paper is not about the relationship between dance and women's studies, I draw your attention to these points in order to construct a framework for understanding what follows. Dance in higher education, like women's studies, is still in the process of becoming and does not enjoy the comfort of unquestioned acceptance that other academic disciplines share. In dance, this basic fact has been largely unexamined. Instead, dance academics have been grateful for any support they can generate in order simply to get on with the business of studying dance. While I support my colleagues in their determination to ignore the larger obstacles that dance in higher education must continue to face, my own work (which has clearly been influenced by my experiences as a dance academic at The University of Calgary) is concerned with understanding why dance is so little valued by our universities. Until we, i.e., dance academics, can see more clearly what we are up against, and what factors keep dance a 'minor' field of study, dance will remain a relatively unexplored area.

This is an enormously complex task. It is necessarily an ongoing process which will require the work of many individuals over time, and which will need to be studied from a variety of perspectives. This paper reflects my thinking over the past two years which has been influenced very much by my study of philosophy of mind and philosophy of science, by feminist analysis, and by interpretive anthropology, as well as by my ongoing experiences as a dancer. As such, I ask that you view the following attempt to construct a broad framework for understanding the low profile of dance study in higher education as a contextually specific and only a partial construction of what is a much larger and almost completely unexplored conceptual landscape.

It may appear that a discussion of dance in higher education is not immediately relevant to the topic of this anthology. My intention is to show that lack of interest in dance as an academic field of study is precipitated by our acceptance of a largely male constructed world-view which is essentially dualistic. This world-view has shaped our thinking about the nature and goals of research, about what we take to be properly 'academic,' and about what we accept as 'legitimate' knowledge.

To begin, I will present a brief overview of dance study in higher education and then move on to a discussion of how a dualist epistemology distorts the way that dance is described and perceived. Dance is a recent addition to university programs. The first degree program in dance in North America was established at the University of Wisconsin in 1926. Currently there are over 200 degree programs offered by American universities and colleges (*College Blue Book* 1985). In Canada, the first degree in dance was offered by York University in 1970. Today there are five universities which offer a minor in dance and most at least offer a few courses.[1]

The introduction of dance into higher education occurred primarily through departments of physical education where dance tends to be viewed as a rhythmic and expressive 'physical' activity comparable to sport, save for the expressive part. Dance programs also emerged in departments of fine arts spurred by the rapid growth of the American modern dance movement. With the exception of a few places where dance can be found in departments of health, recreation, or even humanities, dance programs tend to be housed either in physical education or fine arts departments.[2]

The splitting up of dance study into these departmental categories — constructed with quite different ends in mind — has had extremely negative effects on its development as a field of study. The physical education concept of dance is that dance is largely a 'physical' activity. An unfortunate consequence of this view is the substitution of aerobics for dance, which is happening in many schools today. This view of dance as largely a physical activity has been matched by an equally limited fine arts concept of dance as something that highly trained performers do on a stage in front of an audience. Neither of these concepts comes close to capturing the real activity of dancing as it has existed throughout human history. And further, these concepts have obstructed any sort of meaningful understanding of dance as a cultural construct.

It is not only at the conceptual level that this division of conceptual approaches to dance is present. In a number of universities, including The University of Calgary, dance programs exist in both the Faculties of Fine Arts and of Physical Education. Each program is given a mandate not to wander beyond its territory. Dance in physical education is not to speak about dance as a performing art, and dance in fine arts should not touch the educational, recreational, or sensory aspects of dance. As one might imagine, this situation has led to bitter conflicts over who rightfully possesses which aspects of the study of dance. (On bad days I am given to believing that this is a ploy on the part of the administration to keep dance fragmented and hence seemingly without cohesion.) The tail end of this divisive conflict emerges within the student body as a difference between the 'serious' and 'not-so-serious' study of dance. For the student it amounts to an aesthetic decision about which camp to join.

The structural division of dance into discrete areas of study that has occurred in many universities is one example of how dualist conceptualizations have been imposed on an area which is intrinsically not dualistic.[3] Dance is a complex area, and trying to understand it is not an easy task. Still, it would be better to accept it with all its human complexity than attempt to impose inappropriate theoretical constructions on it for the sake of an ideal of order. Dance is a movement activity, a form of art, an entertainment, and a social/psychological construct or sign. As such, the proper study of dance must be self-consciously pluralistic. It cannot, and should not, be restricted by the territorial outlines of current university structures. There are universities where dance exists autonomously and where the approach to studying dance takes into account the broad nature of the field. But there has been a pattern in higher education of subsuming dance under other supposedly related areas where it is not recognized as an important field of study in and of itself.

Let me explain, in part, what this means in the everyday world of a dance academic. Dancers like myself, who work in physical education departments, are urged to relate dance to sport by choreographing for skaters and gymnasts, and by helping volleyball and basketball players improve their grace and jumping skills by giving them ballet classes. Dancers who work in fine arts departments are asked to choreograph everything from little minuets for eighteenth-century plays to wild scenes of abandon for musicals like Hair. To my knowledge, no one asks theologians to instruct commerce students on how to look pious to achieve better sales, or archeologists to give digging lessons to engineers. Those of us in physical education departments also have to be translators. We hear rehearsals called practices, costumes called uniforms, and choreography called routines or numbers. The pressure is so strong for dance academics to show how dance is valuable to other areas, it is a wonder that we remember anything about dance as dance.

Before getting into a discussion of dualism in relation to dance in higher education, I want to offer one final observation about the development of dance study in universities. The development of master and doctoral programs in dance has been slow. To a large extent the current body of dance scholars has been trained in other disciplines, such as history, philosophy, anthropology, sociology, psychology, kinesiology, education, and criticism. The lack of availability of advanced degree programs in dance, plus the general view held by dance academics that one can more easily gain acceptance into the academic community by holding a degree in one of the more 'traditional' disciplines, has meant that approaches to dance research have been informed by frameworks which were not constructed with dance in mind. I do not want to deny the value of this multidisciplinary approach. The field of dance has benefitted greatly from the work of scholars in the biological and social sciences, as well as the humanities. However, the necessity for dancers to seek advanced training in other disciplines has often led to a practitioner being the lone dancer in an academic community where dance is little understood, if considered at all.

Let me now move on to the question of why dance is relatively undeveloped as a field of academic study, and what I think this has to do with dualist views of the world and of human beings. Dualist labels divide the world up into pairs of polar opposites. These opposites are essentially connected, but they can also be examined and potentially understood independently of one another. The concept of the world as fundamentally divided into nature and culture is one example of dualism. Dualist labels are not only used to describe the world (which is presumed to be "out there" and separate from our human perception of it), but also to describe human beings. The concept of the essential dualism of mind and body, which Descartes so clearly articulated, lives with us today as the standard view of the human being (Churchland 1984). Other familiar dualist concepts include: mind and nature, reason and emotion, subjective and objective, art and science, and, perhaps more fundamentally, man and woman.

The two versions of dualism that I want to mention in this connection are mind/body and gender dualism. I do not want to suggest that other versions of dualism do not bear on the issue of dance. They are all relevant to how we have come to perceive dance. But dealing with all these issues is well beyond the scope of this paper.

A dualist explanation of what has become known in philosophy as the mind/body problem can be traced back in the west to Plato and Pythagoras, and is also to be found in eastern doctrines, but our contemporary version is particularly associated with Descartes and the shift to a mechanistic view of the world that surrounded the development of modern science in the seventeenth century.[4] Descartes' version of dualism which Gilbert Ryle, one of its critics, calls the "official doctrine," essentially states that all human beings are composed of an incorporeal mind and a corporeal body. The body is a physical substance to which mechanical laws apply and which is public and therefore observable. Mind, on the other hand, does not live in the physical world. Its workings are private and its functioning is not observable by others (Ryle 1949: 13). In the post-medieval world, Descartes (1596-1650) was the first major proponent of dualism: his influence was extensive in the seventeenth century, and the effects of his views are with us yet. His continuing effect is not surprising since reaction against his views, until this century, was exclusively reaction within a Cartesian framework of the philosophy of mind. In the sixth of his *Meditations on First Philosophy* which is titled: "Concerning the Existence of Material Things, and the Real Distinction of the Mind from the Body," Descartes argues:

> For this reason, from the fact that I know that I exist, and that meanwhile I judge that nothing else clearly belongs to my nature or essence except that I am a thing that thinks, I rightly conclude that my essence consists in this alone: that I am only a thing that thinks. Although perhaps (or rather, as I shall soon say, to be sure) I have a body that is very closely joined to me, nevertheless, because on the one hand I have a clear and distinct idea of

myself—insofar as I am a thing that thinks and not an extended thing—and because on the other hand I have a distinct idea of a body—insofar as it is merely an extended thing, and not a thing that thinks—it is therefore certain that I am truly distinct from my body, and that I can exist without it (1980: 93).

Cartesian dualism, which was formulated in a social climate dominated by a particular religious outlook, offered support for a systematic objectification and denial of the body. The body was already metaphorically linked up with nature, women, the secretive, the sometimes uncontrollable, and the irrational. Given this context, it is not surprising that Descartes' explanation of mind/body duality would receive support. The body and its correlates needed to be controlled and rendered submissive in the seventeenth-century scheme of things. This need, unfortunately, is the legacy that we still share (Keller 1985). Although dualism as a doctrine is not widespread in philosophy[5] it is still very much a part of how we describe ourselves today. One need not look far for signs of dualist thinking in contemporary culture: the notion of 'physical' education is one example that comes immediately to mind. The recent fitness movement is offering us a million ways to change and rearrange that unfortunate bit of physical baggage below the neck that we call our body. We talk about bodies not as though they are us, but as if they are something we own—something that can be controlled and directed by the mind, in the same way that nature can be controlled and directed by culture. Bodies remind us of our connection to nature and to women, realities that have been rendered submissive in the pursuit of what Henry Oldenburg, one-time secretary of the Royal Society, called a 'Masculine Philosophy' (Keller 1985: 52).

I hope it is obvious what all this has to do with dance. Dance as it is described through dualist lenses is a 'physical' activity involving the body. It is therefore primal, sensual, and potentially corruptive. Dance is associated with emotions, with subjectivity, with the irrational, and, consequently, with women. Since dualism sets up exclusive either/or distinctions, it follows that dance is generally not associated with mind, thinking, or rationality—and hence is not associated with 'real' men and the pursuit of knowledge. Certainly I am stating the extremes. I recognize that dance is not viewed in such absolute terms, and that my analysis is not relevant in all other cultures. My intention is simply to point out that our understanding of dance may be restricted by epistemological structures and, in particular, that dualism does not provide us with a useful way of looking at dance. With its simplistic categorizing, dualism restricts us to a view of dance that bears no relation to the actual experience of dancing and, in addition, trivializes the importance of dance in the history of culture. Our culture has tended to value only one side of our dualist formulations, namely, those qualities ascribed to men.[6] Viewed in this light, the power that dance has to heighten our awareness of ourselves as feeling and sensing human animals has induced a fear of dance which we seek to escape.

We are very careful, even today, to regulate our dancing where we can. In The University of Calgary two out of three dance studios are in the basement, while the third is a large cement-block square room. The message is clear: you can do your dancing but we do not want to see you or hear your music. There is an issue, however, that is more serious than the relegation of our studios to the bowels of the university. Last year, I was involved in a dispute over whether to remove dance from the required core of the Alberta provincial curriculum in response to "the religious objections to dance by some parents and in some communities. These objections center on the term Dance and appear to focus on the 'expressive movement' emphasis in Dance."[7] The worst part of this particular situation was that no member of Alberta's university dance community was informed that this was even an issue. It was being handled by administrators, all men, who knew almost nothing about dance. I am not sure if this says something about dance or about Alberta, but as one who donned her most conservative clothes to attend a meeting with the Associate Director of Curriculum and a few of his colleagues, it said something very powerful to me.

Accepting dualism as a conceptual framework for ordering the world and our experiences means that we have described and based our understanding of dance, among many other things, on misleading concepts. Anyone who dances knows that it is not merely a 'physical' activity, or an unrestrained emotional outburst. Yet we persist in talking about dance as though it has nothing to do with thinking or reasoning. Since traditional images of women largely exclude us from the domains of reason and rationality, it should come as no surprise that the overwhelming majority of individuals who work as dance academics are women. This is a curious fact that has not received much attention in the literature on dance or women, but which, I would like to suggest, is critical to our understanding of the status of dance in higher education.[8]

Dance, in its association with the expression of feelings and emotions, seems properly the domain of women who have traditionally been responsible for nurturing and for keeping the species in touch with our feelings. Dance in higher education has been developed largely by women, and women participate in dance classes in significantly greater numbers than men. The following excerpt from an essay written by a male student for a modern dance course that I taught recently sums up beautifully the prevailing attitude of men towards dance, especially 'expressive' dance.

"I have to take what?!"

"Everyone in the faculty of Physical Education has to take some form of dance."

"Oh, wonderful."

And so it began, way back at registration. At least I had until October before I had to take the dreaded "modern dance" PHAC. Images of tutus and tights and men with questionable sexual preferences rampaged throughout my distraught mind. How would I ever explain it to my family, my friends?

"Mom," I would say, "I've got something to tell you and Dad ... I'm ... I'm taking dance classes — there, I've said it!"

Oh, the grief, the sorrow and pain my parents would go through, the ridicule from their friends when the terrible news got out, as it inevitably would. Oh, the shame of it all!

Then, the day came. Monday. October twentieth. Eleven o'clock. Sob. A small crowd of people were milling about the doorway of the dance studio, looking like they would bolt at the slightest sound. I pushed my way through, determined to keep "a stiff upper lip" and at the same time, keep out of sight of anyone who might recognize me.

The room was bare save for a piano on one corner of the plain hardwood floor. Two of the walls had a wooden bar placed horizontally at about hip height, while a third wall was completely mirrored. The fourth wall had a door and a small window through which only blackness could be seen. This, I imagined, would be where thousands of people would file by on the other side, unbeknownst to us, as we skipped and daintily flitted about in our light cotton print dresses.

At this point I bolted for the door, but too late! In walked the teacher, closing the door and trapping us all inside! Aaagh! Attendance was taken, and my name was irrevocably marked on the list.[9]

This particular student turned out to be extremely receptive to dance. In a matter of weeks he was staying after class to go over material and his final essay reflected an enormous change in his understanding of dance and its importance to the individual. This kind of radical change, which I have been fortunate to witness many, many times, says something, I think, about the power of dance to transform. There is a tendency in this culture to think that dance comes more 'naturally' to women. That dance emphasizes characteristics which women more 'naturally' possess. But this attitude is just another way of ignoring gender as a social construction and hiding behind a biological fortress. There is nothing about dance itself that makes it more suitable to men or women. It is only our misunderstanding of it that makes it appear so. As long as we continue inappropriately to associate dance with the exclusive dualistic domains of the body (the natural, the emotional, and the female), I think that dance will remain an area that is little understood, appearing only marginally relevant to the scholarly enterprise and to the pursuit of knowledge. In addition, any analysis of dance which relies on a dualist epistemology is doomed to failure as a result of making the fundamental methodological mistake of ignoring the real data of dancing, which is revealed when dance is allowed to 'speak' for itself.[10]

I believe that dance has much to offer in the way of insight into human beings and their cultures. Its presence throughout history and across cultures is some indication of its deep connection to human life, and perhaps it is this very fundamental connection which makes dance seem so elusive to analysis. Clearly, we still have much to learn about the meaning of dance to individuals and to the cultures they create. Having said this, let me close by referring back to my analogy between women's studies and dance. It appears that it has only been in the 'doing' of women's studies that we have come to appreciate how important the role of women is to our understanding of the world. This anthology attests to the fact that the inclusion of gender in methodological approaches is producing a very different picture of the world. At this point, we do not know what the study of dance might reveal. However, I think that the meaning and importance of dance can only emerge from the 'doing' of dance study, rather than ignoring it. Feminists seem the most likely candidates for taking up this task because of their nondualistic approach. The rejection of false dichotomies which is characteristic of what I understand to be part of feminist approaches to research is just what is needed if dance is to become a more meaningful part of our collective pursuit of knowledge.

Endnotes

1. See *The Directory of Post Secondary Dance Courses and Programs in Canada* (1979-80).

2. For more information about the development of dance in education see Chapman and Kraus (1981: chaps. 7, 13, 14).

3. In an introduction to a feature on dance in the university/college setting that appeared in the *Journal of Physical Education, Recreation and Dance* (May/June 1986), the feature editor wrote, "The duality of dance is inherent in its very nature. . . ." This way of describing dance is very common and I think it is, in part, a reflection of how comfortable we have become with a dualist world-view.

4. For a discussion of the shift in thinking that accompanied the development of modern science in the seventeenth century, see Keller (1985: chs. 2 & 3).

5. Although dualism is still occasionally discussed in passing, e.g. Gregory (1981: 459-80), the evidence for contemporary philosophers abandoning dualism comes from the absence of such discussions in the literature. For example, the topic scarcely is mentioned in such recent works as: Dennett (1981); Haugeland, ed. (1981); Hofstadter and Dennett (1981); Churchland (1984).

6. This point has received much attention in recent feminist literature. See for example: Harding and Hintikka, eds. (1983); Gilligan (1982); Hartsock (1985); and Keller (1985).

7. Personal correspondence with the Associate Director of Curriculum, Department of Education, Government of Alberta, January 14, 1986.

8. It seems unnecessary, given the nature of this anthology, to go into detail about the lack of power that women have held with regard to the creation of academic policy and curriculum. So let me ask that you imagine what it might be like to be a women and a dancer arguing against a cut in operating funds in a room full of male administrators. I hope the image speaks for itself.

9. Excerpt from an assignment for PHAC 285.01 Modern Dance I, Faculty of Physical Education, The University of Calgary, 1986.

10.   For more on this point see Keller (1985:   ch. 9), where she discusses the work of Barbara McClintock, the geneticist and Nobel Prize winner.

References

_____·

1985   *The College Blue Book*, 20th ed. New York: Macmillan Publishing Co.

Chapman, Sandra, and Kraus, Richard.
1981   *History of the Dance in Art and Education*, 2nd ed. New Jersey: Prentice Hall.

Churchland, Paul M.
1984   *Matter and Consciousness*. Cambridge: M.I.T.

Dennett, Daniel C.
1981   *Brainstorms*. Cambridge: M.I.T.

Descartes, Rene.
1980   *Discourse on Method and Meditations of First Philosophy*. Trans. Donald A. Cress. Indianapolis: Hackett Publishing Co.

Gilligan, Carol.
1982   *In a Different Voice*. Cambridge: Harvard University.

Gregory, Richard L.
1981   *Mind in Science*. Cambridge: Cambridge University.

Harding, Sandra, and Hintikka, Merrill B. (eds.).
1983   *Discovering Reality: Feminist Perspectives on Epistemology, Metaphysics, Methodology, and Philosophy of Science*. Dordrecht, Holland: D. Reidel.

Hartsock, Nancy C.M.
1985   *Money, Sex, and Power*. Boston: Northeastern University.

Haugeland, John (ed.).
1981   *Mind Design*. Cambridge: M.I.T.

Hofstadter, D.R., and Dennett, D.C.
1981   *The Minds I*. New York: Basic Books.

Keller, Evelyn Fox.
1985   *Reflection on Gender and Science*. New Haven: Yale University.

Ryle, Gilbert.
    1949   *The Concept of Mind*. Middlesex: Penguin.

Chapter 10

THE IMPACT OF A FEMINIST PERSPECTIVE ON RESEARCH METHODOLOGIES: SOCIAL SCIENCES

Kathleen Driscoll and Joan McFarland*

Introduction

Feminist scholarship has been in the forefront of the debate over appropriate research methodologies. It is a debate which has been sorely lacking in other areas of research.

Part I is about general issues raised in the social sciences by feminist discussion of the research process. It concludes with an outline of the important characteristics of an evolving feminist research methodology.

The intention of Part II is to discuss the difficulties that feminists encounter in regard to the content and methods of economics, particularly in the neo-classical paradigm, and to illustrate these difficulties with the presentation of the results of a survey of articles on the subject of women in recent economic journals.

The conclusion points to the importance of methodological issues in relation to the kind of policy recommendations made by economists.

PART I: Issues in Research Methodology

Conceptual Framework and Research Techniques

Research methodology is examined according to two interconnected processes: (1) conceptual framework and (2) techniques of data collection and analysis.

Techniques of data collection and analysis are not neutral. They are shaped by the conceptual framework and they may, in turn, further shape that framework. Each technique embodies decisions concerning

---

*The conceptual approach and the organization were co-authored. Kathleen Driscoll (sociologist) was mainly responsible for Part I. Joan McFarland (economist) was mainly responsible for the analysis of economics, and Part II.

appropriate units of study, the important characteristics of the units, and the relationship between units (Graham 1983).   Each technique's usefulness and its limitations are structured by its underlying assumptions.   Adopting a research technique means adopting its conceptual framework.

Feminist research raises profound questions concerning the conceptual framework of the social sciences (Eichler 1985 and Harding 1986: 9).   It thereby questions the research techniques developed in conjunction with that framework.   There are three major areas of focus in this discussion of research methodology:

1.   power relationships between the researcher and the subjects of the research;
2.   validity and importance of women's experiences;
3.   assumptions built into established techniques of data collection and analysis.

Power/Authority Issues

The gender, class, race, and educational status of the researcher as well as her/his institutional affiliation, may all set up patterns of power and subordination which are part of the general society.[1]   For the feminist who is challenging these patterns of power, this raises important ethical questions.   By participating in these divisions the researcher is contributing to women's subordination.

If being 'objective' means that the researcher must separate herself from the people she is studying, a number of further problems arise.   The researcher's participation in the social patterns is denied or ignored.   The complexity and contextual nature of reality and of the research process is not taken into account.   Such denial and omission may also conceal ways in which the social relations of the research process shape the findings.

These ethical and substantive questions are frequently raised by feminist researchers who are uncomfortable in the stance adopted by established researchers.   Can the separation required by demands for 'objectivity' contribute to women's empowerment when it is so firmly tied to their subordination?

The researcher's task, by definition, is the search for greater understanding.   This can establish another authority division between researcher and the people studied—a division based on differences in knowledge.   The researcher acquires more knowledge or is perceived to acquire the objective 'truth' concerning the people and situations being studied (Stanley and Wise 1983). Some of the questions raised by feminist work on this issue are addressed in the next section on the validity of women's experiences.

A related concern is the imposition of inappropriate categories and interpretive frameworks onto women's experiences. The application to women's experiences of concepts and modes of analyses developed in studying men's lives in the public sphere often devalues women's experiences and reinforces women's subordination.

Validity of Women's Experiences

Feminist work starts from assumptions about the importance and validity of women's experiences (Stanley and Wise 1983: 53). The understanding, emerging from the women's movement, that 'personal is political' is central here. The struggle is to find ways to use these experiences as a basis for the development of both theory and method rather than trying to fit women's actions and thoughts into a framework generated outside of their experiences (Du Bois 1980: 108).

This means that women's experiences must be constantly responded to and incorporated into the ongoing research process. Various ways of doing this are being developed. One direction has been an emphasis on the importance of 'qualitative' research involving in-depth contact between the researcher and the people being studied. The importance of qualitative research techniques is that they may, with care, allow greater access to people's experiences. These techniques do this by facilitating the use of those experiences to modify the analysis in an ongoing fashion throughout the research process. There is a reflexive relation between the research method, the subject being researched, and the researcher. Quantitative research, however, clearly remains important, particularly with reference to public debate concerning policy issues.

Qualitative techniques allow us to locate action and experience in its context (Duelli Klein 1980). We are thus better able to incorporate the complexity of the real world. Jayaratne (1980: 154) goes so far as to suggest that:

> Every quantitative research project should include some qualitative data, not only for use by researchers to understand their respondents better, but also to include in presentations and publications so that others may gain a deeper understanding of the quantified results.

An important part of these qualitative techniques is the effort to incorporate both the subject's reactions and the researcher's use of her own experience into the research (Stanley and Wise 1980).

Assumptions/Limitations of Research Techniques

We have referred above to problematic assumptions concerning both the relationship between researcher and subject, and the relative status of their knowledge. In this section we will discuss two other types of assumptions which underlie many research techniques. These are assumptions concerning (1) the separation of life into public and private spheres and (2) the appropriate units of study as well as the relationship between these units.

Public/private. The social sciences have tended to assume the division of life into public and private spheres. These spheres are considered to be separate and distinct. They can thus be examined apart from one another. It has been suggested that the "traditional concerns of sociology have reproduced the gender order through the categories of the public and the private" (Gamarnikov and Purvis 1983: 6). Of the two, the male public sphere is assumed to be the most important.[2] Research methods have tended to operate from assumptions made about the nature of the public sphere (Graham 1983). Study of the private sphere is done (e.g., 'family economics'); however, the assumptions and techniques are those which were developed to examine the public sphere.

When events and relations from the private sphere are brought to light, they are frequently incomprehensible within established research and analytic frameworks. Research techniques developed in examining the public sphere do not provide sufficient information about the private sphere. They also conceal the integral relationship of public and private. Since women are so often assumed to be primarily in the private sphere of family, personal relations and household, these techniques tend to ignore them. Du Bois (1980: 107) suggests that "...things female have tended to be seen...as anomalies, deviations from the male norm and ideal of the 'person'...." The reality of women's lives (and of men's) is that the public and private are part of one another. Separating them obscures the meaning of phenomena in both.

Units of study. Graham (1983: 130), in her critique of the survey method, suggests that there are four assumptions concerning units of analysis. These assumptions are that:

1. surveys deal with social units (which are "single and complete");

2.   these units are equivalent;
3.   units and their products have an object-form which is external to the individual, can be verbalized, is stable;
4.   units and their outputs are measurable.

These assumptions take the individual out of her/his social context. They mask the structure of social relationships and processes of change. They treat patterns of action and attitude as personal characteristics rather than as dimensions of social structure and of power.

Graham (1983: 144-45) argues that measurement is a highly problematic process: "while measurement presumes the precise definition of social phenomena, the social world is inherently ambiguous." She further suggests that "measurement is closely tied to the marketplace, where activities are quantified and regulated through the medium of money." Thus measurement techniques are based on the patterns of the public sphere. "Women's lives, however, lying 'hidden from history,' may conform to different configurations than those assumed in measurement. Their activities and pattern of relationships may thus defy—or be lost within—the process of measurement."

Quantitative methods make assumptions based on the market nature of the public sphere. These assumptions tend to ignore social context and the complexity of social phenomena. They may make it difficult to investigate social structure and the processes of changing interaction. These assumptions may be inappropriate to the private sphere and may conceal the nonduality of public and private occurrences.

Feminist research methodology is oriented toward contextualizing the research process, the researcher, and the subject of research, based on a nondualistic world view. The researcher should be in contact with the people she/he is studying; there should be provision for feedback between researcher and informants; the researcher's own participation and experience should be a consciously used part of the research process; both conceptualization and methods used for getting information should incorporate the interests and insights of the people being studied. The social context and the intricate connections (Messing 1986: 66) between the various aspects of life should be dealt with. A continual self-consciousness focused on the research process itself should be part of the work.

This all means that research methodology must be an on-going process developing in conjunction with the conceptual framework and in response to the interaction of the researcher and the people being studied. Discussion of the research process itself is a significant part of on-going work. The difficulties encountered can be important sources of insight concerning both the subject being studied and the research methodology. Feminist researchers continue to work with these issues and to develop a more thorough understanding of the research process. Their work has implications which should be taken into account in all areas of social science research.

PART II: Research in Economics

Introduction

What impact has feminist discussion of research methodology had on the discipline of economics? In short, none. This is overwhelmingly the case for work in the neo-classical paradigm, but it is also largely the case in the non-mainstream institutional and radical paradigms as well. In this part of the paper, we will try to explain why such a state of affairs is inevitable given the nature of the theory and methodology of economics, particularly neo-classical economics. In demonstration of this state of affairs, we examine the methodologies employed in articles specifically on the subject of women in recent issues of the economic journals. First, however, we will briefly discuss the impact of a feminist perspective on the research content as opposed to the research methodology of work in economics.

Research Content in Economics

At least four papers have been written in Canada on the general topic of women and economics, and a number have been published in the United States and elsewhere (McFarland 1976; Cohen 1982; MacDonald 1984; White 1984; Amsden 1980). The conclusions of these works may be summarized in four basic points.

First, the authors note the general paucity of works on the subject of women. To a large extent, the scarcity of publications on women in economics is a consequence of ideology. Not only are such topics perceived to be unimportant, but also the implications of a feminist perspective would be unacceptable to the male dominated profession. In addition, the problem at one point seemed to be that women did not fit the basic assumption of the analysis, that of "economic man" who "maximizes his gain given the constraints." It was implied that women were motivated in other ways, particularly within the family. This put women outside of the purview of economic analysis (McFarland 1976).

Second, with the development in the sixties of the new area of 'family economics,' the inadequacy of the economist's tools for the analysis of such subjects became increasingly obvious. The conceptual frameworks — utility theory, marginal productivity theory, the individual as the unit of analysis — could not analyse non-market behavior, or as one author has put it, "the methodology cannot 'see' women's economic behaviour" (Cohen 1982). In fact the development of this new area of economics was led by some of the most conservative of the male economists, e.g., Gary Becker. The purpose was not to illuminate women's position but to test out a new theoretical model of time allocation.

Third, there are serious problems with both the scope of models of economic analysis and with their assumptions. The models never deal with the 'why' questions. The model may seek to determine whether women earn less than men, whether women do some jobs and men others, or the value of housework done by women. However, they do not look at why women earn less than men, why women do some jobs and men others, or why women do the housework in the first place. Assumptions made in these models may include prejudices or stereotypical views, or they may be simply erroneous. Some feminist economists have recently presented data which challenges basic assumptions of the Becker-type analyses (White 1984: 11-16). The assumption of a family's joint-utility maximization function (what is best for one, is best for all) and the assumption of an equal balance of power are among those called into question. These assumptions are precisely what need to be examined or explained. Such assumptions can lead to retrogressive policy conclusions. A background paper for the MacDonald Commission proposing a guaranteed annual income program for Canada assumed one earner families. Thus only one member of the family was to be eligible for government training and adjustment programs (Townson 1986).

Fourth, although the neo-classical paradigm is by far the worst offender in the area, alternative paradigms — the institutional and the radical — cannot be exempted from criticism. The institutional paradigm, which takes an institutional, structural approach to the subject matter of economics, has illuminated certain issues such as segmentation and pay differences. However, like the neo-classical paradigm, it fails to deal with the 'why' questions. Radical economics, based on Marxian analysis, deals with gender relations but gives such relations a status secondary to class relations. MacDonald (1984) concludes that we are still a long way from a "feminist economics." She says: "Such an economics must not only explain the role and position of women, but it must analyse *all* economic phenomena from a model that includes the full economy — formal and informal, public and private, male and female" (MacDonald 1984: 173).

Research Methodology in Economics

Although it is difficult to separate content from methodology, specifically research methodology, the rest of this paper will try to do so. This is important, in part, because the impact of a feminist perspective on research methodology in economics is a subject that has not been dealt with elsewhere to date.

The basic argument here is that while there are ideological and conceptual reasons for the very inadequate treatment of the subject of women in economics, there are also important methodological reasons for this situation. Since the 1930s, economics has moved in the direction of elaborate mathematical model building. Complementary to this, and developing mainly since World War II, has been the emergence of the field of econometrics. This is defined as "the application of modern statistical procedures to theoretical models which have been defined in mathematical terms" (Tinter 1965: 3). The methodology required by mathematical and econometric models dictates the types of questions which can be asked, the assumptions which must be made, and the type of data which must be used in the discipline.

Robert A. Solo (1976: 25-26), a founder turned critic of the new economics, traces the recasting of economics into "complex and esoteric mathematical symbolism" from the movement to make economics into a true "science," like physics. He suggests that this development had two aspects. On the one hand, economics was to be made free of values. On the other hand, the attempt to do so took a mathematical direction. Paul A. Samuelson wrote *Foundations of Economic Analysis* (1948) with the aim of recasting economic theory into a set of mathematical propositions in order that those propositions could be tentatively verified or definitely refuted through experimental testing. However, according to Solo, Samuelson and those who followed him "succeeded certainly in recasting the whole of economics in complex and esoteric mathematical symbolism, *but not a single one of the propositions of theory has, as a consequence, been exposed to refutation through experimental test*" (1976: 26). Instead, Solo argues that the mathematization of economics has had the opposite effect. It has shielded the propositions of economics from challenge on the basis of direct observation and experience.

Whatever suited the narrow scope and limited capabilities of mathematical expression was drawn in, and what could not be so encompassed was excluded from consideration. The energies of generations were consumed not in a search for truth but in displays of virtuosity (1976: 27).

The methodological position adopted by the model builder is that it is not necessary to verify assumptions on which the deductive arguments are built provided that the model is technically correct. When assumptions are challenged, the model builder will offer to construct another model, based on other assumptions. In addition, the question of the empirical validity of the assumptions is skirted when it comes to policy-oriented models. The final policy objectives are acknowledged to be based on normative judgments rather than factual analysis. Thus, "the model builder can secure at least some convenient assumptions without running the risk of being asked to justify them on empirical grounds" (Leontief 1976: 34).

Economics' tenuous connection to the real world is also a result of the way that econometrics has developed. Despite being the empirical branch of economics, it is not strictly "empirical." In fact, econometrics has been severely criticized by one of its founders, Wassily Leontief, for "indirect statistical inference as the principal method of empirical research" (1976: 36). Econometrics, like economic theory, is based on assumptions. In the case of econometrics, the assumptions pertain to the stochastic (random) properties of the phenomena which the particular models are intended to explain. These assumptions can seldom be verified (Leontief 1976: 34).

When the econometrician builds a model, there is generally no attempt to verify empirically either the assumptions or the actual shapes of the parameters by providing first-hand data. Instead, the method of testing is to use indirect statistical inference in order to derive the values of the parameters from, for example, price and output information—the variables that were the unknowns for the theorist. Leontief says: "The work can in general be characterized as an attempt to compensate for the glaring weakness of the data base available to us by the widest possible use of more and more sophisticated statistical techniques" (1976: 34). He suggests that a reason for this, besides the weakness of the data, is that a hierarchy has developed in the academic discipline:

Empirical analysis. . .gets a lower rating than formal mathematical reasoning. Devising a new statistical procedure, however tenuous, that makes it possible to squeeze out one more unknown parameter from a given set of data, is judged a greater scientific achievement than the search for additional information that would permit us to measure the magnitude of the same parameter in a less ingenious, but more reliable way (1976: 35).

Leontief notes that there is nothing stopping either the model builder or the econometrician from going back to original data collection. However, it is seldom done. He also notes that there is nothing *formally* wrong with the apparently circular procedure that the model builder and econometrician follow. It is just that the results have little application to the real world. A past president of the Econometrics Society put it this way:

> the achievements in economic theory in the past two decades are both impressive and in many ways beautiful. But it cannot be denied that there is something scandalous in the spectacle of so many people refining the analysis of economic states which they have no reason to suppose will ever, or have ever, come about. . . .It is an unsatisfactory and slightly dishonest state of affairs. (Leontief, 1976: 34)

In practice, the outcome is that economists feel smug and self-sufficient. Thus they do not cooperate or coordinate their investigations with other social scientists who might have much to offer in terms of examining assumptions and making the discipline of economics more relevant. Instead, economists' work goes on in isolation and irrelevance.

Analysis of Selected Journal Articles[3]

The purpose of the analysis was to determine the impact of feminist research methodologies on work in economics. Articles on women's issues, broadly defined, were selected for examination. It was believed the impact of feminist approaches would be more evident in research on women's issues than elsewhere.[4] Eighty-one issues of 36 journals were examined for such articles. Selected criteria included sex of the author, specific subject, kind of model, method of data gathering and of data analysis of the paper. A summary of the results of the survey is presented in Table 1.

In all, there were only sixteen articles on women's issues. A disproportionate number of these were in two journals from the radical paradigm. Not a single one of the sixteen articles was written by a feminist economist. They were written either by nonfeminist economists, mostly male, or by feminist non-economists — the latter writing in the radical paradigm.

There was a considerable contrast in research methodology between the articles in the neo-classical and institutional paradigms and those in the radical paradigm. The methodology in the neo-classical articles was consistent with the pattern in the discipline as a whole (Peters 1986). The articles on women used mathematical models and econometric testing. Theoretically, they were based on conservative neo-classical models such as Becker's family economics and human capital theory. When it came to 'empirical testing,' all of the neo-classical articles used secondary sources: e.g., the census, national income, and labor statistics. None of the researchers collected his/her own information. In fact, given the nature of their models and the size of samples required, such collection would have been impossible.

The methodology used in the articles from the institutional paradigm was similar to that in the neo-classical paradigm (Nord 1986). In contrast, the methodology in the articles from the radical paradigm was noticeably different. The authors used political economy models based on the Marxist dialectic (Lehrer 1985). The articles presented reasoned argument and interpretive analysis of broad current and historical trends. None included any quantitative work.

Even in the papers from the radical paradigm, however, there was no indication of the impact of feminist debate on methodology. Although the papers from that paradigm were qualitative in approach, so is much of political economy. Feminist methodology requires more than simply a qualitative approach. As described earlier, feedback between researchers and informants and a self-consciousness focused on the research process itself are important elements of feminist methodology. Of course, in papers based on historical evidence, there would be no possibility or feedback between researchers and informants. A self-consciousness focused on the research process itself, however, was also lacking.[5]

Conclusion

In terms of the power/authority issues — the ways in which the social science researcher may enter into or set up an authority relation with those being studied — in economics research, there is no direct contact between the researcher and the women studied. The researcher uses secondary data, usually collected by government agencies. The data are therefore shaped by the power structure of the state or other agencies. There are important power/authority issues in the impact of the policy recommendations made by the researcher. The wise or unwise, warranted or unwarranted, policy recommendations of the economist can have an overwhelming impact on the lives of the women who have indirectly provided the data for the research.

Power/authority issues are relevant also for the feminist economist. It is impossible for her to adopt the concepts/categories and models/interpretations developed in the discipline and not have her own sensibilities assaulted. However, she must either choose this or have her work rejected.

Concerning the issue of the validity of women's experience—recognition of which is the foundation of feminist research, economics provides the strongest possible example of the denial of this validity. 'Family economics,' the entry of economic analysis into the private sphere, has been created and sustained by male economists, and the most conservative of those. The models which have been developed are an outrage to the truth of women's experiences. It has not only *not* been an area of qualitative research; research in many cases has been highly quantitative involving elaborate mathematical and econometric models. A feminist economics has not been allowed to develop even in this area.

The question of the assumptions/limitations of research techniques, particularly with regard to the public/private split and the unit of study, also applies to economics. Economics has in the past dealt exclusively with the public sphere and only recently has ventured into the private sphere, but in an inappropriate way.

In addition, in economics, perhaps more than in any other social science, the individual is the unit of analysis (Himmelweit 1977). Utility theory, theory of the firm, welfare theory, human capital theory, just to name a few, are all based on this unit of analysis. The primary reason is ideological—the idea of freedom of choice. The approach ignores the issue of class and the limits that class imposes on freedom of choice and possibilities for change. The premise that the individual ought to be taken as a unit of analysis more easily allows for quantitative measurement and mathematical model building. For macroeconomic analysis, individuals are aggregated as if they were all the same. This technique, used for the family, has been questioned by feminist economists.

In all, economics seems like a pretty hopeless discipline from a feminist perspective. This extends from its ideology, through its theories, conceptualizations, and assumptions to its research methodology. We wish we could just walk away from the depressing situation. Unfortunately this would be both foolish and dangerous.

Economists do more than produce and test irrelevant theories and models. They make policy recommendations. These recommendations are based on theories, models, and testing that no one but themselves can fully understand. While the premises, assumptions, and data adjustments are concealed in the analysis, the policy recommendations are viewed by policy makers and the public as a kind of objective truth.

The purpose of the work that is being done on women's issues also requires serious consideration. On examination, it becomes apparent that few of these topics are researched in order to explore the implications of findings *for women*. Rather, the purpose is to derive a function to insert into the overall model of the economy. Many studies examined for this paper were concerned with labor supply estimates. This also applies to work on the family. The questions asked are peculiar: Is marriage a good investment? Is divorce efficient? Will divorce increase the labor supply of women? Only a few of the topics in the articles examined for this paper appeared to be of any direct relevance for most women's concerns.

As for the work in the radical paradigm, our attitude is one of impatience for the debate on feminist methodology in the political economy of women to begin. The area seems to be having a difficult time breaking away from the malestream pattern of theoretical debates. However, with the tradition of qualitative work already strong, this is a next logical step for feminist political economists to pursue. We feel confident that it is just a matter of time.

Table 1

Summary of Findings on Analysis of Economics Journals
(July 1986)

	No. of journals examined	No. of issues examined	No. of articles on women's issues	No. of articles by women
neo-classical paradigm	31	71	9	1
institutional paradigm	3	5	2	0
radical paradigm	2	5	5	4
	—	—	—	—
Totals	36	81	16	5

Note: For details about the nature of the survey, please see Endnote 3.

Endnotes

1.   McKee and O'Brien (1983), and Stanley and Wise (1979) indicate the difficulties, within established research procedures, of handling and expressing the conflicts that arise from these power differentials.

2.   For discussion of the social and historical background to this assumption see Zaretsky (1973).

3.   The examination was of current issues of economics journals available in the reading room of the Harriet Irving Library, Fredericton, N.B., in the month of July, 1986. A listing of the articles, journals, and specific issues of those journals examined is available from the authors.

4.   Included were articles dealing with the family as well as those specifically on women's issues. We may have found even fewer articles had we defined women's issues more narrowly. In a 1986 survey done by the Social Sciences Federation of Canada, the Canadian Economics Association reported "0" articles "specifically on women's issues" among the 96 articles published in their journal in the period 1982-84. (This information was obtained from private correspondence with the author of the study.)

5.   A 1984 (Spring) issue of *Review of Radical Political Economy*, devoted exclusively to the political economy of women, confirms this picture further. The concern is with theoretical debates. The methodological debate does not come up.

References

Amsden, Alice H.
> 1980 *The Economics of Women and Work.* New York: St. Martin's.

Cohen, Marjorie.
> 1982 The Problem of Studying "Economic Man." Pp. 89-102 in *Feminism in Canada*, ed. Angela R. Miles and Geraldine Finn. Montreal: Black Rose.

Du Bois, Barbara.
> 1980 Passionate Scholarship: Notes on Values, Knowing and Method in Feminist Social Science. Pp. 105-116 in *Theories of Women's Studies*, ed. Gloria Bowles and Renate Duelli Klein. Berkeley: University of California.

Duelli Klein, Renate.
> 1980 How To Do What We Want To Do: Thoughts about Feminist Methodology. Pp. 88-104 in *Theories of Women's Studies*, ed. Gloria Bowles and Renate Duelli Klein. Berkeley: University of California.

Eichler, Margrit.
> 1985 And the Work Never Ends: Feminist Contributions. *The Canadian Review of Sociology and Anthropology.* December 22: 619-44.

Garmarnikov, Eva, and Purvis, June.
> 1983 Introduction. Pp. 1-6 in *The Public and the Private*, ed. Eva Garmarnikov, David H.J. Morgan, June Purvis, and Daphne Taylorson. London: Heinemann.

Graham, Hilary.
> 1983 Do Her Answers Fit His Questions? Women and the Survey Method. Pp. 132-46 in *The Public and the Private*, ed. Eva Gamarnikov, David H.J. Morgan, June Purvis, and Daphne Taylorson. London: Heinemann.

Harding, Sandra.
> 1986 *The Science Question in Feminism.* Ithaca: Cornell University.

Himmelweit, Sue.
    1977   The Individual as Basic Unit of Analysis. Pp. 21-35 in *Economics: An Anti-Text*, ed. Francis Green and Peter Nore. London: Macmillan.

Jayaratne, Toby Epstein.
    1980   The Value of Quantitative Methodology for Feminist Research. Pp. 140-61 in *Theories of Women's Studies*, ed. Gloria Bowles and Renate Duelli Klein. Berkeley: University of California.

Lehrer, Susan.
    1985   Protective Labour Legislation for Women. *Review of Radical Political Economy* 17: 187-200.

Leontief, Wassily.
    1976   Theoretical Assumptions and Nonobserved Facts. Pp. 32-40 in *Economic Relevance: A Second Look*, ed. Robert L. Heilbroner and Arthur Ford. Pacific Palisades, Calif.: Goodyear.

MacDonald, Martha.
    1984   Economics and Feminism: The Dismal Science. *Studies in Political Economy* 15: 151-78.

McFarland, Joan.
    1976   Economics and Women: A Critique of the Scope of Traditional Analysis and Research. *Atlantis* 1: 26-41.

McKee, Lorna, and O'Brien, Margaret.
    1983   Interviewing Men: "Taking Gender Seriously." Pp. 147-161 in *The Public and the Private*, ed. Eva Gamarnikov, David H.J. Morgan, June Purvis, and Daphne Taylorson. London: Heinemann.

Messing, Karen.
    1986   What Would a Feminist Approach to Science Be? *Resources for Feminist Research* 15: 65-66.

Nord, Stephen.
    1986   An Analysis of the Effects of Higher Education on Wage Differentials between Blacks and Whites in the U.S. *Applied Economics* 18: 173-89.

Peters, H. Elizabeth.
> 1986 Marriage and Divorce: Informational Constraints and Private Contracting. *American Economic Review* 76: 437-54.

Samuelson, Paul.
> 1947 *Foundations of Economic Analysis*. Boston: Harvard University.

Social Sciences Federation of Canada.
> 1986 *Sexist Bias in Research: Current Awareness and Strategies to Eliminate Bias Within Canadian Social Science*. Report of the Task Force on the Elimination of Sexist Bias in Research.

Solo, Robert A.
> 1976 New Maths and Old Sterilities. Pp. 24-27 in *Economic Relevance: A Second Look*, ed. Robert L. Heilbroner and Arthur Ford. Pacific Palisades, Calif.: Goodyear.

Stanley, Liz, and Wise, Sue.
> 1979 Feminist Research, Feminist Consciousness and Experiences of Sexism. *Women's Studies International Quarterly* 2: 359-74.

> 1980 "Back into the personal" or: our attempt to construct "feminist research." Pp. 192-209 in *Theories of Women's Studies*, ed. Gloria Bowles and Renate Duelli Klein. Berkeley: University of California.

> 1983 *Breaking Out: Feminist Consciousness and Feminist Research*. London: Routledge and Kegan Paul.

Tinter, Gerhard.
> 1965 *Econometrics*. New York: John Wiley and Sons.

Townson, Monica.
> 1986 Women and the Canadian Economy. Pp. 5-19 in *National Symposium on Women and the Economy*. Canadian Advisory Council on the Status of Women.

White, Margaret A.
> 1984 Breaking the Circular Hold: Taking on the Patriarchal and Ideological Biases in Traditional Economic Theory. *Occasional Papers in Social Policy Analysis*. No. 7.

Department of Sociology in Education, The Ontario Institute for Studies in Education.

Zaretsky, Eli.
    1973 *Capitalism, the Family and Personal Life.* New York: Harper and Row.

Chapter 11

FEMINISM AND SYSTEM DESIGN: QUESTIONS OF CONTROL

Margaret Lowe Benston

Technology as Social Artifact

Central to Marge Piercy's novel *Woman on the Edge of Time* (1976) is a feminist vision of a utopian society. One of the artifacts that people depend on in this society is their 'kenner' — a miniaturized computer terminal that fits on a wrist and allows instant access to computer communication and information services. There is no explanation given for where kenners came from but clearly an important part of Piercy's vision is how, in a truly free society, technology would be used as an integral support for liberation. She does not really discuss the nature of that technology; in particular, she does not tell us how the technology was developed or how it relates to the community she describes. I realize that there is only so much room in one novel, but her approach allows the reader to assume that technology and the process of developing it are givens, outside the scope of a feminist analysis. Piercy leaves unchallenged the common conception of 'technology,' especially microtechnology, as a neutral tool with an effect, for good or evil, that depends only on the intent of the user.[1] Such a belief is often coupled with a (somewhat contradictory) technological determinism in which a given machine, system, or artifact is seen as the inevitable outcome of the latest objective scientific knowhow. Or it is seen as the result of some logic inherent in 'technology' itself, untouched by human intent or social context. Computer communications systems especially have been among those perceived as inevitable products of technological advance, bringing the potential for liberation if only they are put into the right hands. Without further explanation, it would be easy to assume that Piercy might have this view of technology.

Given the destructive or oppressive role of many of the technologies in our society, however, more than uncritical assumptions about their neutrality are needed. A feminist analysis of technology, while still in its early stages, can begin from the work of such critics of the conventional view of 'neutrality' as Braverman (1974), Noble (1977, 1984), and Dickson (1974). These critics argue, in general, that any given technological system is not in fact neutral or inevitable but reflects the society out of which it comes in a variety of ways. In particular, they argue that the technologies of our society reflect the power relations of that society. Those who commission new technology are most often businessmen, the military, or governments. It is their goals and needs that are embodied in the technologies that are developed. There is, of course, a complex interrelation between technical possibility and intention but the driving force behind a new technology is the intention of those with power. Braverman (1974), for example, has shown that one of the basic values embodied in workplace technologies from the industrial revolution to the present has been that of control over the workforce.

The need for alternate technologies which reflect alternate values has been shown (Howard 1985; Wainwright and Elliot 1982; DeBresson, Benston, and Vorst 1987). Though feminist interest in problems around technology has recently increased, most of the work to date has been concerned with women's relationships to existing technology (Zimmerman 1983; Rothschild 1983; Cockburn 1985). There has been almost no work that tries to combine the two streams of criticism and to look at social bias in technology itself from a feminist point of view. In this essay I will try to show that such an analysis provides insights into how it is that the present system is maintained and how new technology might be created.

In analyzing technology, it is useful to think of the technology available at a given time as providing a 'vocabulary' for social action (Dickson 1974). This vocabulary then defines options for both social activity as well as individual action and self-expression. Technologies ranging through those used for warfare, strip mining, travel by car, heart transplants, and assembly lines are well developed but not equally available to all. This available vocabulary also provides limits on what can be 'said.' The technologies that do not exist are as important as the ones that do. Many actions or expressions of self are simply not possible if a supporting technology is not available: you cannot go somewhere on the bus if there is no bus service to that place; women cannot express their sexuality freely if there is no technology to control unwanted reproduction. Similarly, new technologies may present a new and restricted vocabulary where certain previously appropriate questions or ways of being are no longer available. An illustration of this is when amniocentesis, fetal heart monitors, and other medicalizations of birthing become 'required' for certain women; then other options for these women's relationship to birth and to their own bodies are closed off. The range of options reflects social values: the telephone system, for example, makes communication between two people easy but group communication difficult. Such a technology is appropriate in an individualistic society but not necessarily in one in which cooperation is more highly valued.

In a society based on human need and feminist principles, we would certainly want to change this technological 'vocabulary' in many ways. Many existing technologies would be simply scrapped: nuclear weapons, the assembly line, many large-scale agricultural and resource-extraction practices, electronic surveillance systems, among many others. We might want to redesign other technologies to reach a given goal in a different way. Consider computer communications systems as an example. On-line data bases, as we shall see, are useful but the present ones embody a centralized control over the information in them. Computer conferencing systems also have great potential but women find both economic and technical barriers to using them. These existing computer communications systems are not the only ones possible. They are, however, the ones that have arisen from the present structures of power in our society. A change in who has power to create new technologies would almost certainly result in different ideas and different systems.

Computer-based communications media are especially interesting as examples of the way in which technical 'vocabularies' are developed. As will be discussed in detail below, examination of these technologies shows clearly the choices that have been made in their design and implementation that are not strictly technical but reflect the power relations and social structure out of which they came. Those choices were made by businessmen, the military, technical experts, etc. If, instead, the design process for such technologies gave a major role to people who ordinarily have no power, the results would be significantly different.

One of the major ways in which a feminist approach would differ from the conventional design process is the recognition of the need to involve the people who will be using a technology in its design, with the aim of incorporating more humane values in such systems. One of the bases for such an approach is an analysis of the role of experts and authorities in scientific and technical work that comes out of a feminist analysis of masculinity and control in science.

Science, Technology, and Authority

Understanding how modern technological systems are created requires an understanding of the role of experts and their relationship to power in the society. In general an 'expert' is not just someone who has knowledge but also someone with privilege and authority. An expert has been awarded a status and position that are part of the structure of power and control in our society. It is not surprising then that, in all fields, experts are overwhelmingly male, and most often white. This comes about in part because of the general sexism of the society but is especially true in science and technology because of the ways in which scientific and masculine roles interact. Feminists have explored the complex relationships between scientific practice and the norms for male socialization and male roles (Keller 1985; Harding 1986; Bleier 1985; Benston 1982) in order to highlight the fact that it is not just discrimination (which certainly exists) that keeps women out of science but factors in the practice of science itself. One of these factors is a kind of 'scientific world view' that is also quintessentially a masculine one. A central feature of this world view is the reliance on a kind of (pseudo) objectivity in which it is assumed that the scientist uses essentially pure reason, removed from both social context and ethical responsibility. Other features of present scientific practice embody the kinds of values — such as stress on analytic ability, rationality and distance from emotions — that are central to male socialization.

In addition, both science and technology, as presently practiced, have as one of their basic tenets the legitimacy of domination and control over the physical world (Merchant 1980; Leiss 1972). This is clearly a result of the development of scientific and technical knowledge in capitalist, industrial society where those in power seek control over both the physical and the social world. The use of technology, especially, as a means of control over the social as well as physical world, has been well documented (Arditti *et al*. 1980). This is another crucially important place where male socialization is congruent with scientific practice: it is legitimate, and rewarded, for men to exercise control/domination over the physical world and to exercise authority in society.

The situation is quite different for women. The ideal for femininity stresses intuition, emotion, responsibility for others and interaction with them; power over these people or over the physical world is largely excluded. Such characteristics are in general not congruent with the characteristics of the 'scientific/masculine' worldview and this means that women have a different relationship to scientific and technical areas than do men. This is not to say that women cannot become technical experts — but if they want to participate in science or technology as presently practiced they must learn the 'masculine' rules and style that govern that practice. For almost all women this creates difficulties and, coupled with discrimination and socialization, such sex-role typing ensures that these fields remain overwhelmingly male.[2]

Science and technology are used for domination because they are controlled by the powerful in the society. Scientific or technical experts are central actors in the exercise of this control in two ways. First, the authority they represent removes others from a part in decision making. Second, the technological systems the experts create are themselves part of the apparatus of social control. Non-experts have no say at all in scientific and technical matters or in the values that underlie these. Women especially are taught that technology is a male realm and that technical matters are mysterious and difficult endeavors inaccessible to ordinary people. But reliance on (overwhelmingly male) experts in creating or dealing with technology simply reinforces present structures of sexism, hierarchy, and control. Deference to authority, in the form of technical experts, confirms people (particularly women) in a sense of their own powerlessness.

Among the arguments used to support the legitimacy of this kind of authority is one of 'neutrality.' The men in power and the technical people they hire are strong proponents of both the neutrality of technology and the neutrality of technical expertise. In spite of their claims, technical experts are, of course, not independent of their social context. Instead they are carefully chosen people who can be suitably trained for their role. The process of training ensures that, in addition to the proper 'scientific/masculine' worldview, prospective scientists or technical people are willing to act as authorities. It is for this reason that it is not enough to have knowledge in some area—one has to be *credentialed* through the proper training. This in itself puts white women, women and men from ethnic minorities and, to some extent, working class men at a disadvantage, since the training is not equally available to all. Furthermore, the content of the training mirrors the point of view of the men with power in the society. The career paths and sources of funding of most experts further reinforces this identification. All of these factors are a part of the biases and preconceptions which these experts bring to their work.

Part of the content of present science and technology is the devaluing of everyday, 'non-credentialed' knowledge. The institutionalized areas of (white male) expertise are defined by them as the only legitimate areas of concern and expertise. Areas in which nonscientists have special knowledge are dismissed as unworthy of serious notice.

The devaluing of workplace knowledge shows clearly the role that expertise plays in reinforcing hierarchy and control. Computer systems, for example, are introduced into offices from the top down. Usually a technical expert is brought in to figure out how the changes should be done. The women who do the actual jobs are rarely consulted. The expert will talk to management about the way the office functions and will read job descriptions or examine reports and documents. If the workers *are* consulted, a few interviews with them about specific details of their jobs constitute the 'user input' in this process. The knowledge of the clerical staff may be appropriated for inclusion in the new system; but this expert would never dream of treating the clerical staff as colleagues who should also have a say in the goals and design of the system because of their knowledge of the work process. Such collaboration is impossible in the present situation since the goal of this exercise is not to create an environment in which the workers can do their jobs better or more pleasantly. Rather the goal is to create circumstances that management thinks will further its aim to control and make a profit. The values and goals of the expert and the clerical workers are far apart. The point of view of the technical expert is clearly that of management. This approach to office automation stresses control of the work process and a rather simplistic notion of productivity gains. Very little effort is made to find out what would make the work process fulfilling for workers or to incorporate their values into the new systems.

A feminist critique of science highlights the relationship between the 'masculine/scientific' worldview and the uses of science and technology for control and domination. The power relations in the society as well as the 'scientific/masculine' worldview are embodied not only in technology itself but in the relationship between experts and non-experts. As long as technology is created only by credentialed experts operating from this dominant worldview, it will serve only the interests of those in power and will be inaccessible to women. In a new twist, the idea of the personal as political can be applied to technology in its social context. Present technology contains certain values built into it and is political in that sense. The process of creating a new technology involves not only making these present values and assumptions explicit but creating a method by which different values and assumptions can be incorporated. These different values might reflect alternate, feminist visions, personal needs and goals, or whatever was appropriate to the technology under consideration. In that sense, technology needs to be personal. The fact that it is so far from reflecting the needs or values of individuals today is a measure of the extent to which it is out of our control. The people who will be the users of a technology or affected by it need to have a say in what that technology is to be if it is to truly serve their needs. Only when the present male/expert/power dominated process of creating technology is overcome will such a new technology be created.

Alternatives

One of the strongest themes in the women's movement has been that of empowering women – of questioning power and authority as it is exercised in a sexist, unjust society. Suggestions for changing the role of science and scientific authority have been made by both feminist and nonfeminist critics of present day scientific and technical practice.[3] Three main possibilities emerge (Benston 1986): these can be characterized as technology and science 'for the people,' 'with the people,' and 'by the people.'

The first of these, technology and science 'for the people,' presents a model with a sense of social responsibility – one where practicing scientists and technical experts would try to come up with socially responsible kinds of applications or would make their expertise available where needed. These applications might include creating computer networks for community groups, investigating electronic threats to privacy, or engaging in research around socially relevant issues. In this model, technical people try to shed their training and identify with those on the bottom rather than those on top. It is an attempt to counter the false neutrality of present-day science. But it does not deal with the absolute separation between the 'expert' and the 'lay person.' It also leaves the 'everything else' in the present practice of science, including the mystique of technical expertise, unchallenged. Such an approach does nothing to remove the barriers to women's participation that present-day science presents. This approach simply replaces 'bad' experts with 'good' experts, who are still largely male and white. It is probably a necessary first step but certainly not a total solution.

The second approach, which can be characterized as technology and science 'with the people,' attempts to heal the separation between expert and non-expert. In this approach, everyone working on a given problem is seen as having important knowledge to contribute – the technical person simply has one kind of necessary knowledge and is a resource for the other people.

In the case of the clerical workers described above, their knowledge about their work and workplace, their own values in their work, etc. would be recognized by themselves and by the technical expert. Ideally, the workers would initiate the process, would define the problem and goals, and would retain control of the process so that their own values would be the ones embodied in the technology. Their responsibility would be to assess the information they receive, draw conclusions, decide between alternatives, and formulate strategy. The technical person would be there simply to contribute when that specialized knowledge is needed: to say whether a given idea is feasible, how much it would cost, etc.

This implies of course that the clerical workers must be willing to learn a great deal about 'the territory,' i.e., learn basic terminology, learn how to assess technical information, learn generally about the capabilities and options available in new computer systems, and overall learn what questions to ask. Once the confidence to learn is there, one of the most important tasks of the technical people would be to act as guides for the kind of self-learning that would make the experts unnecessary as authorities.

Personal values and ethical concerns can find a place in the technical process through a discussion of goals and values and a search for a technology appropriate to these. As the non-technical people become more generally knowledgeable, the values and assumptions underlying apparently purely 'technical' decisions would become more apparent to everyone. The result of the whole process would most likely lead to quite different choices than those made under the present system. The consequent enlarging of the available technological 'vocabulary' is a crucial step in the direction of creating a technology suitable to a more humane society.

Overall, the technology and science 'with the people' model stresses cooperation and interaction between all of the participants in the process. Hierarchy is minimized and the goal is the participation of all as equals as well as the revaluing of everyday non-credentialed knowledge.

There are of course many problems with such an approach. The non-experts often not only lack confidence in their ability to deal with technical issues but do not have the time to learn the basics they need to then carry out the possibly lengthy process of discussion and development. Freeing up the time required, particularly in the workplace, and providing facilities for the whole process can be very expensive. By and large, there is very little financial support for such efforts. In addition, the technical people not only do not have experience in operating in this mode but they have been carefully trained to reject it. Success in this kind of scientific practice requires them to change radically not just what they do but their whole view of science and themselves. They will require a clear analysis of the reasons why present scientific practice is problematic and, particularly for men, why reflexes around proper masculine behavior may intrude. In both the experts and the non-experts there is a tendency to fall back into old patterns when problems arise. In addition, even when experts can really give up the power that goes with their expertise, they often face penalties in the form of career problems.

In spite of the difficulties, there have been attempts to work this way. The Utopia project in Sweden (Howard 1985) and a project with a clerical union in Vancouver (Hartman and Benston 1987) are two examples of 'workers' initiatives' projects. In both cases workers have been central in creating an alternative process for designing computer-based workplace systems that would result in alternate technologies. The projects have not worked perfectly by any means – the Vancouver project, for example, ended up as much or more on the 'for the people' model as the 'with the people' one. A major problem was the lack of time to deal with the limited technical knowledge of many of the participants. Only a core group of people did manage to get the necessary background and knowledge of options. Even though these people were generally enthusiastic about discussion around alternatives they did not participate fully in the detailed design process. The choices they made, however, were very interesting. They decided that they were not interested in electronic mail, for example, and most attention was focused on the creation of small data bases in a forum mode. This was a clear consequence of the most frequently expressed value of these public service workers about their jobs, which was to give better service to the public. (The explicit objective of management in introducing new equipment, on the other hand, was to have better information available to managers.) Because of limitations of time and facilities there was an overall tendency for everyone involved, both participants and technical people, to fall back on the expertise of the technical consultants and to rely on their good will. These and other projects, such as that at Lucas Aerospace (Wainwright and Elliot 1982), have had only partial success in other respects as well, e.g., when new technologies have been successfully designed it has not been possible to get them used in the workplace. Even as partial successes, however, they are important, showing clearly the differences that result when different assumptions and values are used in the design process.

Feminists who are technically trained might be more comfortable with this approach to technological development than with conventional modes. Women in general might be better at such an approach and more skilled than men since women have less baggage from the present-day practice of science to shed. The process also depends a great deal on group interaction and on successfully encouraging the development of confidence among people who are nervous around technical issues. Again, women have been socialized more to provide psychological support and to be more sensitive to interpersonal dynamics (which is not to say that men cannot also act in this mode).

The final approach is technology and science 'by the people.' It is most usefully seen, I believe, as a possible future goal. It would mean that science is no longer in a completely separate realm but is reincorporated into everyday life. This is the logical extension of the kind of knowledge that would be acquired by the clerical workers discussed above in their work with technically trained people. In this case, someone who is interested in the subject would begin to learn and study to acquire the specialized knowledge previously considered the preserve of the credentialed elite. Such an approach does not mean that there is no specialized knowledge. Rather it means that learning in any area is open to all and that it is the actual knowledge that is recognized, not the social role of expert. Removing the connection, in this way, between knowledge and the exercise of power would open up these areas to individuals now excluded from them.

Choices in Computer Communications Systems

Computer-based communications systems offer particularly interesting examples for a 'technology with the people' approach. This is because, first, human interaction is an inherent part of system design and, second, the systems that now exist give some clear examples of how values and social bias are incorporated into technical systems. Analysis of the existing public computer-base communications media also provides a basis for discussion of the kinds of systems that do not exist and that feminists might want to create.

On-line data bases are stores of computer-readable public information which can be accessed directly by users. Information in the data base is carefully structured. Although there are different ways of organizing the information to allow for different 'information retrieval' procedures, the overall analogue to an on-line data base is an encyclopedia or other reference work. The retrieval procedures allow the system to respond to requests around whatever specific kind of information (stock market reports, entertainment guides, or bibliographies, for example) is contained in the data base.

In most of the existing data bases a distinction is made between basically passive 'information users' and more active and controlling 'information providers.' Information users have much more limited access to the system than do information providers. We can describe these data-base systems as operating in an essentially one-way 'broadcast mode' in the same way that radio, TV, and the daily papers are broadcast media.

The realities of power in our society are reflected in this centralized control of information. These data-bases have been designed by technical experts who never question the need for a separation between information providers and information users. Naturally it is those who run business and government, plus others in privileged positions in the society, who are the information providers. This means that the information in the data bases is almost certainly going to reflect those interests. This will be problematic for all those without power in the society, including feminists, since distortion and omission are inevitable in an economy that is structured around exploitation and domination. Consider, for example, the differences in information on the history of the women's movement available from a feminist source or from a data base containing information sponsored by conservative businessmen.

A common response to this is to ask for access to and control over the information but to leave the technology intact. The freedom of information laws in both Canada and the United States have this aim. A science and technology 'for the people' model also offers 'good' experts who will work to set up safeguards for access to information but who accept the broadcast mode as a given instead of investigating alternatives. It is necessary, however, to question the fundamental division in control and power that is reflected in the design of the system. And it is from a feminist critique of scientific and technical practice that one can see that the way to change this is to change the process by which the technology has been created. To do this, it is necessary to challenge technical authority and the connection of that authority with the 'masculine' practice of science and masculine authority in the society. This follows since these are integral parts of the development of present technical systems.

Broadcast systems are, in fact, not the only alternatives. Some types of computer communications systems with decentralized control over information already exist. Electronic mail, computer bulletin boards, and computer conferences are all examples of decentralized control. These systems are similar in that the user has an equal chance to be either the source or the destination of information. None of them provide the same service that a data base does.

With electronic mail the focus is on individuals sending messages to each other (although a message can be sent to a whole mailing list if desired). Communication is private and, in theory, can only be read by the sender and the recipient(s).

Both computer conferencing systems and computer bulletin boards (BBS), on the other hand, are primarily designed for the exchange and dissemination of public rather than private information. Bulletin boards are usually small scale systems with limited capacity set up on an individual or business's microcomputer. Initially they were set up and used by (mostly male) computer hobbyists to exchange programs, technical information, and messages about equipment for sale. Even though they are now being used more widely, they are extremely limited. There is little overall organization of the information stored in such a system and there is almost no capacity to connect up related items. In order to find items of interest, it is necessary to browse through the electronic bulletin board much as one would browse through an ordinary one. (As a result of these choices about design and unlike many other forms of computer information system, BBSs are generally free of charge. The relatively modest costs of starting and maintaining the system are borne by the people who run the BBS.)

Computer conferencing systems also are designed primarily for the dissemination of public information. In such a system, participants generate a series of organized public messages relevant to the topic of the conference. Typically a computer conference includes information about who reads and contributes to the messages, as well as a brief description of the topic. Like electronic mail, conferences are typically run on large computers and they may be limited to one computer or be part of a network.

Apart from greater capacity when run on large computers, computer conferences are distinguished from computer bulletin boards primarily by the way in which information is organized. Conference messages are grouped by topic and tend to read more like a conversation. Responses to previous remarks include information indicating which previous message is involved and, often, cross references to other contributions.

Both computer bulletin boards and conferences can be seen as 'forum' systems since the information is public and is distributed to all the participants in the system.   In this sense control over information is decentralized but in both of these systems other design decisions have been made that also influence access to and control over information. For example, these systems, along with electronic mail and data base services, are all designed for use by individuals as individuals.[4] Not only that, but access to them, for most people, is 'privatized.' It is necessary for anyone wanting to use them to set up a personal computer, modem, and appropriate software (none of which is exactly straightforward as yet). For conference, database, or mail services, it is necessary to buy an individual subscription to the service. Choices have been made about how it is best to learn to use the system and get help with it. Choices have been made about what kind of 'interface' to develop, i.e., what kind of commands you need to use to get information out or to put information in. These are all as much or more social choices as technical ones and, for many of them, the choices could be made by the users of the system. Instead, the technical authority makes the decisions even though technically it is quite possible to allow small groups of users in a larger system to design their own interface. Indeed, this is the practice in some (very limited) business applications. That it is not done more often is a matter of power and control, not a technical necessity.

One of the choices that has been made is not to pay much attention to creating on-line data bases in the forum mode. By this is meant a system which allows all participants to both enter and receive information from a data base. This would be extremely useful in various kinds of groups—women's centres, for example, could benefit enormously from the ability to share files or information. The major existing public systems do not support this kind of information flow. It is not surprising since support for group efforts and collective action by those without power has not been a priority for the owners and creators of these media.

Embodying Feminist Values in New Technology

As a feminist, I am looking for technologies that embody egalitarian principles and support the collective work that I want to do, that facilitate decentralized decision-making and the freest possible access to and control over information. The broadcast services are designed to achieve quite different goals. The centralized control of information reflects the imbalance of power in society. The overall impact is intended to serve the interests and priorities of the people who design and control them. Even though it is not as obvious, the electronic messaging and computer conferencing services (whether attached to the commercial services or functioning as independent systems) also reflect the interests and assumptions of those who created them. In these systems, even though the logic of control over information allows much more ability to contribute information, they are still privatized and expensive and there continues to be a focus on the individual as user of the system.

Except for some business systems, there is little support for computer communications media which are designed to enable people in groups to work together. These business systems cannot simply be taken over and used by other groups since the hierarchical logic of business as an institution is represented throughout the technology in one-way information flows and very centralized control over information. There are few examples where the technology enables groups to share information and to communicate with each other as equals even though this is exactly the kind of technology most likely to be useful to feminist activists.

One of the differences between feminist activists and existing technical experts is the feminist stress on collective action. This is more than simply a feminist quirk but a recognition of the importance of community and of the institutions that build and structure human interaction. In particular, communications systems useful to any specific group or community must be carefully designed to suit that group or community, taking into account its purposes and characteristics. In order to do this successfully, it is not enough for a technical expert, even a friendly one, to do some investigation and then decide what is needed. Such use of technical expertise not only supports passivity and powerlessness on the part of system 'users' but it also means that the effect of this system may be quite contrary to the intention of the designer. The real experts on a group's needs, values, and process are the people in that group, whether it be at a worksite or in a feminist collective. Creating a technology that suits a given application requires that the people who will be using that technology have control over system design.

At the moment, the science and technology 'with the people' model is probably the most useful one. This means that while technical people are clearly needed as resources, they should not be the arbiters of what is or is not desirable.

There *is* at least one proposal advocating careful attention to group dynamics and group input into system design (Johnson-Lenz and Johnson-Lenz 1983). They propose a design process for creating 'groupware,' by which they mean systems that match group needs with appropriate software. Yet even in this proposal the privileged role of technical expert remains, in that the technical people are still the ones making the major design choices. Johnson-Lenz and Johnson-Lenz also see basically a very simple relationship between group dynamics and a communications system. In their model, there is no consideration of the fact that the system itself will have an impact on the group dynamic. This is clearly the case and offers yet another reason for the people using the system to have control over what happens with it.

Suppose a group or a number of groups want some form of computer conferencing. A major consideration will be hardware choices or constraints. Choices, which interact with the hardware decision, must also be made about the size of the system, expected number of participants, complexity of commands that seems desirable, and sophistication of text editing capability. Feminists probably would choose different words (metaphors) for commands and for referring to software than those usually chosen. For example, they probably would not use master-slave imagery or choose the common usages 'abort' or 'kill.' Common Ground, for example, designed around the metaphor of a house, uses different rooms to represent different parts of the system. It is intended to be small, easy to use, and to run on a microcomputer (Hancock 1985). Whether directions and help should come from a resource person or from written or screen documentation is another necessary decision.

In designing computer conferencing systems, one must also decide who will control both participation and information. Even though computer conferencing systems are basically forum systems, they often have privileged people who may determine eligibility for participation in the conference and who have somewhat more control than others over the information. Such people do serve real needs in the system—a human overseer can keep information flows going well by splitting conference topics when they get too large, for example. But it is possible to make design choices that satisfy those needs in other ways than through one central authority. The responsibility might simply rotate. Or it might be a collective matter with an 'executive' (permanent or rotating) who carries out this policy, subject to review. (In this case the system could be designed with facilities to make such review very easy.) Or, as another alternative, a quite different system might allow for a variety of volunteers, each of whom structures the information in the ways that seem most interesting and useful to them. Those using the system could 'subscribe' in some way to one or more of these 'information shepherds.'

Conclusion

Whether it is the redesign of a computer conferencing system or the creation of a new technology to provide forum data-bases, the key to a 'feminist' technology is the embodiment of the values and goals appropriate to a feminist, caring, human-centered world in the technology that we create. To accomplish this requires that we understand and change the process by which those in power in society now control the creation of technology.

Given the scope of this kind of approach, it is not surprising that it should be hard to do. We are talking about the reintegration of technical knowledge into everyday matters, about returning control over technology to people, especially women, who have been excluded from important decisions in this area and from the confidence and the knowledge that would make such decision-making possible. The willingness to rely on 'good' experts rather than 'bad' ones is a tendency for us all, particularly given the complexity of the issues. Even when women are willing to approach these issues, they may be daunted by the effort required. Realistically, there will probably be few willing to get deeply involved in designing and carrying out technical projects like the development of a computer communications system suitable for feminist purposes. But the goal of feminist efforts should be to encourage those few and to build our own knowledge. Designing new systems will not be easy and leaning how to do it will be a long process. I would like to believe that Marge Piercy's kenners *were* built by feminists and I think we are just now beginning to learn how to begin such a task.

Endnotes

1. The support for the idea that the new microchip technology is in
    fact neutral, rests most conspicuously on the claim that
    "computers can be used for anything." This may be true on the
    level of hardware. Particularly with chips and cathode ray tubes,
    we have a relatively neutral underlying technology — the bits and
    pieces as it were — that can be put together in widely divergent
    ways. At the level of even single microcomputers, however,
    neutrality is not so clear. At the level of business or institutional
    computer systems — and one must understand that all of the
    hardware components, the software, *and* the way in which the
    components are organized must be included in the description of
    such systems — there is no question at all that we are looking at a
    technology that is only usable in the present society (consider the
    present banking system, for example). It is the whole computer
    system or the whole factory system that constitutes the basic
    technology — not a single robot or a single computer.

2. For a number of feminists the question then arises as to whether
    simply getting more women into scientific fields is enough if the
    roles they are to play do not change.

3. Articles in both Rose and Rose (1979) and Arditti, Brennen, and
    Cavrak (1980) are useful sources for such criticism.

4. This is not necessarily true for systems run by businesses for their
    own use, but in this case a whole different set of assumptions
    about power and authority have been made.

References

Arditti, Rita; Brennen, Pat; and Cavrak, Steve.
    1980 *Science and Liberation*. Boston: South End Press.

Benston, Margaret.
    1982 Feminism and the Critique of Scientific Method. Pp. 47-66 in *Feminism in Canada*, ed. Angela Miles and Geraldine Finn. Montreal: Black Rose.

    1986 Questioning Authority: Feminism and Scientific Expertise. *Resources for Feminist Research*. November: 23-25.

Bleier, Ruth.
    1974 *Science and Gender: A Critique of Biology and its Theories on Women*. London: Pergamon.

Braverman, Harry.
    1974 *Labor and Monopoly Capital: The Degradation of Work in the 20th Century*. New York: Monthly Review Press.

Cockburn, Cynthia.
    1985 *Machinery of Dominance*. London: Pluto.

DeBresson, Chris; Benston, Margaret; and Vorst, Jessie, eds.
    1987 *Work and New Technologies: Other Perspectives*. Toronto: Between the Lines.

Dickson, David.
    1974 *Alternative Technology and the Politics of Technical Change*. London: Fontana.

Hancock, Chris.
    1985 Common Ground. *Byte,* 10; 13: 67-75.

Harding, Sandra.
    1986 *The Science Question in Feminism*. Ithaca: Cornell University.

Hartman, Joey, and Benston, Margaret.
    1987 Worker Initiatives around Technological Change. Manuscript.

Howard, Robert.
1985 Utopia: Where Workers Craft New Technology. *Technology Review* 88: 42-49.

Johnson-Lenz, J.R., and Johnson-Lenz, M.M.
1982 Groupware. Pp. 42-56 in *Computer Mediated Communications Systems*, ed. Elaine Kerr and Roxanne Starr. New York: Academic.

Keller, Evelyn Fox.
1985 *Reflections on Gender and Science*. New Haven: Yale University.

Leiss, William.
1972 *The Domination of Nature*. New York: George Braziller.

Merchant, Carolyn.
1980 *The Death of Nature: Women, Ecology and the Scientific Revolution*. San Francisco: Harper and Row.

Noble, David.
1977 *America by Design: Technology and the Rise of Corporate Capitalism*. New York: Oxford University.

1984 *Forces of Production: A Social History of Industrial Automation*. New York: Knopf.

Piercy, Marge.
1976 *Woman on the Edge of Time*. New York: Knopf.

Rose, Stephen, and Rose, Hilary.
1979 *Ideology of/in the Natural Sciences*. Cambridge, MA: Shenkman.

Rothschild, Joan.
1983 *Machina Ex Dea: Feminist Perspectives on Technology*. New York: Pergamon.

Wainwright, Hilary, and Elliot, David.
1982 *The Lucas Plan: A New Trade Unionism in the Making*. London: Allison and Busby.

Zimmerman, Jan.
1983 *The Technological Women*. New York: Pergamon.

Chapter 12

"THE CHILD IS FATHER TO THE MAN": THE IMPACT OF FEMINISM ON CANADIAN POLITICAL SCIENCE

Naomi Black

In short one must tell lies, & apply every emollient in our power to the swollen & inflamed skin of our brothers' so terribly inflamed vanity. Truth is only to be spoken by those women whose fathers were pork butchers & left them a share in the pig factory (Woolf 1982: 298).

The question of the impact of feminist methodology on research is a question about power — about structures of domination and control. Power is the prerequisite for audibility. Political science ought therefore to be a field centrally involved in the feminist re-evaluations that are now occurring. Instead, precisely because it focuses on power, and above all on the power that is the public environment of academic activities, political science has been one of the disciplines most resistant to feminism's impact, methodological or otherwise. This is a field that, historically, has defined women out of politics.

Virginia Woolf's own case shows just how difficult it is for women to get a hearing, especially when they speak of politics. Her eminently political perceptions, as expressed in *Three Guineas* (1938) and elsewhere, were dismissed by her Fabian, political-journalist husband as the responses of "the least political animal that has lived since Aristotle invented the definition" (L. Woolf 1967: 27). Yet the *Diary* entry quoted above indicates how aware this supposedly nonpolitical person was of the realities of power. Only the daughters of the elite have a voice, she wrote, and even they are likely not to be listened to.

In political science, women are still a very small group indeed, even potentially only a small and unpowerful voice (approximately eleven percent of the field in Canada).[1] It is among women that we can expect to find feminists in the academic world; it was by women that questions about sexist bias in political science first began to be raised (Bourque and Grossholtz 1974). And in Canada it is women who do the very small amount of political science research that focuses on women, the area where the impact of feminism can reasonably be expected.

It is not obvious that a feminist *methodology* could be identified even among that small group of women who, working on women and questioning the nature of the field of political science, are unarguably feminists. But it is clear that a feminist *perspective* is possible, a perspective which does not exclude women nor contrast them unfavorably with men. I shall not try here to identify or examine the small group of feminists among political scientists. Rather, my concern is the progress of the field as a whole towards a feminist perspective.

Such a perspective would be a very significant change for a field which defines its main topic in relation to the socially-authorized use of violence against individuals. Because of the male monopoly of public authority, political science has developed as a field which disregards the whole of private life—almost everything most people do. As Irene Diamond and Nancy Hartsock comment, "To include women's concerns, to represent women in the public life of our society might well lead to a profound redefinition of public life itself" (1981: 721).

Political science, let alone society, is far from such a transformation. In this chapter I shall examine the situation in the field, focusing on the study of Canadian politics as the area where social change might optimistically be expected to have the hoped-for impact even for the nonfemale, nonfeminist majority of political scientists.

As a preface, I shall briefly discuss my own experience, as a political scientist who became a feminist. I am in no way typical, for I represent only a fraction of a fraction of practitioners. But I shall use my own academic biography to make some points about the impact of a feminist perspective. The main body of the paper is an examination of the perspective of those who define political science as an academic discipline.

I

In my own case, to move from international relations into the study of women and politics has meant to be seen, even accused of, doing propaganda instead of political science. I have been asked quite seriously—if with unmistakable hostility—how it is possible to do research when I know what answer I want. This is a question I never heard in the days I studied decolonization, when I certainly did have a preference among possible outcomes of the struggles against imperialism. No such queries are posed to colleagues who are convinced socialists or deeply committed opponents of, for instance, apartheid in the case of a scholar who works on South Africa.

The difference seems to be the way in which as a feminist scholar I am also and unavoidably an activist. Most researchers, even those who work on some subject which they see as important for social change, are unlikely to also be engaged in doing something about it. I share with my colleague, the expert on South Africa, the conviction that my research contributes to the struggle; it is not a conviction that can be shared by my colleague who works on Danish politics focusing on constitutional development or the one who studies the Japanese communist party. But even the Africanist is obviously not on the primary battleground; he can push for divestment, but that is a second-best and has little or no connection with his research, even if he studies the effects of foreign economic pressures on domestic policy. Only as a policy advisor or a swayer of public opinion, a leader of a revolt or possibly a journalist, could he hope to affect the course of events.

In contrast, a feminist scholar is by that fact alone an activist. The attempts by women to do different research differently are challenges to the patriarchy. All parts of the enterprise are significant — the attempts by women to participate as equals in the academic enterprise, their different subjects, and their specific, feminist perspectives or preferences in research strategies. My academic work *as such* now represents an attack on androcentrism in intellectual matters, the notion in the narrowest possible sense of man as the measure of all things.

Obviously these are views I did not have some thirty years ago when I went to Yale Graduate School, one of a handful of women, to be told sweetly that they had probably made a mistake giving me a fellowship since women never completed degrees; nothing personal, it is just statistical.[2]

Feminism has certainly had an effect on my perceptions of my own scholarly role. I am more aware of what I am doing, more methodologically self-conscious and wary. It has also changed my subject matter. I now work on women's organizations, not decolonization or comparative decision-making in foreign policy as I used to. And I use somewhat different procedures than I did in the past. For instance, since I now study women's groups which do not have records stored or copied in libraries, I have to travel, to interview, to sort out raw material.

But unlike many born-again feminists I feel a heartening continuity with the professional formation I received. I had an extraordinary training, by an exceptional man. Karl Deutsch taught a cohort of us to be eclectic and adaptive, sensitive and also rigorous: as much precision as is appropriate and in a form which is appropriate. He did this in a context of special respect and support for his women students, whom he was aware were discriminated against. For instance, he noticed, before such facts had much publicity, that when his male students were all full professors, his female students were still associate professors. He taught us to be alert and skeptical about the implications and assumptions of any methodology. None of us were aware of androcentrism in the 1950s. My students are Deutsch's "grand-students" and they are feminists even if, dating from the period when I was unaware of feminism, some of them were not taught explicitly about it any more than I had been.

The biggest difference in my work today is that I am now working on subjects—people—with whom I am connected by more than abstract principle or sympathy. In addition, in some cases my research can now have consequences, not just in possibly affecting research and therefore male domination, but in affecting the reputation and possibly the real-world impact of the persons whom I study. Certainly I can offend or hurt individuals who are often also friends, militants for causes I hold dear. So I do have heightened and more urgent problems with how I phrase, organize, and use my research findings, which implies previous impact on selection of topics, framing of hypotheses, and so on.

These problems are not different in kind from those I am accustomed to. As I said, I was lucky in who trained me. Other political scientists who became feminists were likely to have had less luck as students. They were badly trained, by men who were often stupid and nearly always arrogant and chauvinist. After all, when I went to Yale, the major figure in political science there was Robert Lane, who publicly endorsed the idea that politically active women were taking time from their families (1955: 399). Other women who became feminist political scientists had to retool in a major way. In my view, feminism has often made them far better scholars. It also often brought them hostility far greater than I experienced.

Today we have a new generation of graduate students who can, if they have luck, go directly to feminism. But I am saddened by the sight of some of the women of the intervening generation, who in some cases did pioneering dissertations on women and then shifted research interests away. They encountered the worst stress. I and the rest of my small academic generation of women got jobs relatively easily in our unmenacing prefeminist incarnation. Armed with tenure, we could handle the flak we later encountered; this is not the place to write of the other problems we had, with salary, promotion, and status in their broader senses. The students I now teach have their own cohort which is militant and mutually supportive. Those in between, who finished, say, five years ago, hit job shortages and marginalization and the biological clock; it is understandable that they now enjoy joining the boys.

The main impact of feminism, then, is to bring what looks like a critical mass of young women into graduate training, into work on women and politics, and, I hope, into the academic profession. It has brought them into a field that, by and large, has barely discovered women and is suspicious of and resistant to any feminist critiques. Certain topics are now less risky—in a safe academic setting. There, among women, remarkable discussions are going on, that implicitly (always) and explicitly (sometimes) challenge the whole definition of the field. But I think these developments are still virtually sealed off from the rest of the field.

II

It is not easy to substantiate these views within the empirical tradition I was trained in and still find valid. There is anecdotal evidence, of course. For instance, an episode in 1979 suggests something of the distance that still needed traversing at that point.

The *Canadian Journal of Political Science* of that September included, unusually, a fair amount of material on women. In an article entitled "The Reality versus the Ideal: J.S. Mill's Treatment of Women, Workers, and Private Property," Patricia Hughes presented a socialist-feminist argument that Mill's basic commitment to private property prevented his making the ideological leap necessary for liberation of either workers or women. In a twelve-page comment George Feaver unkindly summed up her article: "Poor Mill's problem, it seems, was that he was not a Marxist" (1979: 546). Many readers, even feminists, might well agree with Feaver's assessment. Certainly Hughes's paper has defects, including its failure to take account of radical-feminist analyses such as those made by Harriet Taylor Mill—a criticism Feaver did not make.[3]

However, Feaver did more than point out the weaknesses of what is obviously the work of a very young scholar; he also launched an astonishing *"ad feminam"* attack on Hughes, beginning with the title: "Comment: Overcoming His-story? Ms Hughes's Treatment of Mr. Mill." In it Feaver accused Hughes of "macramé-and-beads romanticism" (1979: 549) and of adopting a "trendy" combination of feminism and Marxism:

> her aim initially is to combine the smashing of the bourgeoisie
> with trumpeting the cause of feminism—doing away, as it were,

with the britches altogether....a vision purportedly more innovative by far than mere Bloomsburyism, something fusing gender-and-economic revolutionism, transcending even the Mummy State.

He continued in a similar tone to deride Hughes for wanting

a truly Humanized (or rather, Hu-person-ized) Society in which, liberated entirely from gender stereotyping and economic exploitation, we will have achieved at last our full potential as socialized species-beings, accomplished in every which way just as the spirit moves us, making it possible to be hunters in the morning, fishers in the afternoon, herdpersons in the evening, and critics after dinner (1979: 544-5).

Finally, he made some deserved criticisms of Hughes's description of Mill's economic stance and some less accurate ones of her versions of Mill's ideas about woman's nature.

What is striking about this comment is that it was commissioned by the editor of the journal who then defended his initiative on the grounds that "reviews were contradictory: assessors either liked [the article] very much or strongly recommended against publication" and "further reviews by others did not break the logjam." "The decision to publish the comment," he said, "was made in the knowledge that it would engender controversy." He admitted only that the article was "indelicate" (Holsti 1979). At the Canadian Political Science Association's Annual General Meeting in 1980, challenged by the Women's Caucus (Women in Political Science), he conceded that he would have been wiser to submit Feaver's comments to outside review; he promised to do so in similar situations in the future.

The December 1980 issue of the *Canadian Journal of Political Science* included a short critique of Hughes's piece, also from a socialist-feminist point of view, which correctly concluded that Mill must be evaluated as a reformist rather than a flawed or failed revolutionary. Its author, Barbara Cameron, referred to Feaver's comments only to say that Hughes's paper deserved more serious attention. So much for the reaction to a direct attempt at feminist analysis.

The issue of the *Journal* including the Hughes-Feaver dispute also presented a far more conventional article, unusual only in its subject. Jerome H. Black and Nancy E. McGlen's "Male-Female Political Involvement Differentials in Canada" focused on women's lesser role in politics — their "lag" — and the progress they were making in catching up with men's levels. The differences cited were small enough to be within the range of sampling error (Terry 1982: 4-5).[4] But they were taken seriously by the authors, who set their analysis firmly within a discussion of differences in the participation levels of women and men. Black and McGlen mentioned several methodological problems such as the data's focus on electoral behavior, the lack of information on women's marital and work situation, and the possible impact of politics' disregard of issues of particular interest to women. Then, constrained by the data available in election surveys, they retreated to an analysis that indeed showed women backward but improving as their attitudes changed and resources increased. The comforting conclusion was that time, with possibly some help from the women's movement, would take care of things.

In Black and McGlen's article, feminism, as the ideology of the women's movement, therefore appeared as a nonpolitical element uninfluential on anything except women's situations. And Hughes's experience suggested that feminism could expect hostility and ridicule if it insisted on intruding into scholarly concerns.

III

Supported by this indirect and spotty evidence of my views, I proceeded to test them somewhat more systematically by looking at a selection of introductory texts on Canadian politics.[5] It seemed likely that they might, if only for commercial reasons, be under some pressure to include what Feaver would presumably describe as the "trendy" topics related to women in politics. Initially, I hoped to find some reflection of the discussions of "gender gap" that were prominent in the press in 1983 and 1984; this I soon stopped expecting.[6] More generally, I would have liked to see some response to the feminist discussions that have been going on in political science since at least 1974, some realization that women's relationship to politics is different from men's but with a validity of its own. In my most optimistic moments, I had hoped for an awareness that women's distinctive political behavior might have political causes such as the issues presented to them or the way in which political parties and systems ignore them and block their access to positions of authority.

What I found instead was the continued absence of women plus a limited attempt to explain their lesser level of participation. Social, cultural, or attitudinal factors, but rarely political ones, were invoked in relation to women's behavior. Until 1986, there was no reflection of feminist critiques of the assumption that women "lag" behind men. One 1986 volume and one eight-page selection in a 1987 volume incorporated some of the feminist analyses, but with limitations that will be discussed below.

The general perspective can be summed up by a comment of William Christian:

> It is not expected that the ordinary citizen has a comprehensive and conscious view of politics that he could readily articulate. As a child he will learn something about politics from his parents, from his parents' friends, from his school, and from his playmates. . . .Work, marriage, and the aging process will modify these attitudes, but probably not in any fundamental way. The child is father to the man (Redekop 1978: 120).

Christian's comment was published in 1978. It is likely that, some ten years later, his successors would avoid the obviously exclusionary language he used. At least, their editors or publishers would oblige them to rewrite, so that a new lapidary quote would be used, perhaps something like "as the twig is bent, so is the tree inclined." The blatant elitism would be reduced. Instead, today, the language of class would assert in an apparently neutral fashion that most people have a low level of class or political awareness; women, even those with an "occupation," would be assigned the class situation and political awareness, usually pretty low, of their husbands or fathers. In this rather dismal situation, women would be seen to lag even behind their men, largely because in their case "[household] work, marriage, and the aging process" *are* assumed to have a significant impact, further reducing interest in and comprehension of politics; responsibilities for children, not mentioned for "the ordinary citizen," serve as further obstacles.

In short, on the evidence of the texts examined, Canadian political science has discovered Marxism. Though some of the collected volumes appear to segregate class analysis as an "alternate" to mainstream modes of inquiry, sources using this approach are cited frequently and the terminology is widely accepted.

Certainly, class analysis fits very well with an androcentric view of the world. Social identity and political role are defined by workplace occupation, a notion that often omits or misrepresents women. Formal leftist commitment to gender issues does little to mitigate a theoretical barrier of formidable scale.

In contrast, gender never appears, sex does so only rarely, and women remain in their separate sphere. Dennis Forcese even doubted, in 1986, whether women's increased labor force participation was going to continue (Fox and White 1987: 37).

The very concept of "gender," as the socially constructed elements of sexual identity, is missing. To be more accurate, it is missing as a dimension of politics; it appears, unnamed, as the explanation of the absence of women from politics. For instance, in an article dated 1984 (and cited by Jackson *et al.* 1986) William Mishler wrote:

> Traditionally, the most consistent differences in participation have been those based on sex. Because women until quite recently have been viewed as a politically inferior group, politics have been deemed to be a man's world.

Even after the formal grant of access, Mishler noted, "numerous informal barriers persist," the result of continuing "disproportionate responsibilities for managing home and family" and socialization into roles "emphasizing subservience and passivity" (Whittington and Williams 1984: 183-4).

That is, gender serves to act as a boundary or basis of exclusion from politics; it is not a dimension of politics. As a result, issues seen as related to gender—"women's issues"—are not really seen as political, and pressure groups concerned with such issues or made up of women are not seen as truly political. In the texts studied, there is virtually no reference to such issues or organizations. Neither women nor women's organizations are seen as political actors to whom the state need make any response.

Generally speaking, anything characteristic of women is marginalized in these texts as in the real world of politics. For instance, discussion of elites usually elicits a comment that the leaders of the economy and the polity do not include women; no-one feels the need to speculate on reasons or to note that women comprise half of the other groups slow to have access. Thus, Dennis Olsen supplied a list of the powerless that includes, along with women, members of the working class, and "non-British, non-French ethnicities" (Panitch 1977: 217). Are women then not part of the working class, of ethnicities?

Another example of the marginality of women, in the same 1977 collection, is Hugh Armstrong's "The Labour Force and State Workers in Canada," which mentioned day care in an introductory list of areas of state intervention but relegated discussion of women's labor-force participation to footnotes (Panitch 1977: 307). Armstrong, with Pat Armstrong, is something of a specialist on women's labor-force participation, and cites his own published work. But women do not play any role in his argument about the state as employer even though they predominate among low-paid state employees.

IV

In 1978 Hugh Armstrong co-authored a book called *The Double Ghetto: Women's Segregated Work in Canada*. It provides a useful metaphor: in the texts discussed there is a triple ghettoization and segregation of women.

First, any direct study of women is shut off somewhere discontinuous with mainstream political science, as Hugh Armstrong showed in his piece discussed above. When women do, briefly, get some mention, it is in the context of nonpolitical dimensions of politics or nonpolitical influences on politics. The second segregation takes the form of limiting the discussion of women to documentation and possibly explanation of their absence or lag. Finally, any specificities of women's political behavior, such as distinctive patterns of opinion or vote, are allotted nonpolitical causes, that is, social or attitudinal causes.

The most recent text examined (Fox and White 1987) shows good will by including an entire selection on women; it manages to do so in a way that epitomizes the three segregations. Fox and White is the sixth edition of a respected and widely used text, a classic. It now takes the form of an anthology, including selections by the majority of senior scholars in the field of Canadian politics.

In Fox and White, the selection on women is from a recent (1985) volume by M. Janine Brodie, reporting a study of the recruitment processes of women candidates for office. Its focus is the familiar one: why women do not get nominated and elected. The book's title: *Women and Politics in Canada*. This is in a series where the forthcoming titles announced are the following: *Government in Canada, The Revised Canadian Constitutions, Canada's Judicial System, Canada's Parliamentary System, Canada's Foreign Policy*, and *Federal Condition in Canada*. The implication is clear: women play no role in any of the significant areas or dimensions of Canadian politics.

The same marginalization from politics is seen in the placement of the chapter in Fox and White. Women appear in the section on "Culture and Constitution," under the sub-heading "Socio-political Issues in Canadian Politics" along with political philosophy, Native rights, class analysis, and free trade. If we combine the two very brief free trade pieces, Brodie's is the shortest article in the section. Eight pages long, it is given a title combining the title of Brodie's book with the heading of its first chapter: "Women in Politics—Many Participate but Few are Selected." Its impeccable academic language and format may possibly keep it from being grouped with the statement of the Native activist (female) following it, as merely a statement of a pressure group stance.

The second ghettoization—the concentration on women's absence from politics—is already evident in the topic of Brodie's book, which is less about recruitment than about barriers to recruitment. Here of course both Brodie and Paul Fox, who selected her material to reproduce, follow the field.

In Brodie's book, however, she went on to propose an explanation for the scarcity of women in political office that is at least potentially feminist: "Our findings suggest. . .that the roots of recruitment biases run deep in the social structures of all liberal democracies." She also referred to political parties' "historical legacy of gender bias" (1985: 125, 124).

Early in her book, Brodie presented with some care the feminist critiques of social science in general and political science in particular; this was the subject of the final section of her eleven-page first chapter. We can wonder at the editorial decision that excluded the final three pages on "Male Theories and Female Politicians." Here Brodie indicted recruitment literature in political science for "employing concepts formulated solely on the basis of male experience" (1985: 10). Her argument was that these studies generalized inappropriately to both genders from a single-gender sample, thus failing to meet scientific standards.

In these pages Brodie lined herself up squarely with feminist critiques of political science research, quoting Thelma McCormack gently enough to say that "male biases" in the literature are "more puerile than prejudicial, more accidental than intentional" (1985: 11). She distinguished her views from those of "radical feminists" epitomized by Shulamith Firestone, whom she dismissed as believing in "a male conspiracy that subjugates women to a subordinate and dependent social status" (1985: 7, n. 23); this misleading attribution, incidentally, is in the section included by Fox. Hers is the critique of male science by its own alleged standards, which comes early in feminist criticism (Black 1988).

The mutilation of Brodie's chapter excised her feminist critique. It left her presenting merely the fact of women's lesser power and numbers in "elite politics" along with the arguments that have been given by mainstream theorists to explain this absence. These are, of course, the familiar notions of the impact of socialization and women's roles as constraints—the third ghetto of confinement to the nonpolitical as an explanation of women's political specificity. Setting the discussion in the context of political recruitment was not enough to escape the traps.

V

Fox and White showed how little the study of women, carried on by feminists, even feminist political scientists, has been integrated into the mainstream of political science in Canada. One other recent text showed, however, that such integration is possible.

Jackson *et al.*, published in 1986, managed repeatedly to give attention to women. Women appeared in the context of all the logical sections such as Issues, Political Culture, and Political Socialization. The impact of mothers' political beliefs on children's was mentioned, citing a 1976 study by Canadian political scientists which seems to have been overlooked by everyone else (Jabbra and Landes 1976). The authors were prepared to make judgments: "The record [of representation of women in parliament] is dismal." They were also aware that the reasons for women's "dismal but improving record" are not established: "one can only speculate on the reasons" (1986: 458). Here they reflected interestingly the state and stance of formal research about women's low level of participation, research which was also summarized in the sections of Brodie's work reprinted in Fox and White: uncertainty about even the social reasons usually cited, but no alternative explanation available.

At the same time, the discussions of women in politics, as given by Jackson *et al.*, imply a more radical or at least more feminist assessment. A cartoon shows a constituency selection committee, accurately represented as nine men and one woman, listening happily as their Chair says, "Our next candidate has a Ph.D. in Economics, is vice president of a large corporation and has long been active in community affairs...." "Pity it's a woman!" he concludes, tossing away the sheet he had been reading from. On the same page there is a reference to how women were "diverted" to the women's auxiliaries of the parties and "effectively barred from any significant part" in the national organization (1986: 456).

Similarly, discussing women in the public service in a section two and one-half pages long, Jackson *et al.* commented that "in direct contradiction of the merit principle, anti-female prejudice was built into the very fabric of civil service legislature and personnel practice." The authors specifically noted the contrast with the "informal bias" that affected francophones. They concluded, "While the just application of the merit principle might permit women to increase their representation very gradually in the long term, in the short term there is manifestly a need in the public service for serious commitment to continued and expanded affirmative action programs" (1986: 397, 396, 398). Bias, prejudice, male dominance of structures of power, refusal to admit even "qualified" women, the need for systemic remedies: the components of a feminist perspective are present even though they are not made explicit.

From a feminist point of view, this book is not perfect. As noted, Jackson *et al.* do not go so far as to identify and condemn systemic discrimination against women. There are problems of interpretation, as when Native peoples, but not women, are cited in the discussion of minority rights in relation to the Charter (1986: 203). The authors may not have read the most recent feminist studies of women in politics: the analyses of Canadian women's candidacies by Jill Vickers and Janine Brodie are cited only from an article in a mainstream collection (Penniman 1981). Nevertheless, one of Vickers's *Atlantis* articles is cited; what a pleasure to see a feminist journal noticed! And individual women, ranging from Margaret Atwood to Iona Campagnolo and Lorna Marsden, actually appear in the index and meaningfully in the text.

Jackson *et al.*, in short, were responsive to the demand not to omit women where they exist and matter in politics and in relation to politics. They were also prepared to see policy implications in the absence of women. Aware of affirmative action, they probably made special efforts to include discussion of women where it has customarily been omitted. And we need hardly note that they avoided all sexist language. This is certainly the text, out of those examined, that a feminist should select. In all this, it is a text very different from the others.

VI

The threat for the present generation of students in political science is, in practical terms, the nonfeminist, nearly always male teachers who still dominate the study of politics. Having discovered class analysis, they filter the study of women through their Marxism. Easily recognizable by their references to the "Woman Question," they have no difficulty with the conundrums of dual systems theory. Nor do they doubt their authority to dismiss women's organizations as destructive of the progress of the working class, to condemn part-time work or regulation of violent pornography as not being "objective" interests of women, to dictate the proper role of feminism or of women. And they are not ready to give serious consideration to the essential theoretical questions about a possible feminist methodology or perspective.

Reading Jackson *et al.*, I have the uneasy feeling that the authors are out of step with the field. From a feminist perspective, they are well ahead of it. I wonder if or how the field as a whole will catch up. But I am now sure of one thing: it will not be political science that will lead the way in integrating the perspectives and findings of feminist research into the mainstream.

Endnotes

1.　This is the figure given by Brodie (1982). Joan Pond, the Administrator of the Canadian Political Science Association, assured me in September 1987 that rough, annual hand-counts indicate that, until December 1986, this figure has remained a relatively stable eleven to thirteen percent.

2.　No woman had completed the doctorate in political science at Yale since the 1920s; I am happy to say that no less than three of us did in 1964, two of us married and having produced three children between us as well as the dissertations.

3.　Reprinted in the edition of John Stuart Mill's feminist writing cited by Hughes (Rossi 1970).

4.　Black and McGlen found significant differences in *means* of reported frequency of various sorts of participation over the past two elections; they did not find significant differences of turn-out in any given election (1979: 476).

5.　The following texts were examined: Panitch (ed.) 1977; Redekop (ed.) 1978; Clarke *et al.* 1979; Brodie and Jenson 1980; Van Loon and Whittington 1981; Kornberg and Clarke (eds.) 1983; Whittington and Williams (eds.) 1984; Jackson *et al.* 1986; Fox and White (eds.) 1987. Susan Ferguson, a graduate student in political science at York University, assessed all but Fox and White (1987) which I did myself. Our procedure was as follows:
　　　1 - selected representative texts used or recommended in introductory courses in Canadian Politics at York University and the University of Toronto;
　　　2 - noted any direct references to feminism and feminists in Table of Contents and Indexes;
　　　3 - noted and checked any references in Tables of Contents and Indexes that might deal with or present feminist perspectives, women's issues or women;
　　　4 - in collections, read all pieces by women;
　　　5 - watched for intersection of gender/class/race throughout;
　　　6 - bibliographies and reading lists were also checked for inclusion of feminist analyses, and sections on political socialization were examined for discussion of women's role.

6.   In 1984 women in both Canada and the United States were the majority of the electorate, voting at the same rate as men, but showing persistent differences in respect to partisan and public policy choices; it was thought these might translate into different voting patterns. See Terry (1984), Black (1985).

References

Armstrong, Pat, and Armstrong, Hugh.
  1978 *The Double Ghetto: Women's Segregated Work in Canada*.
     Toronto: McClelland and Stewart.

Black, Jerome H., and McGlen, Nancy E.
  1979 Male-Female Political Involvement Differentials in
     Canada. *Canadian Political Science Review* 12: 471-98.

Black, Naomi.
  1980 Of Lions and Mice: Making Women's Politics Effective.
     Canadian Women's Studies/Les cahiers de la femme 2: 62-
     64.

  1985 Where does the Gender Gap? Or: The Future Influence
     of Women in Politics. *Canadian Women's Studies/Les
     cahiers de la femme* 6: 33-35.

  1988 Where All the Ladders Start. Pp. 167-89 in *Gender Bias in
     Scholarship: The Pervasive Prejudice*, ed. Winnifred Tomm
     and Gordon Hamilton. Waterloo: Wilfrid Laurier
     University.

Bourque, Susan, and Grossholtz, Jean.
  1974 Politics An Unnatural Practice: Political Science Looks at
     Female Participation. *Politics and Society* 4: 255-66.

Brodie, M. Janine.
  1982 Report on the Status of Women in the Discipline. Ottawa:
     Canadian Political Science Association.

  1985 *Women and Politics in Canada*. Toronto. McGraw-Hill
     Ryerson.

Brodie, M. Janine, and Jenson, Jane.
  1980 *Crisis, Challenge and Change: Party and Class in Canada*.
     Toronto: Methuen.

Cameron, Barbara.
  1980 Mill's Treatment of Women, Workers, and Private
     Property. *Canadian Political Science Review* 13: 775-84.

Clarke, Harold D.; Jenson, Jane; LeDuc, Lawrence; and Pammett, Jon H., (eds.).
> 1979 *Political Choice in Canada*. Toronto: McGraw-Hill Ryerson.

Diamond, Irene, and Hartsock, Nancy.
> 1981 Beyond Interests in Politics: A Comment on "When are Interests Interesting? The Problem of Political Representation of Women." *American Political Science Review* 75: 717-21.

Feaver, George.
> 1979 Comment: Overcoming His-story? Ms Hughes's Treatment of Mr. Mill. *Canadian Political Science Review* 12: 543-54.

Fox, Paul W., and White, Graham (eds.).
> 1987 *Politics in Canada*. 6th ed. Toronto: McGraw-Hill Ryerson.

Holsti, Kal J.
> 1979 Letter dated October 19.

Hughes, Patricia.
> 1979 The Reality versus the Ideal: J.S. Mill's Treatment of Women, Workers, and Private Property. *Canadian Political Science Review* 12: 523-42.

Jabbra, J.C., and Landes, R.G.
> 1976 Political Orientations among Adolescents in Nova Scotia: An Exploratory Analysis of a Regional Political Culture in Canada. *Indian Journal of Political Science* 34: 75-96.

Jackson, Robert J.; Jackson, Doreen; and Baxter-Moore, Nicholas.
> 1986 *Politics in Canada: Culture, Institutions, Behaviours and Public Policy*. Scarborough, Ont.: Prentice-Hall Canada.

Kornberg, Allan, and Clarke, Harold D. (eds.).
> 1983 *Political Support in Canada: The Crisis Years. Essays in Honor of Richard A. Preston*. Durham, N.C.: Duke University.

Lane, Robert E.
> 1965 *Political Life*. New York: The Free Press.

Panitch, Leo (ed.).
  1977 *The Canadian State: Political Economy and Political Power.* Toronto: University of Toronto.

Penniman, Howard J. (ed.).
  1981 *Canada at the Polls, 1979 and 1980.* Washington, D.C.: American Enterprise Institute.

Redekop, John H. (ed.).
  1978 *Approaches to Canadian Politics.* Scarborough, Ont.: Prentice-Hall of Canada.

Rossi, Alice S. (ed.).
  1970 *John Stuart Mill and Harriet Taylor Mill: Essays on Sex Equality.* Chicago: University of Chicago.

Terry, John.
  1982 Male-Female Differences in Voting Turnout and Campaign Activities in Canada and Ontario. Ottawa: Library of Parliament Research Branch.

  1984 The Gender Gap: Women's Political Power. Ottawa: Library of Parliament Research Branch.

Van Loon, Richard J., and Whittington, Michael S.
  1981 *The Canadian Political System.* 3rd ed. Toronto: McGraw-Hill Ryerson.

Whittington, Michael S., and Williams, Glen (eds.).
  1984 *Canadian Politics in the 1980s.* 2nd ed. Toronto: Methuen.

Woolf, Leonard.
  1967 *Downhill all the Way: An Autobiography of the Years 1919 to 1939.* London: Hogarth.

Woolf, Virginia.
  1938 *Three Guineas.* London: Hogarth.

  1982 *The Diary of Virginia Woolf,* vol. IV: 1931-35, ed. Anne Olivier Bell, assisted by Andrew McNeillie. London: Hogarth.

NAME INDEX

SUBJECT INDEX

Also published by Wilfrid Laurier University Press
for The Calgary Institute for the Humanities

RELIGION AND ETHNICITY
Edited by Harold Coward and Leslie Kawamura

Essays by: Harold Barclay, Harold Coward, Frank Epp, David Goa, Yvonne Yazbeck Haddad, Gordon Hirabayashi, Roger Hutchinson, Leslie Kawamura, Grant Maxwell, Cyril Williams

1978 / pp. x + 181 / ISBN 0-88920-064-5

THE NEW LAND
Studies in a Literary Theme
Edited by Richard Chadbourne and Hallvard Dahlie

Essays by: Richard Chadbourne, Hallvard Dahlie, Naïm Kattan, Roger Motut, Peter Stevens, Ronald Sutherland, Richard Switzer, Clara Thomas, Jack Warwick, Rudy Wiebe

1978 / pp. viii + 160 / ISBN 0-88920-065-3

SCIENCE, PSEUDO-SCIENCE AND SOCIETY
Edited by Marsha P. Hanen, Margaret J. Osler, and Robert G. Weyant

Essays by: Paul Thagard, Adolf Grünbaum, Antony Flew, Robert G. Weyant, Marsha P. Hanen, Richard S. Westfall, Trevor H. Levere, A. B. McKillop, James R. Jacob, Roger Cooter, Margaret J. Osler, Marx W. Wartofsky

1980 / pp. x + 303 / ISBN 0-88920-100-5

CRIME AND CRIMINAL JUSTICE IN
EUROPE AND CANADA
Edited by Louis A. Knafla

Essays by: J. H. Baker, Alfred Soman, Douglas Hay, T. C. Curtis and F. M. Hale, J. M. Beattie, Terry Chapman, André Lachance, Simon N. Verdun-Jones, T. Thorner and N. Watson, W. G. Morrow, Herman Diederiks, W. A. Calder, Pieter Spierenburg, Byron Henderson

1985, Revised Edition / pp. xxx + 344 / ISBN 0-88920-181-1

DOCTORS, PATIENTS, AND SOCIETY
Power and Authority in Medical Care
Edited by Martin S. Staum and Donald E. Larsen

Essays by: David J. Roy, John C. Moskop, Ellen Picard, Robert E. Hatfield, Harvey Mitchell, Toby Gelfand, Hazel Weidman, Anthony K. S. Lam, Carol Herbert, Josephine Flaherty, Benjamin Freedman, Lionel E. McLeod, Janice P. Dickin McGinnis, Anne Crichton, Malcolm C. Brown, Thomas McKeown, Cathy Charles

1981 / pp. xiv + 290 / ISBN 0-88920-111-0

IDEOLOGY, PHILOSOPHY AND POLITICS
Edited by Anthony Parel

Essays by: Frederick C. Copleston, Charles Taylor, John Plamenatz, Hugo Meynell, Barry Cooper, Willard A. Mullins, Kai Nielsen, Joseph Owens, Kenneth Minogue, Lynda Lange, Lyman Tower Sargent, Andre Liebich

1983 / pp. x + 246 / ISBN 0-88920-129-3

DRIVING HOME
A Dialogue Between Writers and Readers
Edited by Barbara Belyea and Estelle Dansereau

Essays by: E. D. Blodgett, Christopher Wiseman, D. G. Jones, Myrna Kostash, Richard Giguère, Aritha van Herk, Peter Stevens, Jacques Brault

1984 / pp. xiv + 98 / ISBN 0-88920-148-X

ANCIENT COINS OF THE GRAECO-ROMAN WORLD
The Nickle Numismatic Papers
Edited by Waldemar Heckel and Richard Sullivan

Essays by: C. M. Kraay, M. B. Wallace, Nancy Moore, Stanley M. Burstein, Frank Holt, Otto Mørkholm, Bluma Trell, Richard Sullivan, Duncan Fishwick, B. Levy, Richard Weigel, Frances Van Keuren, P. Visonà, Alexander G. McKay, Robert L. Hohlfelder

1984 / pp. xii + 310 / ISBN 0-88920-130-7

FRANZ KAFKA (1883-1983)
His Craft and Thought
Edited by Roman Struc and J. C. Yardley

Essays by: Charles Bernheimer, James Rolleston, Patrick O'Neill, Egon Schwarz, Ernst Loeb, Mark Harman, Ruth Gross, W. G. Kudszus

1986 / pp. viii + 160 / ISBN 0-88920-187-0

GENDER BIAS IN SCHOLARSHIP
The Pervasive Prejudice
Edited by Winnifred Tomm and Gordon Hamilton

Essays by: Marlene Mackie, Carolyn C. Larsen, Estelle Dansereau, Gisele Thibault, Alice Mansell, Eliane Leslau Silverman, Yvonne Lefebvre, Petra von Morstein, Naomi Black

1988 / pp. xx + 206 / ISBN 0-88920-963-4

BIOMEDICAL ETHICS AND FETAL THERAPY
Edited by Carl Nimrod and Glenn Griener

Essays by: Carl Nimrod, Alan Cameron, Dawn Davies, Joyce Harder and Stuart Nicholson, Ruth Milner, Sydney Segal, David Hoar, David J. Roy, David Manchester, William Clewell, Michael Manco-Johnson, Dolores Pretorius and Paul Meier, Edward W. Keyserlingk, William Ruddick

1988 / pp. xii + 122 / ISBN 0-88920-962-6

THINKING THE UNTHINKABLE
Civilization and Rapid Climate Change
Lydia Dotto

Based on the Conference
Civilization and Rapid Climate Change
University of Calgary, August 22-24, 1987

1988 / pp. viii + 73 / ISBN 0-88920-968-5

THE EFFECTS OF FEMINIST APPROACHES
ON RESEARCH METHODOLOGIES
Edited by Winnie Tomm

Essays by: Margaret Lowe Benston, Naomi Black, Kathleen Driscoll and Joan McFarland, Micheline Dumont, Anne Flynn, Marsha Hanen, Jeanne Lapointe, Hilary M. Lips, Pamela McCallum, Thelma McCormack, Rosemary Nielsen and E. D. Blodgett, Lynn Smith

1989 / pp. x + 259 / ISBN 0-88920-986-3